THE ART OF KNITTED LACE

THE ART OF
KNITTED LACE

With Complete Lace How-to and Dozens of Patterns

Includes Patterns From:

Lisa Lloyd,

Annie Modesitt,

Berta Karapetyan,

Melissa Matthay,

Phoenix Bess,

and More

edited by Potter Craft

POTTER
CRAFT

New York

CONTENTS

INTRODUCTION

by Kristin Omdahl

Lace is a journey, not a destination. And if you can knit, you can knit lace. There is no elusive secret! Simply put, it is a combination of knit, purl, increases, and decreases—just like any other type of knitting. Chart reading is sometimes required, but it is an easy task to learn. Getting comfortable with lace requires only time and experience.

Unlike other types of knitting, you cannot always see the "big picture" until your stitches are bound off and pinned out to block. In my opinion, one of the greatest challenges of lace knitting is the blind faith required to believe that the ball of fluff on your needles will transform into an exquisite, ethereal masterpiece! Yet the first time you see your lace in all its glory is one of the most rewarding moments you will experience as a knitter.

My advice: Start with a small project, and watch your skills grow! Embrace the complex stitch patterns and the delicate touch of holding the blocked beauty in your hands. Fall in love with the beautiful marriage of positive and negative space that only the increases and decreases of lace can create.

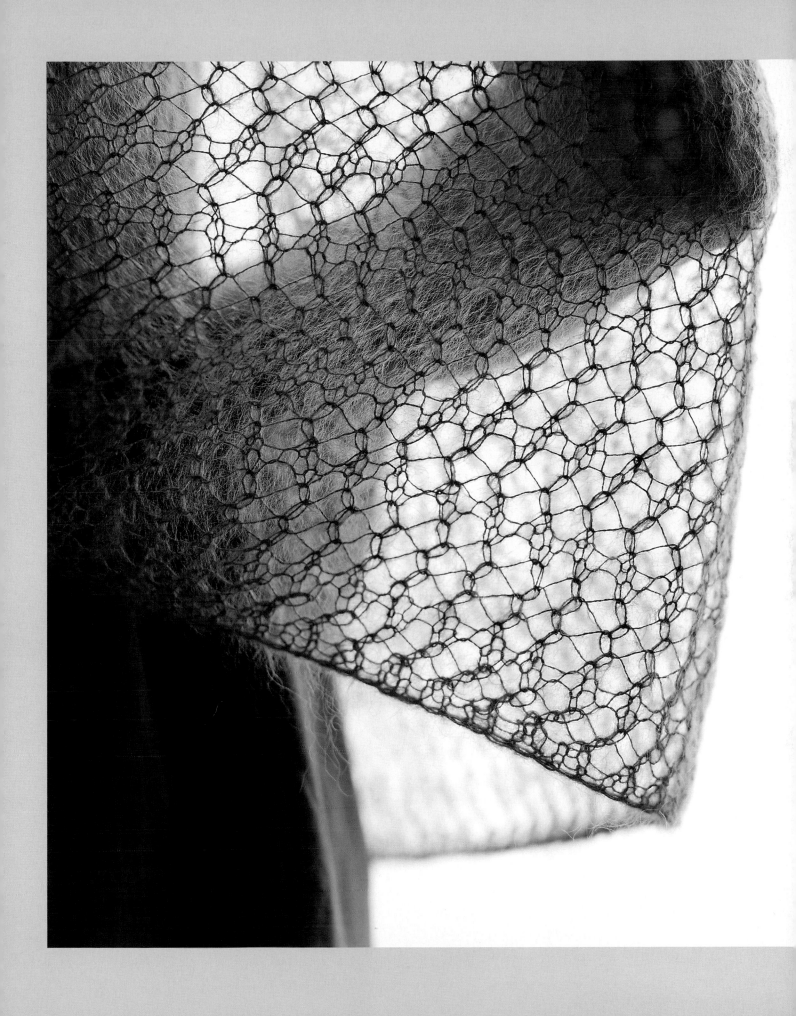

CHAPTER 1

Lace Basics

Before You Begin: Selecting Needles and Fibers for Lace

Lacework requires knitting at a loose gauge, so the piece has room to grow in the blocking process. In order to accomplish this, you must use a needle that is several sizes larger than is recommended from the yarn manufacturer—generally the size of needle called for in a pattern will be the correct size. Getting used to knitting at such a loose gauge is one of the toughest challenges when you begin to knit lace. The stitches can be difficult to differentiate on the needles, and it is hard to fix mistakes along the way. With that in mind, it is important to pick the right needles and yarn to give yourself an edge.

Start Large

Start with a DK- or worsted-weight yarn to get a firm understanding of the stitch pattern. It will be far easier to recognize the stitches and make sure you are knitting the stitch pattern correctly.

Use Wood

Use bamboo or wood needles, as they tend to grip the yarn more than other types of needles. Their grip will help you hold the stitches. Super-slick metal needles are great for speed, and you may enjoy them as you gain experience and confidence, but they make your stitches slippery and thus harder to control. You can lose a whole section of stitches in the blink of an eye with one false move!

Stay Sharp

The sharpness of the needle tips is also an important factor to consider when choosing lace needles. A sharper point will help you find the loop made by thinner yarns and work the various stitch manipulations, including single and double decreases and working into the front and back of stitches.

Use Circular Needles

If you love your straights, you can definitely find lace patterns that accommodate them. However, there are times when you will have hundreds of stitches on your needles at one time. Circular needles can hold large stitch counts—even when you are knitting flat rows. Circulars come in many sizes: from 16" (40.5cm) to 60" (152.5cm). For the body of a sweater worked in the round, 24" (61cm) is a good medium length to handle all the stitches. For triangular shawls, I prefer 36" (91cm) or longer to hold the very large number of stitches required for the lower edge. For circular

Confusing Lace Terms

Fagoting is a style of lace work in which almost every stitch is either an increase or a decrease on every row. There are several types of fagoting. Often they have a vertical geometric design and look similar or identical on both the right and wrong side. All fagoting patterns are extremely open, lacy, and stretchy. A loose cast-on and bind-off are necessary to allow the nature of this stitch pattern to open up properly when blocked.

Fagoting, left; eyelet, right.

Eyelet is a pattern in which yarn overs are generally separated by more stitches than other types of lace knitting. But they should still be well-blocked to open up the pattern details. This is a subtle style of openwork; take special care to choose the right combination of large needles and thin yarn, otherwise the openings can get lost in a dense fabric.

Knitted lace is a type of open stitchwork in which the stitch pattern rows are alternated with rows of plain knit or purl stitches.

Lace knitting is a type of open stitchwork in which the stitch pattern rows are worked on both right- and wrong-side rows. This is the more advanced style and requires more finesse when fixing mistakes.

shawls, you will need to start with either the magic loop technique or double-pointed needles and then switch to a long circular needle (36"–60" [91–152.5cm]) as you reach the outer perimeter.

For smaller items worked in the round, like socks, hats, and gloves, you can either use double-pointed needles, small circular needles, use the magic loop technique on a longer circular needle, or work with 2 circular needles at the same time, alternating one half of the stitches on one circular and the other half on a second.

Magic loop is a technique of knitting a small circumference of stitches on one large circular needle with a flexible cable that is 3 to 4 times longer than the circumference of the knitting. Generally a flexible cable length of 32" (81cm) or longer will work.

Keep It Natural

Blocking is different for natural and synthetic fibers because animal fibers have elasticity and memory. I have learned that synthetic fibers do not have the memory of natural fibers and will not hold their blocked lace shapes. That's the main reason I prefer natural fibers for lace. However, one of the most dramatic transformations I ever witnessed included steam blocking and a bamboo/acrylic blend yarn, so sometimes a test swatch is the only way to tell!

Color Me Simple

To best display your fine stitchwork, choose a yarn that does not overpower. A solid or semi-solid yarn complements all types of lace knitting and complements intricate stitch detail very nicely. Variegated yarns work best with simple stitches, like eyelets and fagoting. If you are planning a multi-directional project, long self-striping yarns can add to the geometric design.

How to Read Line-by-Line Instructions

Line-by-line instructions are the words that spell out every stitch and instruction of a pattern. Oftentimes a chart can express the same instructions in a more concise way, but not all instructions are (or can be) written in chart form.

Line-by-line symbols, such as parentheses, brackets, and asterisks, are used to explain the repeating of certain stitches. This is helpful to reduce extreme repetition of the same terms and keep the instructions concise. If the stitch pattern repeat is complicated, it may have several sets of repeated commands within the repeat. If multiple symbols are required, you may find sets of parentheses within to explain a repeat of certain stitches. Brackets and/or asterisks may then be used to repeat a larger series of stitches or the whole pattern repeat.

For example, let's say we have the following pattern in a single row, with 3 knit stitches on each side. This is how the actual stitches would be worked in each repeat (not including the border of knit stitches):

k2tog, k2tog, k2tog, yo, k1, yo, k1, yo, k1, yo, k1, yo, k1, yo, k1, ssk, ssk, ssk.

Now let's look at the same instructions with parentheses used to mark the small section of stitches within the pattern repeat (including the border stitches):

K3, [k2tog x3, (yo, k1) x6, ssk x3]. Repeat from [to] to last 3 stitches. K3.

Last but not least, here is the same line written as a multi-symbol pattern row:

K3, *[k2tog] 3 times, [yo, k1] 6 times, [ssk] 3 times; repeat from * to last 3 stitches, k3.

The symbols of line-by-line instructions are universal to all knitting and crochet patterns. If the line of instructions includes more than one repeat of a stitch pattern, the repeat will be contained in brackets, parentheses, or asterisks. The instructions should tell you how many times to repeat.

HOW TO READ CHARTS

Charts are an even more concise way to view stitch instructions. They're a great tool because they're universal and can be read regardless of the language you speak. Additionally, the more you use charts, the more you can "see" what the pattern will look like before you actually begin knitting! Here is an example of the same instructions from the previous page, but concisely drawn in chart form:

be charted. Also, if the chart is written for a project that is circular (worked in rounds), all rounds of the chart are read from the right to the left.

If the lace pattern is stockinette based, it means that you purl on the wrong-side rows.

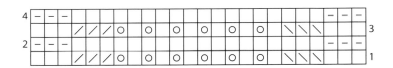

If the lace pattern is garter based, it means you knit on the wrong-side rows.

	Knit 1 on RS, Purl 1 on WS		Ssk
	Knit 1 on WS		Yarn over
	K2tog		

Charts should be read in the same direction as the knitting in your hands: from the bottom up, from the right to the left (the perspective of the right side facing). On wrong-side rows, you read the chart from left to right because you have turned your work around.

Note that if the stitch pattern is alternated with rows of plain stitches (knitted lace), sometimes only the pattern stitch rows will

This sample demonstrates a stitch pattern worked on both right- and wrong-side rows.

Here are many of the common symbols used in charts:

	K1 (st st)		Sl 1 (purlwise) wyib		K2tog (right slant dec)		K3tog
	P1 (rev st st)		Sl 1 (purlwise) wyif (for float)		SKP (left slant dec) - sl 1, k1, psso		P3tog
	Selvage (edge) st		K1-b (k1 in row below)				SK2P - sl 1, k2tog, psso
	Yo (yarn over)		P1-b (p1 in row below)		SSK (left slant dec) - sl 2 tog knitwise, knit 2 sts in front		S2KP2 - sl 2, k1, p2sso
	K1-b (twisted st)		M1 (Make One) - lift running thread bet st just worked and next st, knit-tbl		P2tog		K4tog
	P1-b (twisted st)				P2tog-tbl		MB Make bobble
	Sl 1 (knitwise) wyib		Inc 2 - (k1, p1, k1) in same st				

CAST-ON AND BIND-OFF TECHNIQUES

There are dozens of techniques for casting on and binding off your knitting. We all have our favorites, but it is important to know that they don't all work the same. Oftentimes if a pattern requires a special cast-on or bind-off, it will be noted within. Depending on the amount of stretch the designer intended for the lace, specific techniques can be called out.

For example, for a triangular lace shawl that begins small at the top and is worked down toward the bottom "V," ample stretch is a must to allow the open stitch work to blossom. Whereas for a rectangular shawl that is worked in one piece, you must have cast-on and bind-off techniques that are not only stretchy to accommodate the blocking growth but also are identical in the amount of stretch.

Helpful Cast-Ons for Lace

Double-Needle Cast-On
For ample stretch, cast on using the method of your choice with double needles: Hold two needles together and wrap the yarn around them, as you would normally do with just one. When all the stitches are cast on, simply slip the second needle out of the loops. Working your first row of stitches is a breeze with the large loops.

Provisional (Invisible) Cast-On
First, knot your working yarn to a contrasting yarn. Then, with needle and knot in your right hand, pull both strands with your left hand until you achieve tension. Make sure to separate the strands using the fingers of your left hand. Yarn over with working yarn in front of waste yarn.

Crochet Cast-On
Make a slipknot in the cotton contrast color yarn and place it on the crochet hook. *Hold the needle and yarn in your left hand and the crochet hook with the slipknot in the right hand as though to crochet. Place the needle on top of the yarn held in the left hand. Holding the hook over the needle, crochet a chain stitch over the top of the knitting needle. Move the yarn under the knitting needle and back toward the left. Repeat from * for required number of stitches. Cut the yarn and fasten off. Tie a knot in the end of this tail to remember from which end to remove the chain.

Helpful Bind-Offs for Lace
(For Maximum Stretch in Blocking):

K1, yo, k1
Pick up the first knit stitch and yarn over, and pass both off the needles, leaving 1 stitch remaining on the right-hand needle. *Yarn over, knit 1. Pick up first knit stitch and yarn over, and pass both off the needles, leaving 1 stitch remaining on right-hand needle. Repeat from * until only 1 stitch remains on the right-hand needle. Fasten off. The extra yarn over between bind-off stitches adds extra length to your final stitches and gives you extra stretch for blocking.

Picot Bind-Off
Bind off 2 stitches; place remaining stitch on right needle back on left needle as if to purl; *cast on 1 stitch using a cable cast-on; bind off 3 stitches; place remaining stitch on right needle back on left needle as if to purl. Repeat from * until all stitches are bound off.

Crochet Chain Bind-Off
With a crochet hook, *insert hook into the next 4 stitches, yarn over hook, pull through all stitches, chain 8. Repeat from * to last 4 stitches, insert hook into last 4 stitches, yarn over hook, pull through all stitches. Fasten off. This technique gives you a very stretchy edge as well as a delicate scallop. This technique works very well for an edge that will be fringed, as each scallop is shaped well for spacing out sections of fringe evenly.

Everyone's tension is unique, but I find that the double-needle cast-on and the "yo, k1" bind-off techniques are very compatible for a rectangular shawl where the length of the cast-on edge must equal the length of the bound-off edge.

The Knitting

Simply put, lace patterns are created with increases (usually yarn overs) and their corresponding decreases. The number of increases equals the number of decreases, unless you are shaping. The art lies in the ability to manipulate the increases and decreases to create texture, geometry, pattern, images, and more.

Increases

Most increases are created with yarn overs, but there are also right-leaning, left-leaning, and center increases. It is helpful to learn how each increase looks so you can use the right method.

Yarn Over (yo)

This is the basis of most lace patterns and is very simple to make. On a knit row, you simply bring yarn to the front before the next knit stitch. An extra loop will be on the right needle. On a purl row, you simply bring yarn to the back before the next purl stitch. An extra loop will be on the right needle.

Knit Into the Front and Back of Same Stitch (kfb)
(also called Bar Increase)

Knit into the front of specified stitch, but before you slip the stitch off of the left needle, knit into the back loop of the same stitch. This technique will show a small bump on the right side of the fabric.

Make 1 (m1)

This increase is worked by knitting into the horizontal strand between the right stitch (just worked) and the left stitch (not yet worked). For a left-leaning increase, insert the left needle from front to back under the strand. With the right needle, knit into the back of the strand. Slip the strand off of the left needle. For a right-leaning increase, insert the left needle from back to front under the strand. Knit into the front of the strand. Slip the strand off the left needle.

Decreases

There are many different types of decreases.

Single decreases, i.e., ssk, k2tog, decrease the stitch count by 1. Double decreases, i.e., k3tog, sk2p, s2kp2, decrease the stitch count by 2.

Right-leaning, left-leaning, and center decreases:

Right-Leaning Decreases	Left-Leaning Decreases	Center Decreases
Single: k2tog RS P2tog WS	Single: Ssk RS P2tog tbl WS	
Double: K3tog RS P3tog WS	Double: Sk2p RS Sp2p WS	Double: S2kp2 RS S2pp2 WS

Note: The wrong-side decrease equivalents are written for purl wrong-side rows. If knit wrong-side rows are used, use the right-side decreases.

K2tog: Knit 2 stitches together.

P2tog: Purl 2 stitches together.

Ssk: Slip 2 stitches, one at a time, to the right-hand needle. Knit them together.

Psp: Purl 1 stitch, slip stitch back to left needle, pass the second stitch over the first stitch.

Skp: Slip 1 stitch, knit 1 stitch, pass the slipped stitch over.

P2tog tbl: Purl 2 stitches together through the back loop.

Sk2p: Slip 1 stitch, knit 2 stitches together, pass the slipped stitch over.

Sp2p: Slip 1 stitch, purl 2 stitches together, pass the slipped stitch over.

K3tog: Knit 3 stitches together.

P3tog: Purl 3 stitches together.

S2kp2: Slip 2 stitches, knit 1 stitch, pass the 2 slipped stitches over.

S2pp2: Slip 2 stitches purlwise, one at a time, purl next stitch, pass the 2 slipped stitches over (p2sso).

Symbol	Description of Decrease	Right-Side Row	Wrong-Side Row
/	Right-leaning single decrease	K2tog	P2tog
\	Left-leaning single decrease	Ssk or Skp	P2tog tbl or Psp
⟋ leaning left	Left-leaning double decrease	Sk2p	Sp2p
⟍ leaning right	Right-leaning double decrease	K3tog	P3tog
⋀	Vertical double decrease	S2kp2	S2pp2

SWATCHING, BLOCKING, AND MEASURING

Swatch It

As we all know, swatching is crucial for garments. Lace or otherwise, it is so important to determine your gauge for anything that must be a certain size upon completion. For lace, I suggest working a gauge swatch that is two pattern repeats wide by two pattern repeats tall.

Block It

Whenever you knit lace, you must block the swatch, since the size changes so drastically in the blocking process. If the finished project will be blocked, the swatch must be blocked to determine blocked gauge! A gauge swatch can sometimes double in size!

Make sure that you block the swatch in the same fashion you will be blocking the finished item to ensure exact measurements. Here are the three recommended ways to block lace:

Wet Blocking

Soak the finished item in lukewarm water (preferably with a gentle wool wash) until it is completely wet. Wait 30 to 45 minutes to allow the water to absorb thoroughly. It will float until the trapped air releases and water is completely absorbed. Remove the item from the bath and gently press the water out. Do not wring! Wringing your swatch or finished piece can unevenly stretch or warp the stitches—and even felt it. Place the item on a blocking surface and gently stretch it into shape. A blocking surface could be a carpeted floor covered in fresh towels, a mattress, or a purchased blocking board. Use pins and/or blocking wires to secure your desired shape. Leave the piece to dry. Once dry, your lace will maintain its blocked shape.

Steam Blocking

Some irons have a steam setting, or you can find handheld steamers (my favorite) to purchase. Once you have pinned out your item, lay a towel or other cotton cloth over the surface to be steamed. Direct the steam over the covered area for a few seconds. While steam blocking is nearly as effective as wet blocking for natural fibers, it takes a lot more time because you have to evenly steam every stitch. However, for synthetic fibers such as acrylic, the transformation is phenomenal. Steam blocking alters the fibers dramatically and creates incredible drape and shine.

Mist Blocking

For a minimal stretch, you can place your item on a blocking surface, stretch to desired size and shape, and pin in place. Lightly mist the surface with a spray bottle of water or a combination of water and gentle wool wash. Leave to dry. Once dry, your lace will maintain its blocked shape.

Measure It

Basically you have two options for measuring your gauge swatch. The easiest method is to simply take a measurement over the repeats of the stitch pattern and then plan everything around the measurement of the stitch repeat. For example, if a repeat is 6" wide x 6" tall (15cm x 15cm) and you want your piece to be 30" wide x 60" tall (76cm x 152.5cm), you would cast on stitches for five repeats and knit ten sets of the pattern repeat rows.

Most of the time, you will have to figure out your measurements per stitch, which is often difficult with lace because a blocked yarn over, knit stitch, and decrease stitch can all vary greatly in size! I suggest taking an average of the measurement over a large area to get an approximate measurement per stitch. Again, this is where the two-pattern repeat block comes in handy: Taking an average over a larger area will give you a more accurate estimate. For example, if your repeat is 12 stitches and your measurement is 6" (15cm) for two repeats (24 stitches), the average is simply 24 ÷ 6, which is 4 stitches per inch.

Blocking can dramatically alter the look of a lace stitch pattern.

Once you have your swatch blocked and measured, ask yourself a few questions:

- Is the stitch pattern pleasing to the eye with this size needle?
- Would the stitch definition "pop" if I reduced/increased the needle size?

- Would a different texture or color of yarn show the stitchwork better?
- Does the pattern flow from one repeat to another?
- Is this how I want my finished lace to look?

LACE TIPS AND TRICKS

Mark It

Stitch markers are extremely helpful with lace. If you place a marker between each repeat of the stitch pattern, it is a gentle reminder to stay focused on your stitches. If a problem arises, e.g., stitch count is off, it is easy to determine where in the row the mistake occurred: in the section where the repeat's stitch count is incorrect. Note: when working in the round, use a different color or style of stitch marker to denote the beginning/end of the round.

Insure It

A lifeline is a piece of contrast yarn that is temporarily inserted through an entire row or round of stitches to ensure that you can return to that point unharmed if a problem arises. If you run into a problem that requires you to rip out and re-knit several rows of knitting, the lifeline allows you the luxury of having the stitches held in place at whatever point you positioned it.

First, decide on a row to use for your lifeline. If possible, choose a row of plain knit or purl stitches. If that is not possible, choose a row at the end of a full pattern repeat. Next, choose a smooth, tightly twisted piece of contrast yarn or thread that is finer than the one you are knitting with. A cotton crochet thread or other thin cotton yarn works well. Thread your lifeline onto a tapestry needle and insert it into every stitch, just under your needle, being careful not to thread through any stitch markers. Make sure to use plenty of thread and have a generous length at the beginning and end of the row before cutting the lifeline (I like to loosely tie the ends of the lifeline together.)

If you run into a problem that requires ripping back to the lifeline, remove your stitches from the needles and unravel back to your lifeline. Insert a knitting needle back into the top of each stitch being held by the lifeline (do not pick up the lifeline itself). Count your stitches to be sure you picked up every one, and double check that you have alleviated the problem. Do not remove the lifeline yet. Resume your knitting. When you have reached a point where you need a new lifeline, remove the original and repeat the steps above to create a new lifeline at your current row.

Join It

Joining new yarns and weaving in ends, while inevitable in any knitting project, can be especially challenging for lace. Here are a couple techniques that may make things easier for you:

Spit join

If you are using a natural fiber that can felt, vigorously rub 4" of the strands overlapping between your hands after moistening them with a little water. The friction of your hands and a little moisture will felt the strands together, and you can continue as though you are still knitting from the original ball of yarn.

Temp Knot

With a 5" tail on each yarn end, tie both yarns together with a loose single knot. Continue knitting as before, but with the new yarn. At the end, carefully untie the loose knot and weave in each end separately with a tapestry needle.

Hide It

Always join yarn or weave in ends in the most inconspicuous place possible. If it is a garment, try to place joins and ends near seams, underarms, sides, etc. If it is a shawl or scarf, always try to join at the end of a row. Weaving in ends at the edge is easier and less noticeable than the middle of a row. In the event you have to join in the middle of a row, weave in the loose ends with a tapestry needle, following the direction of the loops and stitches. If you follow a couple of stitches on one row, weave your way diagonally to the next stitch on an adjacent row. A woven-in end that travels diagonally seems to blend into the fabric better than if you work the whole tail across one row.

Fix It

If your mistake is minor, you can probably isolate and repair without ripping back to your lifeline. If you need to drop down to fix one stitch a few rows down, you can drop the stitches one at a time in a vertical line. Insert the left-hand needle into the stitch below on the right-hand needle. Move this stitch to the right needle and pull the working yarn to unravel the above stitch that was on the right needle. Repeat these steps for every row up to and including the row with the stitch you need to fix (you will have wide ladder rungs). Once you fix your stitch (e.g., make a knit a purl, change a ssk to a k2tog, etc.) you will need to re-knit the dropped stitches up the "ladder" back to your current working row.

Depending on whether your background is knit or purl, the direction of your loops will vary. In knit, insert a crochet hook into the live stitch from front to back and *bring hook under ladder (vertical bar) of yarn. Hook ladder yarn and pull through stitch, forming a new stitch on the hook. Repeat from * for each ladder and slide last stitch from crochet hook back to live stitches on right hand knitting needle. In purl, insert crochet hook into the live stitch from back to front and *bring hook under ladder (vertical bar) of yarn. Hook ladder yarn and pull though stitch, forming a new stitch on hook. Repeat for each ladder, and slide last stitch from crochet hook back to live stitches on right hand knitting needle.

Next Steps: Design a Shawl

Design a Shawl

It is fairly simple to design your own two-dimensional lace project. Think of a rectangular shawl or scarf simply as a swatch that keeps going and going and going . . . you get the picture!

Follow these easy steps to create your own one-of-a-kind masterpiece:

Choose Your Yarn

How many yards do I need? If you have an unlimited supply of yarn for your project, you may not need to estimate yardage. However, if you would like to splurge on a luxury fiber, estimated yardage will help you figure out what is within your budget. You may be surprised to find a luxurious fiber fits into your budget when you know your approximate yardage.

Calculate Yardage

To determine estimated yardage of your finished projects, we need to know the measurements and yardage of your gauge swatch. From your swatch we can calculate the yardage used per gauge of the swatch and then calculate yardage for your desired size. We already know how to measure the swatch. Yardage can be measured in two different ways:

1. Unravel your gauge swatch and measure the length of yarn used.

2. With a postage scale, weigh the swatch and calculate the yardage based on the yarn's label. For example, if you used 3 grams of yarn for your swatch and your yarn is 50g/400yd per skein, you can use simple math to find how many yards of the skein you actually used.

In this equation, y represents the unknown yardage:

$$\frac{3 \text{ grams}}{y \text{ yards}} = \frac{50 \text{ grams}}{400 \text{ yards}}$$

Then you can cross-multiply, and divide to find y.

3 x 400 (grams x yards) = 50 x y (grams x yards)

(grams x yards) are on both sides, canceling each other out, so:

3 x 400 = 50 x y

Divide each side by 50 to isolate the y:

(3 x 400) ÷ 50 = y

1200 ÷ 50 = y

24 = y

You can now apply the yardage of your swatch toward calculating the yardage required for your shawl.

Determine Shawl Size

To figure out the size of the shawl you want to make, follow these simple geometric equations. Just plug in your numbers to determine your yardage:

For a rectangle, the area is equal to the length multiplied by the width.

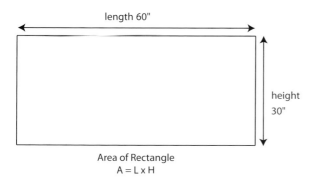

length 60"

height 30"

Area of Rectangle
A = L x H

So let's say you want to make a rectangular shawl that is 30" wide x 60" long. That would have an area of 30 multiplied by 60 = 1,800 square inches.

If your swatch is 6" x 6", it would have an area of 36 square inches. Let's say it is the same swatch we calculated yardage for above: 24 yards.

Divide the total area of the shawl (1,800 square inches) by the area of the swatch (36 square inches) = 50, or the equivalent of 50 swatches.

Since we know that one swatch requires 24 yards of yarn, multiply 50 swatches by 24 = 1,200 yards of yarn.

For a circular shawl, the area is a bit trickier to calculate, relying on first finding the radius of the circle and making a calculation using pi (π). Pi is a mathematical constant that is approximately equal to 3.14.

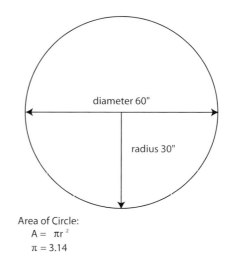

diameter 60"

radius 30"

Area of Circle:
A = πr^2
π = 3.14

Let's say you want a circle that is 60" wide. The width is the diameter, but for our equation we need the radius, which is just half of the diameter: 60 divided by 2 = 30" radius.

Let's use the same swatch as above: 6" x 6" = 36 sq in and 24 yards of yarn.

The full equation for area of a circle is,

Area = πr^2

This equation reads as "area equals pi r squared." R stands for the radius of the circle. "Squaring" a number means that you must multiply it by itself; for example, four squared (4^2) equals 4 x 4, or 16s.

Since we now know the radius of the circle, we can do the simple math. Below, *a* equals area of the circle:

$$a = \pi r^2$$
$$a = 3.14 \times (30 \text{ inches} \times 30 \text{ inches})$$
$$a = 3.14 \times 900 \text{ square inches}$$
$$a = 2{,}826 \text{ square inches}$$

Now that we know the full area of the circle, we can divide it by the area of our swatch to find out how much yarn is required.

2,826 square inches (total) ÷ 36 square inches (of the swatch) = the equivalent of 78.5 swatches.

And since we now know that one swatch equals 24 yards of yarn:

78.5 swatches x 24 yards = 1,884 yards of yarn to make a circular shawl.

For a triangular shawl, the area = ½ (base x height).

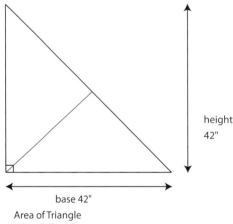

height
42"

base 42"
Area of Triangle
A = ½ (B x H)

Most triangular shawls, unless extra shaping is used, are right triangles. The base is one of the diagonal lines of the lower "V" of the shawl and the height is the other diagonal line of the lower "V" of the shawl. Note: In the illustration, notice the shawl is rotated to show the normal view of a right triangle.

For a 60" wide by 30" long shawl, the lower "V" edge will be 42" on each side of the point. We will use the same swatch as above: 6" x 6" = 36 square inches and 24 yards of yarn.

With *a* as the area of triangle,

$$a = \tfrac{1}{2} \text{ (base x height)}$$
$$a = \tfrac{1}{2} \text{ (42 inches x 42 inches)}$$
$$a = \tfrac{1}{2} \text{ (1,764 square inches)}$$
$$a = 882 \text{ square inches}$$

And now that we know the full area of the triangle, we can divide it by the area of our swatch to find out how much yarn is required.

882 square inches (total) ÷ 36 square inches (of the swatch) = the equivalent of 24.5 swatches.

And since we now know that one swatch equals 24 yards of yarn:

24.5 swatches x 24 yards = 588 yards of yarn to make a triangular shawl.

Skill levels for Knitting

Beginner   Projects for first-time knitters using basic knit and purl stitches. Minimal shaping.

Easy   Projects using basic stitches, repetitive stitch patterns, simple color changes, and simple shaping and finishing.

Intermediate   Projects with a variety of stitches, such as basic cables and lace, simple intarsia, double-pointed needles and knitting in the round needle techniques, mid-level shaping and finishing.

Experienced   Projects using advanced techniques and stitches, such as short rows, fair isle, more intricate intarsia, cables, lace patterns, and numerous color changes.

CHAPTER 2

ROMANTIC LACE

NINOTCHKA TANK

by Annie Modesitt

SKILL LEVEL
Intermediate

SIZE
To fit bust: 28 (32, 36, 40, 44, 48)" (71, [81, 91, 101.5, 112, 122]cm)

Directions are for smallest size, with larger sizes in parentheses.

FINISHED MEASUREMENTS
- Bust: 30 (34, 38, 42, 46, 50)" (76, [86, 96.5, 106.5, 117, 127]cm)
- Length: 16 (17, 18, 19, 20, 21)" (40.5 [43, 45.5, 48.5, 51, 53.5]cm)

MATERIALS

Yarn A
- 2 (3, 3, 3, 3, 3) skeins Silk Rhapsody by Artyarns (each approximately 3½ oz [100g], 260 yd [238m], 100% silk and 70% mohair, 30% silk), in color #RH245 Raspberry Pink (3) light, or 589 (653, 717, 781, 845, 909)yd/(537 [595.5, 654, 712.5, 770.5, 829]m) of worsted-weight yarn (4) medium

Yarn B
- 1 (2, 2, 2, 2, 2) balls Fixation by Cascade (each approximately 1¾ oz [50g], 100 yd [92m], 98.3% cotton, 1.7% elastic), in color #7219 Red (3) light, or 139 (155, 171, 185, 202, 215) yd/ (127 [141.5, 155, 168.5, 182.5, 196]m) of sportweight yarn (2) fine

Yarn C
- 1 (1, 1, 2, 2, 2) skeins Regal Silk 101 by Artyarns (each approximately 1¾ oz [50g], 163 yd [149m], 100% silk), in color #RS245 Raspberry Pink (3) light, or 199 (222, 242, 263, 285, 307) yd/(181.5 [200.5, 220.5, 242, 262, 280]m) of sportweight yarn (2) fine

Yarn D
- 1 (1, 1, 2, 2, 2) skeins Silk Mohair by Artyarns (each approximately 8.8 oz [25g], 230 yd [210m], 70% super kid mohair, 30% silk), in color #MS413 Pinks, or 280 (311, 341, 372, 402, 432) yd/(255.5 [283.5, 311, 339.5, 366.5, 394] m) of laceweight yarn (1) super fine

Yarn E
- 1 (1, 1, 1, 1, 1) skein Silk Rhapsody by Artyarns, in color #RI1113 Browns (4) medium, or 91 (101, 112, 131, 140, 150) yd/(83 [91, 100.5, 109.5, 118.5, 127.5]m) of worsted-weight yarn (4) medium
- Size 4 (3.5mm) circular needle, 24" (61cm) long
- Size 5 (3.75mm) circular needle, 24" (61cm) long, *or size needed to obtain gauge*
- Size 8 (5mm) circular needle, 24" (61cm) long
- Stitch markers
- Yarn needle
- ⅜" (9mm) elastic, cut to rib cage measurement plus 2" (5cm)
- Sewing needle and thread

GAUGE
24 stitches and 32 rows = 4" (10cm) in stockinette stitch using size 5 (3.75mm) needles. *To save time, take time to check your gauge.*

SPECIAL STITCHES
(see Glossary on page 162)

3-needle bind-off; I-cord bind-off; k2togR; k2, p2 rib; m1; provisional cast-on; pick up and knit; stockinette stitch; twisted cord; vdd (vertical double decrease); w&t (wrap & turn); join; yo

INSTRUCTIONS

BODICE

Using a provisional cast-on, with medium needle and yarn A, cast on 180 (204, 228, 252, 276, 300) stitches. Join, placing marker to note start of round.

Knit 2 rows.

Eyelet Round: *K2togR, yo, k2; repeat from * around all stitches.

Next Round: Purl.

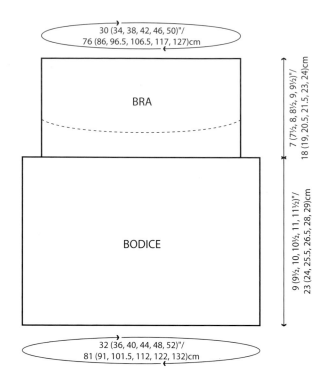

30 (34, 38, 42, 46, 50)"/
76 (86, 96.5, 106.5, 117, 127)cm

BRA

7 (7½, 8, 8½, 9, 9½)"/
18 (19, 20.5, 21.5, 23, 24)cm

BODICE

9 (9½, 10, 10½, 11, 11½)"/
23 (24, 25.5, 26.5, 28, 29)cm

32 (36, 40, 44, 48, 52)"/
81 (91, 101.5, 112, 122, 132)cm

Next Round: Knit.

Continue in stockinette stitch until piece measures 7 (7½, 8, 8½, 9, 9½)" (18 [19, 20.5, 21.5, 23, 24]cm) from cast-on. Do not bind off; set stitches aside.

SHELF BRA

With smallest needles and yarn B, cast on 168 (192, 216, 240, 264, 288) stitches.

Work back and forth in stockinette stitch for ½" (1.25cm), ending with a right-side row.

Next Row (WS): Knit, join stitches, and place marker to note start of round (this will mark the left side of the body).

Next Round (RS): *K2, p2; repeat from * around all stitches.

Continue in k2, p2 rib as established for 1" (2.5cm).

Next Round: *K15 (17, 19, 21, 23, 25), m1; repeat from * 6 times more for front, place second marker at side seam, knit to end of round (back)—180 (204, 228, 252, 276, 300) stitches.

Next Round (front short-row shaping): Knit to 2 stitches before second marker, w&t, work back to 2 stitches before first marker, w&t.

Next Round: Knit all stitches.

Repeat last 2 rounds until piece measures 5⅛ (5⅛, 6⅛, 5¼, 6¼, 7¾)" (13.1 [13.1, 15.7, 13.5, 16, 19.5]cm) from start of rib when measured across non-short-row (back) area.

Note: For larger cup sizes, you may want to work the entire front short-row shaping again in part or in its entirety.

JOINING BRA TO BODICE

Place pieces with right sides together and wrong sides facing out.

With medium needle and yarn E, join pieces with 3-needle bind-off.

Turn joined piece inside out so that bra is to the inside and stockinette stitch of Bodice is facing out. Steam-block join gently.

TOP EDGE TRIM

With medium needle and yarn E, pick up and knit 180 (204, 228, 252, 276, 300) stitches around top of work at join, knit 1 round, then bind off all stitches using I-cord bind-off.

PEPLUM

Slip provisional stitches onto circular needle; place marker to note center back.

Next Round: With largest needle and yarn C, *k15 (17, 19, 21, 23, 25) stitches, m1; repeat from * 12 times around all stitches—192 (216, 240, 264, 288, 312) stitches.

Next Round: Knit all stitches.

Next 10 Rounds: Work Rows 1 and 2 of Lace Chart 3 times, then change to yarn D and work Rows 3 and 4 of Lace Chart twice.

Repeat these 10 rounds until piece measures approximately 8 (8½, 9, 9½, 10, 10½)" (20.5 [21.5, 23, 24, 25.5, 26.5]cm), then change to yarn E and work Rows 1 and 2 of Lace Chart 3 more times.

Knit 1 round, purl 1 round.

Bind off all stitches loosely.

FINISHING

Steam-block piece through outer layer and bra.

With yarn B and a yarn needle, turn bottom (stockinette stitch section) of bra up and sew in place, creating a casing. Slip the elastic into the casing through the unjoined edge stitches from the first rows of the bra. Tack the ends of the elastic together using sewing needle and thread.

Try on the top to determine the length of the shoulder ties from the top edge of the tank to the top of the shoulder. With yarn E, make 2 twisted cord ties that measure twice this length. Tack in place on front and back of bodice.

With yarn E, make a twisted cord to measure around rib cage plus 8" (20.5cm). Draw this cord through the eyelets at the top of the lace section and arrange the cord so the ties hang down in the center front.

With yarn E, make a 10" (25.5cm) piece of I-cord and tie it into a bow. Tack this to the I-cord bind-off at the center front of the tank.

Lace Chart

−	−	−	−	−	−	−	−	4
								3
								2
O			⋀			O		1

8   5   1

☐ Knit 1

− Purl 1

O Yarn over

⋀ VDD

FERN AND WAVES SCARF

by Anne Lorenz-Panzer
of Arlene's World of Lace

SKILL LEVEL
Intermediate

SIZE
One size

FINISHED MEASUREMENTS
- Width: 12" (30.5cm)
- Total length: 70" (180cm)—including 3" (7.5cm) border for each side.

MATERIALS
- 1 skein Lace by Wollmeise (each approximately 10½ oz [300g], 1717yd [1570m], 100% wool superwash), in color Pesto **1** super fine
- Size 4 (3.5mm) straight needles, *or size needed to obtain gauge*
- Yarn needle

GAUGE
22¾ stitches and 30 rows = 4" (10cm) in pattern stitch. *Exact gauge is not important for this project.*

SPECIAL STITCHES
(see Glossary on page 162)
garter stitch; k2tog; kfb; sl2-k1-p2sso; sl2-k2tog-p2sso; sl1-k2tog-psso; yo

NOTES
1. Wrong-side rows are not shown in chart. Always purl wrong-side rows.
2. Selvedge stitches are included in chart.

INSTRUCTIONS

SCARF
Cast on 68 stitches loosely.

Knit 3 rows garter stitch.

Row 1 (RS): Begin and work Row 1 of Chart 1 (beginning), repeating 16-stitch pattern 4 times.

Row 2 and all wrong-side rows: Purl.

Rows 3–12: Work Rows 3–12 of Chart 1.

Next, begin Chart 2 (center) and work Rows 13–24, maintaining 4 repeats of the 16-stitch pattern.

Repeat Rows 13–24 until the work measures approximately 63" (160cm) from beginning without being stretched, ending with Row 24 of chart pattern (Row 24 is the last row of the row repeat and will be purled).

Now, work Rows 1–3 of Chart 3 (ending). Knit the last wrong-side row (Row 4) of Chart 3.

Knit 2 more rows of garter stitch.

Bind off all stitches loosely and at the same tension as the cast-on.

Border
With scarf right side facing you, pick up and knit 69 stitches along bound-off side of the scarf. Purl 1 wrong-side row and all subsequent wrong-side rows.

Row 1 (RS): K3, *[kfb] twice, k3; repeat from *, ending last repeat with k4—95 stitches.

Row 3 (RS): K4, *[kfb] twice, k5; repeat from * to end—121 stitches.

Row 5 (RS): K5, *[kfb] twice, k7; repeat from *, ending last repeat with k6—147 stitches.

Row 7 (RS): K6, *[kfb] twice, k9; repeat from *, ending last repeat with k7—173 stitches.

Row 9 (RS): K7, *[kfb] twice, k11; repeat from *, ending last repeat with k8—199 stitches.

Row 11 (RS): K8, *[kfb] twice, k13; repeat from *, ending last repeat with k9—225 stitches.

Row 13 (RS): K9, *[kfb] twice, k15, repeat from *, ending last repeat with k10—251 stitches

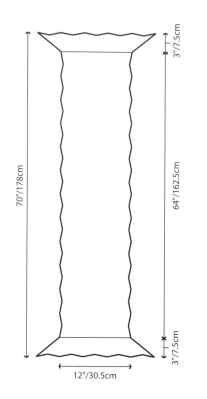

70"/178cm

64"/162.5cm

3"/7.5cm

3"/7.5cm

12"/30.5cm

Final Lace Section

Row 15 (RS): K1, *yo, sl2-k1-p2sso*; repeat from * to * 6 times, yo, sl2-k2tog-p2sso, **[yo, sl2-k1-p2sso] 5 times, yo, sl2-k2tog-p2sso** repeat from ** to ** 11 times, *yo, sl2-k1-p2sso*; repeat from * to * 6 times, end with yo, k1—161 stitches.

Row 16 (WS): Knit.

Row 17: K3, yo, k1, *yo, sl1-k2tog-psso, yo, k1*; repeat from * to * 39 times, end with k1—162 stitches.

Row 18 (WS): Purl.

Work a very loose decrease bind-off as follows:

*K2tog, slip new stitch back onto left needle without twisting; repeat from * to end.

Work a second border along the cast-on side of the scarf.

FINISHING

To block scarf, soak in lukewarm water until the fabric is fully saturated; carefully roll in a towel to squeeze out excess water.

Stretch and pin out scarf to the dimensions specified. Do not pin out the border exactly, just arrange it slightly ruffled and only use pins to block at the tip of each spike. Allow to dry completely before removing the pins. Weave in ends.

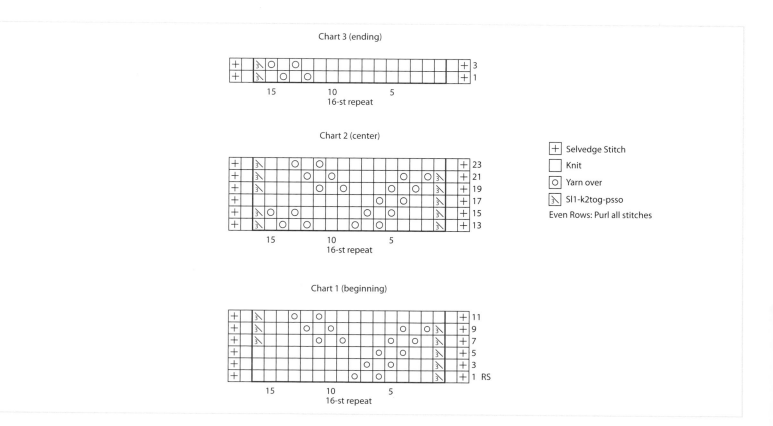

Chart 3 (ending)

Chart 2 (center)

Chart 1 (beginning)

+ Selvedge Stitch

□ Knit

○ Yarn over

Sl1-k2tog-psso

Even Rows: Purl all stitches

A STREETCAR NAMED DESIRE CARDIGAN

by Annie Modesitt

SKILL LEVEL
Intermediate

SIZE
To fit bust: 28 (32, 36, 40, 44, 50)" (71 [81, 91, 101.5, 112, 127]cm)

Directions are for smallest size, with larger sizes in parentheses.

FINISHED MEASUREMENTS
- Bust: 30¼ (37¾, 37¾, 45¼, 45¼, 52¾)" (77 [96, 96, 115, 115, 134]cm)
- Length: 22¾ (23½, 24¼, 25½, 26, 26¾)" (58 [59.5, 61.5, 65, 66, 68]cm)

MATERIALS
- 11 skeins Royal Bamboo by Plymouth Yarns (each approximately 1¾ oz [50g], 93 yd [85m], 100% bamboo), in color #04 Pink (4) medium, or 722 (783, 846, 917, 976, 1063) yd (658 [714, 771, 836, 899, 970]m) worsted-weight yarn (4) medium
- Size 6 (4mm) circular needle, at least 24" (61cm) long
- Size 7 (4.5mm) circular needle, at least 24" (61cm) long, *or size needed to obtain gauge*
- Yarn needle
- Stitch holders
- Stitch markers

GAUGE
18 stitches and 24 rows = 4" (10cm) over Chart B using size 7 (4.5mm) needle. *To save time, take time to check your gauge.*

SPECIAL STITCHES
(see Glossary on page 162)

I-bobble; I-cord; k2togL; k2togR; pick up and knit; shirr (gather); slip stitch (knit); slip stitch (crochet); vdd; yo

INSTRUCTIONS

BODY

With smaller needle, cast on 137 (171, 171, 205, 205, 239) stitches.

Knit 2 rows.

Work Rows 1–6 of Chart A once.

Work Rows 1–4 of Chart C once, decreasing 1 stitch on last row of chart—136 (170, 170, 204, 204, 238) stitches.

Next Row (RS): Change to larger needles and work Chart B across all stitches, placing a marker after each repeat.

Work Chart B as established to Row 24, then work 4 rows of Chart C.

Next Row (RS): Work Chart D across all stitches, placing a marker after each repeat.

Continue working Chart D until piece measures 12¾ (12¾, 13½, 14, 14¾, 14¾)" (32.5 [32.5, 34.5, 35.5, 37.5, 37.5]cm) from eyelet row—Row 3 of Chart A.

Divide Fronts and Back

Next Row (RS): Continuing in Chart D as established, work 34 (42, 42, 51, 51, 59) stitches for right front, put these stitches on a holder. Work across 68 (86, 86, 102, 102, 120) stitches for Back. Put remaining 34 (42, 42, 51, 51, 59) stitches for left front on holder.

Back Armhole Shaping

Working only with Back stitches, work armhole shaping as follows:

Bind off 2 (2, 2, 4, 4, 4) stitches at beginning of next 2 rows, then bind off 2 (2, 2, 2, 2, 3) stitches at beginning of next 4 rows—56 (74, 74, 86, 86, 100) stitches remaining.

Continue working Chart D as established across remaining Back stitches until armhole measures 9 (9½, 9½, 10, 10, 10½)" (23 [24, 24, 25.5, 25.5, 26.5]cm.) End with a wrong-side row.

Shoulder Shaping

Bind off 5 (5, 5, 8, 7, 9) stitches at beginning of next 2 rows, then bind off 4 (8, 8, 10, 10, 12) stitches at beginning of next 4 rows. Bind off remaining 30 (32, 32, 30, 32, 34) stitches for back neck.

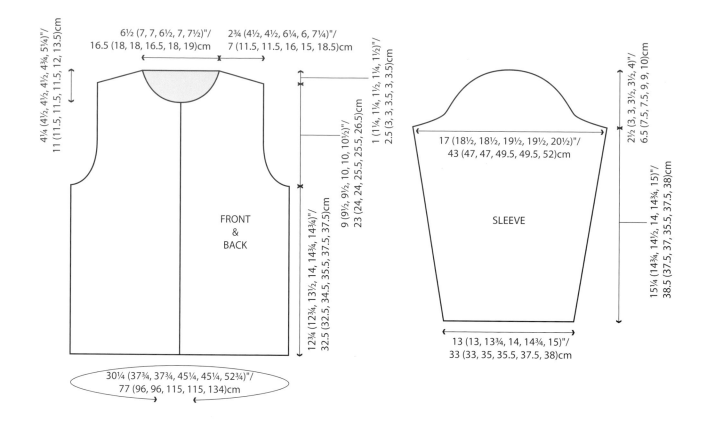

Front Armhole Shaping

Working on 34 (42, 42, 51, 51, 59) stitches for Front, and using two skeins of yarn, work both sides at once as follows:

Bind off 2 (2, 2, 4, 4, 4) stitches at armhole edge once, then bind off 2 (2, 2, 2, 2, 3) stitches at armhole edge twice—28 (36, 36, 43, 43, 49) stitches remain on each Front.

Continue working Chart D as established across remaining Front stitches until armhole measures 5¾ (6⅛, 6⅛, 7, 6½, 6⅞)" (14.5 [15.5, 15.5, 18, 16.5, 17.5]cm).

Neck Shaping

At each neck edge, working both Fronts at the same time, bind off 6 (6, 6, 6, 7, 7) stitches once, then bind off 1 (1, 1, 1, 1, 1) stitches at neck edge every row 3 times, then bind off 2 (2, 2, 2, 2, 2) stitches at neck edge every other row twice, then bind off 1 (1, 1, 1, 1, 1) stitches at neck edge every fourth row twice—13 (21, 21, 28, 27, 33) stitches remain in each shoulder.

Continue working Chart D as established across remaining stitches until armhole measures 9 (9½, 9½, 10, 10, 10½)" (23 [24, 24, 25.5, 25.5, 26.5]cm). End with a wrong-side row.

Shape Shoulders

Bind off 5 (5, 5, 8, 7, 9) stitches at armhole edge once, then bind off 4 (8, 8, 10, 10, 12) stitches at armhole edge twice.

SLEEVES (MAKE 2)

With smaller needle, cast on 49 (53, 53, 57, 57, 61) stitches.

Knit 2 rows.

Work Rows 1–6 of Chart A once.

Work Rows 1–4 of Chart C once, decrease 1 (0, 0, 0, 0, increase 4) stitches in last row of chart—48 (53, 53, 57, 57, 65) stitches.

Next Row (RS): Change to larger needle, and starting with stitch 11 (17, 17, 15, 15, 11) of Row 1 of Chart D, work across all stitches, placing a marker after each repeat of chart and ending with stitch 7 (1, 1, 3, 3, 7). Increase 1 stitch at each end every 6 rows 14 (15, 15, 15, 15, 13) times—76 (83, 83, 87, 87, 91) stitches.

Work even until Sleeve measures 13 (13, 13¾, 14, 14¾, 15)" (33 [33, 35, 35.5, 37.5, 38]cm from eyelet row. End with a wrong-side row.

Cap Shaping

Bind off 7 (7, 7, 8, 8, 8) stitches at beginning of next 6 rows, then bind off 3 (4, 4, 3, 3, 3) stitches at beginning of next 4 rows, then bind off 2 (3, 2, 3, 2, 3) stitches at beginning of next 2 (2, 4, 4, 4, 4) rows.

Bind off remaining 18 (19, 17, 15, 19, 19) stitches.

FINISHING

Block all pieces. Sew Sleeves into armholes, then sew underarm and side seams. If the shoulder droops a little down the arm, turn the sweater inside out and work a row of slip stitch crochet along the shoulder seams to tighten them up and slightly shirr (gather) the seam. Turn up hem and sleeve cuffs and stitch the cast-on edge to the wrong side.

Neck

With smaller needle, pick up and knit 65 (65, 69, 69, 73, 73) stitches around neck opening.

Knit 2 rows.

Work Rows 1–6 of Chart A once.

Bind off all stitches loosely. Sew bound-off edge to wrong side of neck opening where stitches were picked up.

Plackets

With smaller needle (circular), pick up and knit 70 (70, 74, 74, 79, 79) stitches up right front edge, including along the edge of neck binding.

Knit 2 rows.

Work Rows 1–6 of Chart A once.

Bind off all stitches loosely. Sew bound-off edge to wrong side of right front where stitches were picked up.

Repeat for left front placket.

Belt

Create a 60" (152.5cm) piece of I-cord (or longer, if desired) and thread through the series of eyelet holes that falls nearest your natural waist. Tie loosely like a negligee to wear.

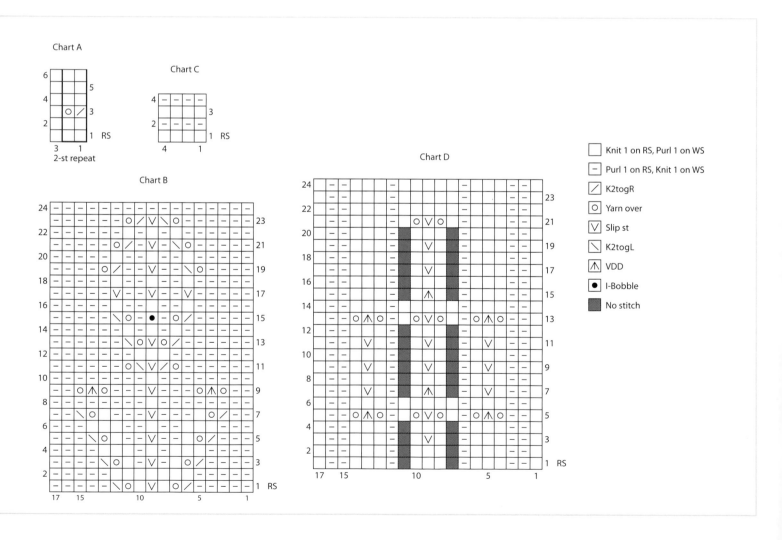

REBECCA TANK

by Melissa Matthay

SKILL LEVEL
Experienced

SIZE
S (M, L, XL)

Directions are for smallest size, with larger sizes in parentheses.

FINISHED MEASUREMENTS
- Bust: 37 (40, 43, 46)" (94 [101.5, 109, 117]cm)
- Length: 22½ (24, 25½, 26)" (57 [61, 65, 66]cm)

MATERIALS
- 5 (6, 7, 8) skeins Scarlett by GGH (each approximately 1¾ oz [50g], 115 yd [105m], 100% Egyptian cotton), in color #35 Turquoise (3) light
- Size 6 (4mm) straight needles, *or size needed to obtain gauge*
- Size 10 (6mm) straight and circular needles, *or size needed to obtain gauge*
- Yarn needle

GAUGE
19 stitches and 24 rows = 4" (10cm) in stockinette stitch using size 6 (4mm) needles and 1 strand of yarn.

15 stitches and 18 rows = 4" (10cm) over stockinette stitch using size 10 (6mm) needles and 2 strands of yarn.

To save time, take time to check your gauge.

SPECIAL STITCHES
(see Glossary on page 162)

k2tog; pick up and knit; stockinette stitch; sl1-k1-psso; yo

SPECIAL PATTERN
Lattice-Lace Pattern (multiple of 13 stitches + 2)

Row 1: K1, *k2, sl1-k1-psso, k4, k2tog, k2, yo, k1, yo; repeat from * to last stitch, k1.

Row 2 and all even rows: Purl.

Row 3: K1, *yo, k2, sl1-k1-psso, k2, k2tog, k2, yo, k3; repeat from * to last stitch, k1.

Row 5: K1, *k1, yo, k2, sl1-k1-psso, k2tog, k2, yo, k4; repeat from * to last stitch, k1.

Row 7: K1, *yo, k1, yo, k2, sl1-k1-psso, k4, k2tog, k2; repeat from * to last stitch, k1.

Row 9: K1, *k3, yo, k2, sl1-k1-psso, k2, k2tog, k2, yo; repeat from * to last stitch, k1.

Row 11: K1, *k4, yo, k2, sl1-k1-psso, k2tog, k2, yo, k1; repeat from * to last stitch, k1.

Repeat Rows 1–12 for pattern.

INSTRUCTIONS

FRONT AND BACK

With size 6 needles, cast on 93 (106, 106, 119) stitches. Begin and work in lace pattern until piece measures 12 (13, 14, 14)" (30.5 [33, 35.5, 35.5]cm) from beginning, ending with wrong-side row. Change to size 10 needles and 2 strands of yarn. Decrease 25 (32, 26, 33) stitches evenly across row—68 (74, 80, 86) stitches. Continue in stockinette stitch for 1" (2.5cm), then on next right-side row k1, (k2tog, yo) to end, k1. Work until piece measures 15 (16, 17, 17)" (38 [40.5, 43, 43]cm).

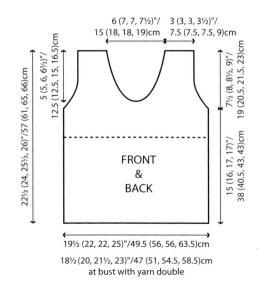

6 (7, 7, 7½)"/ 15 (18, 18, 19)cm   3 (3, 3, 3½)"/ 7.5 (7.5, 7.5, 9)cm

5 (5, 6, 6½)"/ 12.5 (12.5, 15, 16.5)cm

22½ (24, 25½, 26)"/57 (61, 65, 66)cm

7½ (8, 8½, 9)"/ 19 (20.5, 21.5, 23)cm

15 (16, 17, 17)"/ 38 (40.5, 43, 43)cm

FRONT & BACK

19½ (22, 22, 25)"/49.5 (56, 56, 63.5)cm

18½ (20, 21½, 23)"/47 (51, 54.5, 58.5)cm at bust with yarn double

Shape Armhole

Bind off 3 stitches at beginning of next 2 rows, then decrease 1 stitch at each edge every other row 4 (5, 6, 7) times.

Shape Neck

When piece measures 17 (18, 19, 19)" (43 [45.5, 48.5, 48.5]cm), work 16 (19, 21, 22) stitches. Join a second ball of yarn and bind off center 18 (20, 20, 22) stitches, work to end. Working both sides at once, bind off at beginning of each neck edge 2 stitches 1 (1, 1, 2) times, then decrease 1 stitch every other row 3 (4, 4, 4) times. Work even on remaining 11 (13, 14, 14) stitches until armhole measures 7½ (8, 8½, 9)" (19 [20.5, 21.5, 23]cm). Bind off.

FINISHING

Sew shoulder and side seams. Weave in drawstring ribbon.

Neckband

With size 10 circular needle and 2 strands of yarn, pick up and knit 110 (114, 118, 122) stitches around neck edge. Join and knit 1 row. Bind off all stitches.

Armbands

With right side facing, pick up 56 (62, 64, 66) stitches evenly around armhole and knit 1 row. Bind off.

CHARADE TOP

by Annie Modesitt

SKILL LEVEL
Experienced

SIZE
To fit bust: 30 (40, 50)" (76 [101.5, 127]cm)

Directions are for smallest size, with larger sizes in parentheses.

FINISHED MEASUREMENTS
- Bust (wrapped with ease): 34 (44, 54)" (86 [112, 137]cm)
- Hem (unwrapped): 91¼ (121¼, 141¼)" (231.8 [308, 384.2]cm)
- Length: 30½ (31½, 32½)" (77.5 [80, 82.5]cm)

MATERIALS
- 7 (9, 10) balls Zen by Berroco (each approximately 1¾ oz [50g], 111 yd [101m], 60% nylon, 40% cotton), in color #8241 Shiseido Blue (4) medium, or 758 (826, 960) yd (684 [753.5, 875.5]m) worsted-weight ribbon yarn (4) medium
- Size 6 (4mm) circular needle, 36" (91cm) long
- Size 8 (5mm) circular needle, 36" (91cm) long, *or size needed to obtain gauge*
- Size G/6 (4mm) crochet hook
- Yarn needle
- Stitch holders
- Stitch markers, including two markers in contrasting colors

GAUGE
16 stitches and 26 rows = 4" (10cm) over Lattice Lace Pattern (Chart A) using size 8 (5mm) needle.
Note: It is essential to work a rather large swatch containing at least two repeats of the 15-stitch Lattice Lace Pattern in Chart A. *To save time, take time to check your gauge.*

SPECIAL STITCHES
(see Glossary on page 162)
3-needle bind-off; k2togL; k2togR; k3togL; k3togR; long-tail cast-on; p2togl; p3tog; p2tog tbl; yo

INSTRUCTIONS

BODY
With larger needle and using the long-tail cast-on method, cast on 365 (485, 605) stitches.

Note: Use one strand from each of two separate balls of yarn to make this easier. Cut one strand of yarn at the end of cast-on.

Knit 1 row.

Next Row (RS): K1, *k2togR, yo; repeat from * to end of row, end k2.

Next Row (WS): Knit.

Next Row (RS): Work Row 1 of Chart B, place contrasting marker, k2, (work Row 1 of Chart A, place marker) 9 (12, 15) times, place a double marker to note right side of garment, (work Row 1 of Chart A, place marker) 4 (6, 8) times, place a double marker to note left side of garment, (work Row 1 of Chart A, place marker) 9 (12, 15) times, k3, place contrasting marker, work Row 1 of Chart C.

Next Row (WS): Work in charts as established.

Next Row (RS): Work Chart B as established, slip contrasting marker, k2togL (k3togL, k3togL), work in Lattice Lace Chart A as established, slipping side markers as you pass them, to 2 stitches before contrasting marker*, k2togR, sm, work Chart C as established.

Next Row (WS): Work Chart C as established, p2tog (p3tog, p3tog), purl to 2 stitches before next contrasting marker, slipping side markers as you pass them. P2tog tbl, slip contrasting marker, work Chart B as established.

Repeat last 2 rows, decreasing 1 (2, 2) stitches after first contrasting marker and decreasing 1 before second contrasting marker every row until piece measures 19½ (20, 20½)"/(49.5 [51, 52]cm) from cast-on edge. End with a wrong-side row.

Note: When working decreases at contrasting marker every right-side row, be sure to omit incomplete yo/k2tog pairings as you work. Only work a yo if it has a partner k2tog and vice versa. Be prepared to move markers when necessary to work decreases affecting stitches on either side of marker.

Divide for Armholes

Next Row (RS): Work as established and continue with decreasing at contrasting marker to double marker. Slip stitches just worked (Right Front) onto holder to work later. Continue with Back stitches and work in pattern as established to next double marker. Join second ball of yarn and work remaining stitches in row, decreasing at contrasting marker and working

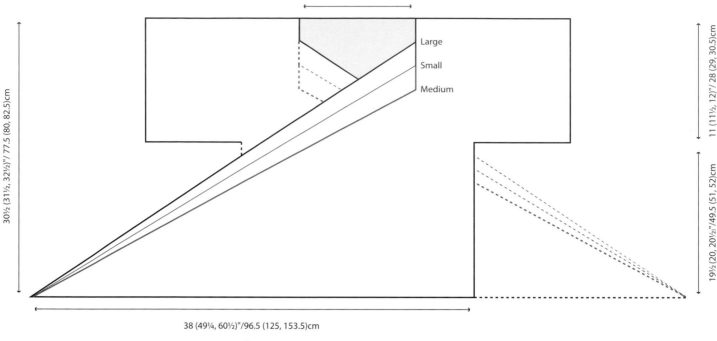

5¾ (6, 6½)"/14.5 (15, 16.5)cm

Large

Small

Medium

30½ (31½, 32½)"/ 77.5 (80, 82.5)cm

11 (11½, 12)"/ 28 (29, 30.5)cm

19½ (20, 20½)"/49.5 (51, 52)cm

38 (49¼, 60½)"/96.5 (125, 153.5)cm

17½ (22, 27½)"/44.5 (56, 70)cm

edge stitches as established. Slip this last group of stitches (Left Front) onto holder to work later.

BACK

Next Row (WS): Returning to Back stitches, cast on 30 sleeve stitches and work across 60 (90, 120) Back stitches in charted pattern as established, then cast on 30 sleeve stitches—120 (150, 180) stitches.

Next Row (RS): Knit new cast-on stitches, work Back stitches in pattern as established, continue in pattern as established across last newly cast-on 30 stitches for sleeve.

Next Row (WS): Work across new cast-on stitches in pattern as established, work across Back, then continue on to left sleeve cast-on stitches, incorporating new stitches into pattern as established across Back.

Work even, incorporating new stitches into pattern as established and with no shaping until piece measures 11 (11½, 12)" (28 [29, 30.5]cm) from armhole divide.

End with a right-side row and slip stitches onto holder to work 3-needle bind-off at shoulders later.

FRONTS

Working both Fronts at the same time using separate balls of yarn, add stitches for left and right sleeves as follows:

Return to Front stitches and cast on 30 stitches at each armhole edge.

Left Front

Next Row (RS): Work across all stitches, decrease at neck edge and working in pattern as established.

Next Row (WS): Work to armhole edge, cast on 30 stitches.

Next Row (RS): Work in stockinette stitch across cast-on stitches, work across remaining stitches in pattern as established, decreasing at neck edge.

Next Row (WS): Work to cast-on stitches, work across new left sleeve stitches in pattern as established.

Continue working sleeve in pattern as established for Left Front, decreasing at neck edge as established.

Right Front

Next Row (RS): Decrease at neck edge as established and work across all stitches in pattern as established, then cast on 30 stitches.

Next Row (WS): Work in pattern as established across all stitches to neck edge.

Next Row (RS): Decrease at neck edge as established and work across all stitches, incorporating sleeve stitches into pattern as established.

Next Row (WS): Work in pattern as established to neck edge.

Continue working sleeve in pattern as established for Right and Left Fronts, decreasing at neck edges as established until 58 (59, 60) stitches remain at Right Front, and 59 (60, 61) stitches remain at Left Front. Work one more row, decreasing 1 stitch at Left Front—58 (59, 60) stitches remain for each Front. Work even until Front measures same as Back, ending with a right-side row.

JOINING

Slip lace neck edge stitches to holder.

Starting at sleeve edges, with right sides together, join Fronts to Back using 3-needle bind-off.

Bind off 26 (28, 30) at center Back.

Return to Front lace edge and continue working in patterns as established until both sides reach center Back (end right lace neck edge with a right-side row and left lace neck edge with a wrong-side row). With right sides together, join with a 3-needle bind-off. Sew bottom edge of lace to Back neck opening

FINISHING

Weave in ends. Steam-block.

Wear garment by tying long ends in front or pulling them around the back and tying them, ballet style.

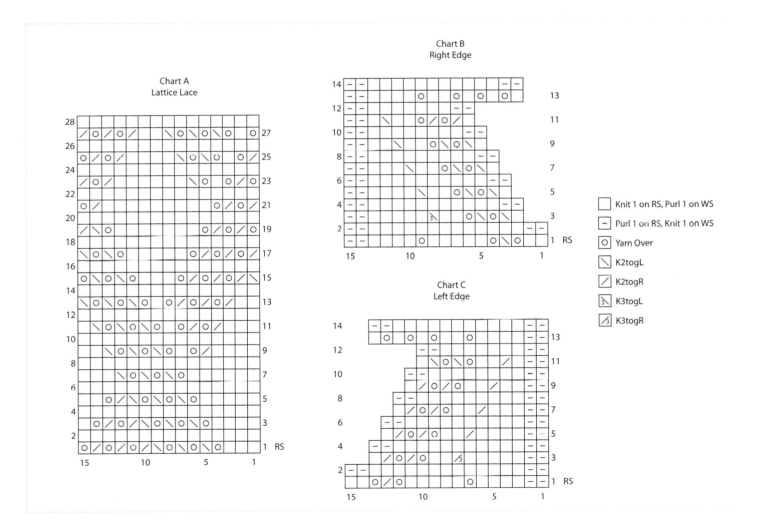

KRISTINA SHELL

by Melissa Matthay

SKILL LEVEL
Experienced

SIZE
S (M, L, XL)

Directions are for smallest size, with larger sizes in parentheses.

FINISHED MEASUREMENTS
- Bust: 34 (39, 44, 50)" (86 [99, 112, 127]cm)
- Length: 20½ (22, 22½, 24)" (52 [56, 57, 61]cm)

MATERIALS
- 9 (10, 13) balls Filatura Di Crosa Cashmere by Takhi Stacy Charles (each approximately 1¾ oz [50g], 154 yd [140m] 100% cashmere), in color #06 Ecru (ⓐ) light
- Size 6 (4mm) needles, *or size needed to obtain gauge*
- Size F/5 (3.75mm) crochet hook
- Yarn needle

GAUGE
19 stitches and 24 rows = 4" (10cm) in stockinette stitch. *To save time, take time to check your gauge.*

SPECIAL STITCHES
(see Glossary on page 162)

bind off loosely; k2tog; shrimp stitch; stockinette stitch; sl1-k1-psso; yo

SPECIAL PATTERN
Lattice-Lace Pattern (multiple of 13 stitches + 2)

Row 1: K1, *k2, sl1-k1-psso, k4, k2tog, k2, yo, k1, yo; repeat from * to last stitch, k1.

Row 2 and all even rows: Purl.

Row 3: K1, *yo, k2, sl1-k1-psso, k2, k2tog, k2, yo, k3; repeat from * to last stitch, k1.

Row 5: K1, *k1, yo, k2, sl1-k1-psso, k2tog, k2, yo, k4; repeat from * to last stitch, k1.

Row 7: K1, *yo, k1, yo, k2, sl1-k1-psso, k4, k2tog, k2; repeat from * to last stitch, k1.

Row 9: K1, *k3, yo, k2, sl1-k1-psso, k2, k2tog, k2, yo; repeat from * to last stitch, k1.

Row 11: K1, *k4, yo, k2, sl1-k1-psso, k2tog, k2, yo, k1; repeat from * to last stitch, k1.

Repeat Rows 1–12 for pattern.

INSTRUCTIONS

BACK
Cast on 80 (93, 106, 119) stitches. Begin and work in Lattice-Lace Pattern until piece measures 15 (16, 17, 17)" (38 [40.5, 43, 43]cm).

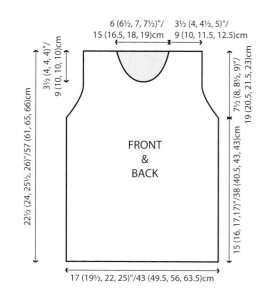

6 (6½, 7, 7½)"/   3½ (4, 4½, 5)"/
15 (16.5, 18, 19)cm   9 (10, 11.5, 12.5)cm

3½ (4, 4, 4)"/
9 (10, 10, 10)cm

7½ (8, 8½, 9)"/
19 (20.5, 21.5, 23)cm

22½ (24, 25½, 26)"/57 (61, 65, 66)cm

FRONT & BACK

15 (16, 17,17)"/38 (40.5, 43, 43)cm

17 (19½, 22, 25)"/43 (49.5, 56, 63.5)cm

Shape Armhole

Bind off 8 stitches at beginning of next 2 rows, then decrease 1 stitch at each edge every other row 3 (5, 7, 9) times—58 (67, 76, 85) stitches. Continue and work even in pattern until piece measures 22½ (24, 24, 26)" (57 [61, 61, 66]cm). Bind off loosely.

FRONT

Work the same as Back until piece measures 19½ (21, 21, 23)" (49.5 [53.5, 53.5, 58.5]cm).

Shape Neck

Work 21 (24, 23, 31) stitches. Join a second ball of yarn and bind off center 16 (19, 20, 23) stitches; work to end of row. Working both sides at once, decrease 1 stitch at neck edge every other row 5 (6, 5, 7) times—16 (18, 18, 24) remaining stitches for each shoulder. Work even in pattern until piece measures same as Back. Bind off loosely.

FINISHING

Sew shoulder and side seams.

Neckband and Armhole Edging

With crochet hook, work shrimp stitch around the neck and armholes.

A DAY IN VENICE STOLE

by Anne Lorenz-Panzer
of Arlene's World of Lace

SKILL LEVEL
Intermediate

SIZE
One size

FINISHED MEASUREMENTS
- Width: 28" (71cm)
- Length: 75½" (192cm)
- Measurements include the 2½" (6.5cm) edging

MATERIALS
- 3 skeins Lace Baby Merino by Malabrigo (each approximately 1¾ oz [50g], 470 yd [430m], 100% baby merino wool), in color Burgundy (2) fine
- Size 7 (4.5mm) circular needle, 48" (122cm) long, *or size needed to obtain gauge*
- Stitch marker (optional)
- Yarn needle

GAUGE
21 stitches and 26 rows = 4" (10cm) in lace pattern.
To save time, take time to check your gauge.

SPECIAL STITCHES
(see Glossary on page 162)
bind off loosely; m1 (eyelet); yo

INSTRUCTIONS

CENTER OF STOLE

Cast on 93 stitches.

Set-Up Row (WS): Purl.

Row 1 (RS): K1, *k4, k2tog, yo; repeat from * 15 times, end k2.

Row 2: P2, *yo, p1, p2tog, p3; repeat from * 15 times, end p1.

Row 3: K1, *k2, k2tog, k2, yo; repeat from * 15 times, end k2.

Row 4: P2, *yo, p3, p2tog, p1; repeat from *15 times, end p1.

Row 5: K1, *k2tog, k4, yo; repeat from * 15 times, end k2.

Row 6: P3, *p4, yo, p2tog; repeat from * 15 times.

Row 7: K1, *k1, yo, k3, k2tog; repeat from * 15 times, end k2.

Row 8: P2, *p2tog, p2, yo, p2; repeat from * 15 times, end p1.

Row 9: K1, *k3, yo, k1, k2tog; repeat from * 15 times, end k2.

Row 10: P2, *p2tog, yo, p4; repeat from * 15 times, end p1.

Work Rows 1–10 for a total of 38 times.

Bind off loosely on the following right-side row.

EDGING

Note: There are 380 rows; skip every 4th stitch when you pick up stitches for edges 1 and 3.

Edge 1: Start at stitch 3 and pick up 290 stitches.

Corner 1: Pick up 6 stitches from the 3 corner stitches (3 stitches increased).

Edge 2: Pick up 94 stitches evenly.

Corner 2: Pick up 6 stitches from the 3 corner stitches (3 stitches increased).

Edge 3: Pick up 290 stitches evenly.

Corner 3: Pick up 6 stitches from the 3 corner stitches (3 stitches increased).

Edge 4: Pick up 94 stitches evenly.

Corner 4: Pick up 6 stitches from the 3 corner stitches (3 stitches increased)—792 stitches.

Place stitch marker (optional) to mark beginning of round.

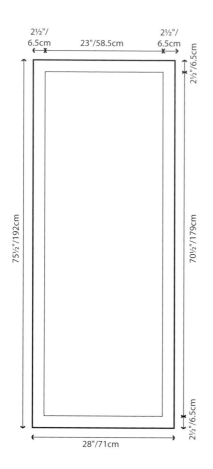

Round 6: *P2, k4; repeat from * to end of round.

Round 7: *P2, k4; repeat from * to end of round.

Round 8: *P2, k4, m1 (eyelet); repeat from * to end of round—1,386 stitches.

Round 9: *P2, k5; repeat from * to end of round.

Round 10: *P2, k5; repeat from * to end of round.

Round 11: *P2, k5, m1; repeat from * to end of round—1,584 stitches.

Round 12: *P2, k6; repeat from * to end of round.

Round 13: *P2, k6; repeat from * to end of round.

Round 14: *P2, k6, m1; repeat from * to end of round—1,782 stitches.

Round 15 (bind off): *P2, k7; repeat from * to end of round AND AT THE SAME TIME bind off very loosely in pattern.

FINISHING

Weave in all ends.

To block stole, soak in lukewarm water until the fabric is fully saturated; roll in a towel to squeeze out excess water carefully.

Stretch out and pin stole to the dimensions specified. Block only the center piece, not the edging. Allow the stole to dry completely before unpinning.

Round 1

Edge 1: Starting at stitch 3, *p2, k2; repeat from * to end of edge, p2.

Corner 1: K2, p2, k2.

Edge 2: *P2, k2; repeat from * to end of edge, p2.

Corner 2: K2, p2, k2.

Edge 3: *P2, k2; repeat from * to end of edge, p2.

Corner 3: K2, p2, k2.

Edge 4: *P2, k2; repeat from * to end of edge, p2.

Corner 4: K2, p2, k2.

Round 2: *P2, k2, m1 (eyelet); repeat from * to end of round—990 stitches.

Round 3: *P2, k3; repeat from * to end of round.

Round 4: *P2, k3; repeat from * to end of round.

Round 5: *P2, k3, m1 (eyelet); repeat from * to end of round—1,188 stitches.

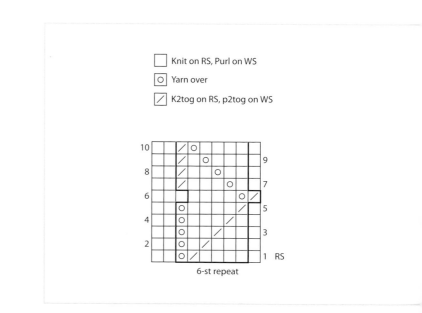

CASABLANCA CORSET

by Annie Modesitt

SKILL LEVEL
Intermediate

SIZE
To fit bust: 28 (40, 52)" (71 [101.5, 132]cm)
Directions are for smallest size, with larger sizes in parentheses.

FINISHED MEASUREMENTS
- Neck Opening: approximately 28 (40, 52)" (71 [101.5, 132]cm); exact size determined by tension of crochet edging
- Bust: 30 (42, 54)" (76 [106.5, 137]cm)
- Length: 22¾ (23¾, 24¾)" (58 [60, 63]cm)

MATERIALS
- 7 (9, 11) balls Zodiac by Karabella (each approximately 1¾ oz [50g], 98 yd [90m], 100% mercerized cotton), in color #413 Sage Green (④) medium
- Size 5 (3.75mm) circular needle, one at least 24" (61cm) long and one 12" (30.5cm) long, *or size needed to obtain gauge*
- Size 6 (4mm) circular needle, 12" (30.5cm) long
- Size 7 (4.5mm) circular needles, one at least 24" (61cm) long and one 12" (30.5cm) long
- Stitch markers
- Waste yarn
- Safety pin
- Size F/5 (3.75mm) crochet hook
- Yarn needle

GAUGE
20 stitches and 24 rows = 4" (10cm) in rib (slightly stretched) using size 5 (3.75mm) needle. *To save time, take time to check your gauge.*

SPECIAL STITCHES
(see Glossary on page 162)

bind off loosely; join; k2togL; k2togR; m1; pick up and knit; single crochet; slip stitch (crochet); slip stitch (knit); vdd; w&t; waste yarn; yo

INSTRUCTIONS

NECKLINE
With smallest 24" (61cm) needle, cast on 150 (210, 270) stitches.

Join for round, making sure not to twist stitches on needle.

Knit 1 round.

Purl 1 round.

Next Round: Work Row 1 of Chart A (Scalloped Edge) around all stitches 10 (14, 18) times. Place a contrasting marker to note start of round.

Next Round: Work Row 2 of Chart A around all stitches.

Repeat last 2 rounds 2 more times—6 rounds of Chart A.

Next 7 Rounds: Change to largest 24" (61cm) needle and work Rows 1–7 of Chart B (Lace Panel Corset Edge) around all stitches.

ARMHOLES
Next Round: Working Row 8 of Chart B, create armhole placement as follows:

K9 (23, 30) stitches. With a piece of waste yarn, k28 (29, 30) stitches (right armhole). Slip these waste yarn–worked stitches back to left-hand needle and work them again with the sweater yarn.

K46 (76, 105) stitches (Back). With a piece of waste yarn, k28 (29, 30) stitches (left armhole). Slip these waste yarn–worked stitches back to left-hand needle and work them again with the sweater yarn. K9 (23, 30) stitches. Place marker, k30 (30, 45) stitches.

You now have 30 (30, 45) stitches in the center front panel between the markers and 120 (180, 225) stitches outside of the markers.

BODY
Next Round: Work Chart D (Rib) 8 (12, 15) times around corset sides and back, then work Chart C (Lace Panel) 2 (2, 3) times across center front stitches between markers.

Continue working charts as established until piece measures 18½ (19½, 20½)" (47 [49.5, 52]cm) from armhole waste yarn, ending with Row 8 or 18 of Chart C.

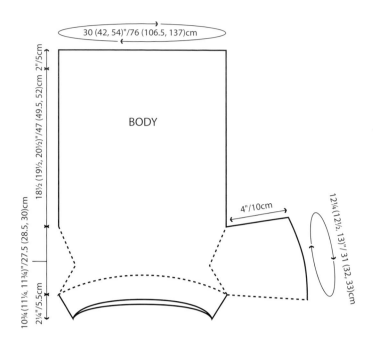

30 (42, 54)"/76 (106.5, 137)cm

BODY

18½ (19½, 20½)"/47 (49.5, 52)cm 2"/5cm

10¾ (11¼, 11¾)"/27.5 (28.5, 30)cm 2¼/5.5cm

4"/10cm

12¼ (12½, 13)"/ 31 (32, 33)cm

CAP SHAPING

Row 1 (RS): Starting at center top and working center stitch as stitch 8 of Chart D (Rib) work 2 stitches (working Chart D stitches 8 and 9), w&t.

Row 2 (WS): Work in rib back to center stitch, then continue in charted pattern, work 2 stitches, w&t.

Row 3 (RS): Continue in chart pattern as established, working to next wrapped stitch, lift wrap to needle and work together with wrapped stitch, then continue in chart working 3 stitches, w&t.

Row 4 (WS): Continue in chart pattern as established, working to next wrapped stitch, lift wrap to needle and work together with wrapped stitch, then continue in chart working 3 stitches, w&t.

Row 5 (RS): Continue in chart pattern as established, working to next wrapped stitch, lift wrap to needle and work together with wrapped stitch, then continue in chart, working 2 stitches, w&t.

Row 6 (WS): Continue in chart pattern as established, working to next wrapped stitch, lift wrap to needle and work together with wrapped stitch, then continue in chart working 2 stitches, w&t.

Next Row: Continue in chart pattern as established, working to next wrapped stitch, lift wrap to needle and work together with wrapped stitch, then continue in chart working 3 (2, 2) stitches, w&t.

Work last row a total of 2 (4, 4) times, ending with a wrong-side row—34 (32, 34) stitches remain unworked at underarm.

HEM

Work Rows 1 and 2 of Chart A around all stitches twice (4 rounds total), then work Rows 1–8 of Chart B once (8 more rounds).

Next Round: Knit.

Next Round: Purl.

Bind off all stitches loosely.

SLEEVES (MAKE 2)

With smallest 12" (30.5cm) needle, pick up all stitches above and below waste yarn—28 (29, 30) stitches at the neck side and 29 (30, 31) stitches at the body side of the waste yarn.

Pick up an additional 2 stitches on either edge of the armhole opening to close the gap created when moving from upper to lower stitches in opening (mark any one of these stitches with a safety pin)—61 (63, 65) stitches total. Remove waste yarn.

Slip stitches onto largest 12" (30.5cm) needle, arranging them so you are starting at the center stitch on the neck side of the opening (15 [15, 16] stitches from sleeve edge where the stitch is marked with a safety pin). This center stitch is the center top stitch of the sleeve cap.

SLEEVE

From this point you will be working in the round.

Continue with sleeve cap after last w&t and, working on the right side of the piece, work across all cap stitches to last w&t, work wrap as for previous wrapped stitches, place marker, k34 (32, 34) stitches, place marker, work in rib as established to marker.

(K2 [2, 3] stitches, m1), 14 (12, 10) times, knit to marker—75 (75, 75) stitches.

Begin working Chart B around all stitches, matching chart placement with rib stitch placement around all stitches.

Work 8-row repeat of chart with smallest 12" (30.5cm) needle, then work 8-row repeat with medium 12" (30.5cm) needle and end by working 8 rows of chart with largest 12" (30.5cm) needle.

Next Round: Knit.

Next Round: Purl.

Bind off loosely.

FINISHING
Steam-block piece.

Crochet Edging
Single crochet around all stitches at neck edge for 2 rounds, then work 1 round of slip stitch crochet, tightening up the neck opening so the garment sits comfortably. Adjust tension, depending on how wide or narrow you prefer the neck opening.

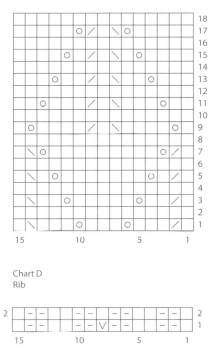

Chart A
Scalloped Edge

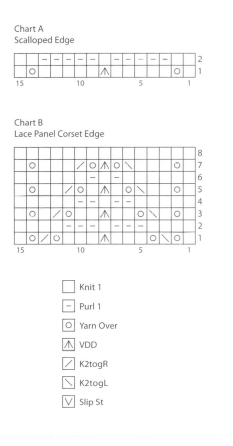

Chart B
Lace Panel Corset Edge

Knit 1
Purl 1
Yarn Over
VDD
K2togR
K2togL
Slip St

Chart C
Lace Panel

Chart D
Rib

URSULA SHRUG

by Melissa Matthay

SKILL LEVEL
Easy

SIZE
S (M, L, XL)
Directions are for smallest size, with larger sizes in parentheses.

FINISHED MEASUREMENTS
- Bust: 18 (18, 19, 20)" (45.5 [45.5, 48.5, 51]cm)
- Length: 51 (53, 55, 57)" (128.5 [134.5, 140, 145]cm)

MATERIALS
- 8 (9, 10, 12) skeins Cashmerino Chunky Yarn by Debbie Bliss (each approximately 1¾ oz [50g], 72 yd [64m], 55% merino wool, 33% microfiber, 12% cashmere), in color #09 Rose ⑤ bulky
- Size 10½ (6.5mm) needles, *or size needed to obtain gauge*
- Yarn needle

GAUGE
14 stitches and 17 rows = 4" (10cm) over stockinette stitch. *To save time, take time to check gauge.*

SPECIAL STITCHES
(see Glossary on page 162)
bind off; k2tog; k2tog tbl; k1, p1 rib; yo

SPECIAL PATTERN

Lace Pattern
Row 1: K1, *k3, k2tog, yo, k1, yo, k2tog tbl, k2, repeat from *, end k2.
Row 2 and all even rows: Purl.
Row 3: K1, *k2, k2tog, yo, k3, yo, k2tog tbl, k1, repeat from *, end k2.
Row 5: K1, *k1, k2tog, yo, k5, yo, k2tog tbl, repeat from *, end k2.
Rows 7, 9, and 11: K1, *p1, k2tog, k2, yo, k1, yo, k2, k2tog tbl, repeat from *, end k2.
Row 13: K1, *k1, k2tog, yo, k5, yo, k2tog tbl, repeat from *, end k2.
Row 15: K1, *k2, k2tog, yo, k3, yo, k2tog tbl, k1, repeat from *, end k2.
Row 17: K1, *k3, yo, k2tog, k1, k2tog tbl, yo, k2, repeat from *, end k2.
Row 19, 21, and 23: K1, *k1, yo, k2, k2tog, p1, k2tog tbl, k2, yo, * end k2.
Row 24: Purl.
Repeat Rows 1–24 for Lace Pattern.

INSTRUCTIONS

BODY
The body is one piece, worked cuff to cuff.

Cast on 53 stitches and work in Lace Pattern until piece measures 51 (53, 55, 57)" (128.5 [134.5, 140, 145]cm). Bind off all stitches.

FINISHING
Fold in half lengthwise. Beginning at cuff, sew 15 (16, 16, 16)" (38 [40.5, 40.5, 40.5]cm) underarm seam, leaving a 21 (21, 23, 23)" (53.5 [53.5, 58.5, 58.5]cm) opening.

Pick up 80 (80, 88, 88) stitches along upper edge and 80 (80, 88, 88) stitches along lower edge. Join work in k1, p1 rib for 3½" (9cm). Bind off.

51 (53, 55, 57)"/128.5 (134.5, 140, 145)cm

18 (18, 19, 20)"/45.5 (45.5, 48.5, 51)cm

SILK STOCKINGS

by Annie Modesitt

SKILL LEVEL
Experienced

SIZE
Women's S (M, L)

Directions are for smallest size, with larger sizes in parentheses.

FINISHED MEASUREMENTS
- Foot Circumference: 7 (7¾, 8½)" 18 [19.5, 21.5] cm)
- Foot Length: 7½ (8½, 9½)" (19 [21.5, 24]cm)
- Leg Length: 19⅛ (21¾, 24⅜)" (49 [55, 62]cm)

MATERIALS
- 2 (2, 2) skeins Regal Silk 101 by Artyarns (each approximately 1¾ oz [50g], 163 yd [149m], 100% silk), in color #221 White/Pink **(3)** light, or 289 (326, 381) yd/(263.5 [297.5, 347.5]m) sportweight yarn **(4)** medium
- Two size 5 (3.75mm) circular needles, each 12" (30.5cm) long, *or size needed to obtain gauge*
- Yarn needle
- Stitch markers

GAUGE
24 stitches and 28 rows = 4" (10cm) in stockinette stitch. *To save time, take time to check your gauge.*

SPECIAL STITCHES
(see Glossary on page 162)

garter stitch, k2togR, k2togL, kfb; slip stitch (knit); stockinette stitch; vdd; w&t; yo

NOTE
This pattern is written to be worked on 2 circular needles. For ease of comprehension, one needle is designated as the "Sole" and the other as the "Instep" needle.

INSTRUCTIONS

TOE
Holding 2 circular needles parallel in your right hand, cast on 12 (12, 12) stitches by casting on 1 stitch on one needle, then casting on 1 stitch on the other needle 6 times. Work back and forth, holding the circulars close together, until all stitches are cast on.

Round 1: Always working the stitches on circular #1 with the opposite end of circular #1, k1, kfb, knit to the last 2 stitches on circular #1, kfb, knit the last stitch. Move to circular #2 and repeat.

Round 2: Always working the stitches with the opposite end of the same needle on which they sit, knit all stitches.

Repeat the last 2 rounds until there are 44 (48, 52) stitches total, then repeat only Round 2, working even with no shaping until sock reaches just past pinky toe—22 (24, 26) stitches on each needle.

Designate one needle as the instep, and decrease 1 stitch in center of instep needle in final "toe round"—21 (23, 25) stitches.

Slip 2 (1, 0) stitches from each edge of sole needle onto instep needle—18 (22, 26) sole stitches and 25 (25, 25) instep stitches.

LACE INSTEP
Begin with Stitch 1, Row 1 of Chart A (Instep Lace Top/Front Panel), work 25 instep needle stitches in pattern while working remaining 18 (22, 26) stitches on sole needle in stockinette stitch.

Continue in patterns as established until piece measures 5¼ (6, 6¾)" (13.5 [15, 17]cm), or until piece reaches center point of ankle bone.

SHORT-ROW HEEL, PART I
(Worked Only on Sole Needle, Stockinette Stitch Section)
Row 1 (RS): On sole needle only, knit to last stitch, w&t.

Row 2 (WS): On sole needle only, purl to last stitch, w&t.

Row 3: Continuing in stockinette stitch as established, work to 1 stitch before last wrapped stitch, w&t.

Repeat Row 3 until 6 stitches remain unwrapped in center of sole needle, ending with a right-side row.

Next Row (WS): Knit to end of sole needle, slipping the wrap from each stitch up onto left-hand needle and working it, along with the stitch it was wrapped around, together as a purl stitch. Turn work.

Next Round (RS): Knit to end of sole needle, working wraps as in previous row, knitting all stitches on needle. Continue around stitches on instep needle in lace pattern as established.

SHORT-ROW HEEL, PART II
(Worked Only on Sole Needle)

Row 1 (RS): Work 12 (14, 16) stitches, w&t.

Row 2 (WS): P6 stitches, w&t.

Row 3: Continuing in stockinette stitch, work to 1 stitch past last wrapped stitch, working wrap along with stitch as previously done, w&t.

Repeat Row 3 until all stitches have been worked, ending with a wrong-side row.

ANKLE

Next Round: Work around all stitches, working stitches on instep needle in lace pattern as established and working stitches on sole needle as follows:

Work 3 stitches in Row 1 of Chart C (Side Edges), place marker, work 12 (16, 20) in Chart B (Sole/Back of Leg Ribbing), starting and ending where directed for your size, place marker, work last 3 stitches on sole needle Chart C.

Continue in patterns as established until sock reaches just beyond narrow portion of ankle—3⅜ (3¾, 4⅛)" (8.5 [9.5, 10.5]cm) from end of heel shaping.

Next Round: Work to marker, slip marker, yo, work to marker, yo, slip marker, work remaining stitches in patterns as established.

Next 3 Rounds: Work in patterns as established, working increase stitches into leg back ribbing.

Continue increasing in this manner, increasing 2 stitches every 4 rounds, until there are 120 (132, 144) stitches total.

LEG
Work even until stocking reaches mid-thigh—19⅛ (21¾, 24⅜)" (48.5 [55, 62]cm) from end of heel shaping.

GARTER TOP
Work 6 rounds in garter stitch (knit 1 round, purl 1 round) twice.

Preparation Round: (K1, slip 1) around all stitches.

Bind-Off Round: Bind off all stitches loosely using a larger needle.

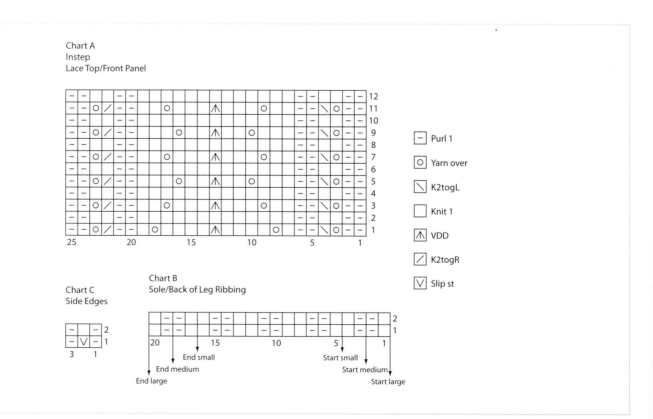

SOME LIKE IT HOT OPERA GLOVES

by Annie Modesitt

SKILL LEVEL
Intermediate

SIZE
Women's S (M, L)

Directions are for smallest size, with larger sizes in parentheses.

FINISHED MEASUREMENTS
- Bicep: 12½ (13½, 14¾)" (32 [34.5,37.5]cm)
- Wrist: 6½ (7½, 8¾)" (16.5 [19, 22]cm)
- Cuff Length: 11 (13,15)" (28 [33, 38]cm)

MATERIALS
- 3 (3, 3) balls Fixation by Cascade (each approximately 1¾ oz [50g], 100 yd [92m], 98.3% cotton, 1.7% elastic), in color #8990 Black, or 266 (303, 337) yd/(242.5 [273.5, 307.5]m) sportweight yarn (3) light
- Size 3 (3.25mm) double-pointed needles
- Size 4 (3.5mm) double-pointed needles, *or size needed to obtain gauge*
- Waste yarn
- Stitch holders
- Stitch markers
- Yarn needle
- ¼" (6mm) elastic
- Sewing thread for tacking ends of elastic cuffs

GAUGE
20 stitches and 26 rows = 4" (10cm) in stockinette stitch using size 4 (3.5mm) needles. *To save time, take time to check your gauge.*

SPECIAL STITCHES
(see Glossary on page 162)

k2togL; k2togR; m1; p2togL; p2togR; pick up and knit; slip stitch; stockinette stitch; vdd; yo

INSTRUCTIONS

CUFF
With smaller needles, cast on 63 (69, 75) stitches, dividing stitches evenly -21 (23, 25) stitches on each needle. Join to work in the round.

Knit 6 rounds. Change to larger needles and purl 1 round.

Starting with Row 17 (9, 1), work Chart A (Glove Lace Back) on needle 1, then work Row 17 (9, 1) of Chart B (Glove Front) across needle 2 and needle 3.

Continue in patterns as established, working decrease as directed until 11 (13, 15) stitches remain on each needle—33 (39, 45) stitches.

Working even with no further decreasing, continue in Chart A pattern on needle 1 and work in ribbing as established on needles 2 and 3 until piece measures 11 (13, 15)" (28 [33, 38]cm) from cast-on or desired length to wrist.

Next Round: Continue in pattern as established on needle 1; on needles 2 and 3 work to center stitch (VDD stitch from previous round), m1, work to end of needle—35 (41, 47) stitches.

Continue working needle 1 in lace pattern with no decreases (Chart C [Lace]), and begin working needles 2 and 3 in stockinette stitch for 4 rounds.

Next Round: Continue in pattern as established on needle 1; on needles 2 and 3 work to center stitch (VDD stitch from previous round), m1, work to end of needle—37 (43, 49) stitches.

Repeat last 4 rounds once more—39 (45, 51) stitches.

THUMB OPENING

Right Thumb: Continuing as established on needle 1, work 4 (4, 5) stitches on needle 2, with a piece of waste yarn k7 (8, 9) stitches, slip these back to needle and knit to end of needle 2. Knit to last 4 (4, 5) stitches on needle 3, place marker, work to end of round.

Left Thumb: Continuing as established on needle 1, work 4 (4, 5) stitches on needle 2, place marker and knit to end of needle 2. Knit to last 11 (12, 14) stitches on needle 3, with a piece of waste yarn k7 (8, 9) stitches, slip these back to needle, work to end of round.

You now have 19 (22, 25) stitches for the palm and 20 (23, 26) stitches for the back of the hand. Continue working lace as established and all other stitches in stockinette stitch until hand measures 1½ (2, 2½)" (3.8 [5, 6.5]cm) from start of thumb, or until hand portion reaches base of fingers.

PALM TOP

Divide stitches in half at marker and outside of thumb—19 (22, 25) palm stitches, 20 (23, 26) hand back stitches. Place stitches from each section on a separate piece of waste yarn.

THUMB

Insert double-pointed needle into 7 (8, 9) stitches above and below thumb-marking waste yarn, and remove yarn. Pick up 1 additional stitch on either side of thumb—16 (18, 20) stitches.

Divide stitches between three double-pointed needles and work in stockinette stitch for approximately 1¼" (3cm) until thumb reaches knuckle.

Decrease 1 stitch at palm side of thumb, continue until thumb is desired length, k1, (k2tog) to end.

Break yarn, leaving an 8" (20.5cm) tail, and draw through all stitches.

INDEX FINGER

Slip 5 (6, 7) stitches from palm waste yarn and 6 (7, 8) stitches from hand back waste yarn onto double-pointed needles. Knit to space between fingers, cast on 2 stitches, knit to end of round—13 (15, 17) stitches.

Knit until finger reaches first knuckle, then decrease 1 stitch at palm side of finger. Knit until finger reaches second knuckle, then decrease 1 stitch at back side of finger.

Knit until finger reaches just below tip of finger, k1, (k2togR) to end.

Break yarn, leaving an 8" (20.5cm) tail, and draw through remaining stitches.

MIDDLE FINGER

Slip 5 (6, 7) stitches from each waste yarn onto double-pointed needles. Knit across back of finger, cast on 3 stitches, knit across front of finger, pick up and knit 2 stitches from previous cast-on stitches, knit to end of round—15 (17, 19) stitches.

Knit around until finger reaches first knuckle, then decrease 1 stitch at palm side of finger. Knit until finger reaches second knuckle, then decrease 1 stitch at back side of finger.

Knit until finger reaches just below tip of finger, k1, (k2togR) to end.

Break yarn, leaving an 8" (20.5cm) tail and draw through all remaining stitches.

RING FINGER

Slip 5 (5, 6) stitches from each waste yarn onto double-pointed needles. Knit across back of finger, cast on 3 stitches, knit across front of finger, pick up and knit 3 stitches from previous cast-on stitches, knit to end of round—16 (16, 18) stitches.

Knit until finger reaches first knuckle, then decrease 1 stitch at palm side of finger. Knit until finger reaches second knuckle, then decrease 1 stitch at back side of finger.

Knit until finger reaches just below tip of finger, k1, (k2togR) to end.

Break yarn, leaving an 8" (20.5cm) tail, and draw through all stitches.

PINKIE FINGER

Slip 4 (5, 5) stitches from each waste yarn onto double-pointed needles. Knit across back of finger, knit across front of finger, pick up 3 stitches from previous cast-on stitches, knit to end of round—11 (13, 13) stitches.

Knit until finger reaches first knuckle, then decrease 1 stitch at palm side of finger. Knit until finger reaches second knuckle, then decrease 1 stitch at back side of finger.

Knit until finger reaches just below tip of finger, k1, (k2togR) to end.

Break yarn, leaving an 8" (20.5cm) tail and draw through all stitches.

FINISHING

Turn cast-on edge under and sew in place to create facing, leaving a ½" (13mm) space. Insert ¼" (6mm) elastic, cut to the circumference of bicep plus 1" (2.5cm), and sew the ends together.

With a darning needle, draw ends into fingers and weave in place.

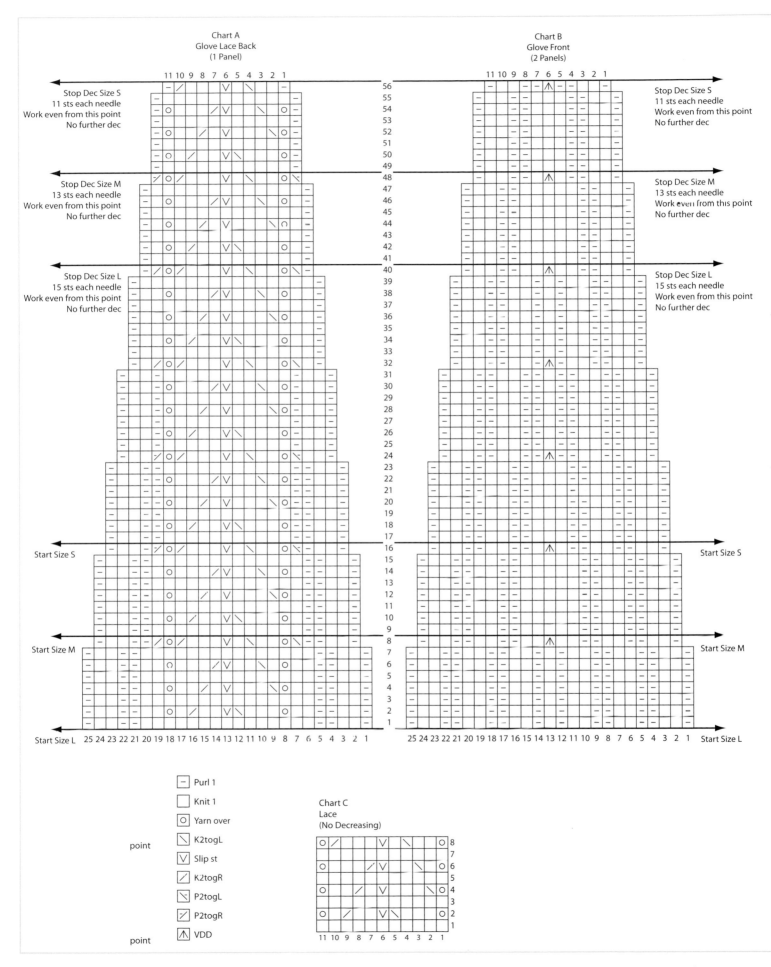

Chart A
Glove Lace Back
(1 Panel)

Chart B
Glove Front
(2 Panels)

Stop Dec Size S
11 sts each needle
Work even from this point
No further dec

Stop Dec Size M
13 sts each needle
Work even from this point
No further dec

Stop Dec Size L
15 sts each needle
Work even from this point
No further dec

Start Size S

Start Size M

Start Size L

Stop Dec Size S
11 sts each needle
Work even from this point
No further dec

Stop Dec Size M
13 sts each needle
Work even from this point
No further dec

Stop Dec Size L
15 sts each needle
Work even from this point
No further dec

Start Size S

Start Size M

Start Size L

point — Purl 1

Knit 1

O Yarn over

point ⟍ K2togL

V Slip st

⟋ K2togR

⟍ P2togL

⟋ P2togR

point ⋀ VDD

Chart C
Lace
(No Decreasing)

JUNE BRIDE MITTS

by Annie Modesitt

SKILL LEVEL
Intermediate

SIZE
Women's S (M, L)

Directions are for smallest size, with larger sizes in parentheses.

FINISHED MEASUREMENTS
- Wrist: 6½ (7½, 8¾)" (16.5 [19, 22]cm)
- Palm: 5¼ (6½, 7¾)" (13 [16.5, 20]cm)

MATERIALS
- 1 (1, 1) skein Cashmere 2 by Artyarns (each approximately 1¾ oz [50g], 255 yd [233m], 100% Cashmere and 30% Silk), in color #128 CS ⓸ medium
- Note: Use only 2 strands to create the mitts.
- Size 5 (3.75mm) double-pointed needles, *or size needed to obtain gauge*
- Size F/5 (3.75mm) crochet hook
- Stitch markers
- Waste yarn
- Yarn needle
- Safety pin

GAUGE
24 stitches and 30 rows = 4" (10cm) in stockinette stitch using 2 strands of yarn. *To save time, take time to check your gauge.*

SPECIAL STITCHES
(see Glossary on page 162)

garter stitch; k2togL; k2togR; k2tog; k2, p2 rib; picot bind-off; stockinette stitch; slip stitch (knit); vdd; yo

INSTRUCTIONS

MITT CUFF
Cast on 80 (96, 112) stitches.

Work 4 rows in garter stitch. Join, place marker to note start of round—this will be the center of the palm.

Next Round: (K2togR) across work—40 (48, 56) stitches.

Next 10 Rounds: Knit.

Next Round: K1, (p2, k2) 2 (3, 4) times, p2, k2togR, knit to last 13 (15, 17), k2togL, p2, (k2, p2) 2 (3, 4) times, k1—39 (47, 55) stitches

Continue in patterns as established for 3 more rounds.

ESTABLISH LACE PATTERN

Next Round: Work in ribbing as established across first 11 (15, 19) stitches, work Lace Mitts Chart across next 17 stitches, work in rib pattern as established to end of round. Continue in patterns as established until rib section measures 1¼ (1½, 1¾)" (3 [3.8, 4.5]cm).

Next Round: Knit to start of chart, work in chart pattern as established, knit to end of round.

Continue working chart as established, working all other stitches in stockinette stitch until piece measures 1¼ (1½, 1¾)" (3 [3.8, 4.5]cm) from end of rib section.

LEFT THUMB OPENING

Next Round: K3 (5,6) stitches, with a piece of waste yarn k5 (6, 7) stitches, slip these waste yarn stitches back to left-hand needle and knit them again, work to chart and complete round as established.

Continue working as established, working center stitches in charted pattern and all other stitches in stockinette stitch, until piece measures 1½ (1¾, 2)" (3.8 [4.5, 5]cm) from start of work or it reaches to base of fingers.

RIGHT THUMB OPENING

Next Round: Work 32 (37, 43) stitches in pattern as established, with a piece of waste yarn k5 (6, 7) stitches, slip these waste yarn stitches back to left-hand needle and knit them again, knit to end of round.

Continue working as established, working center stitches in charted pattern and all other stitches in stockinette stitch, until piece measures 1½ (1¾, 2)" (3.8 [4.5, 5]cm) from start of work or it reaches to base of fingers.

TOP OF HAND

Next 2 Rounds: Knit all stitches.

Next 4 Rounds: Work in garter stitch.

Work k2tog picot bind-off, chaining 3 stitches between each bind-off stitch.

THUMB

Slip 6 (7, 8) stitches from top of thumb opening waste yarn and 5 (6, 7) stitches from bottom of thumb opening waste yarn onto double-pointed needles—11 (13, 15) stitches total.

Knit 8 rounds (or until thumb reaches knuckle).

Next 2 Rounds: Knit all stitches.

Next 4 Rounds: Work in garter stitch.

Bind off as for Hand.

FINISHING

Steam-block piece. Weave in ends. If desired, single crochet around cast-on and bound-off edges to add extra dimension to the ruffled edges.

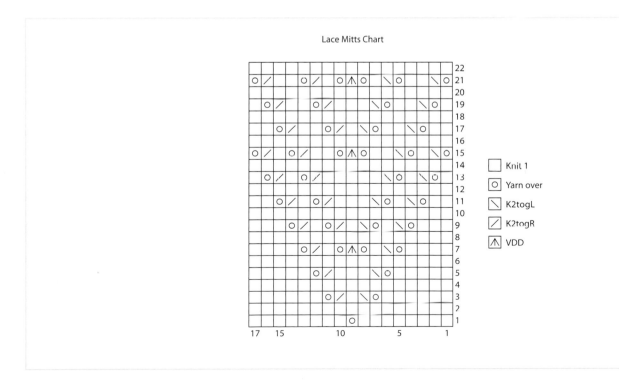

Lace Mitts Chart

ZINFANDEL BLANKET

by Bethany Kok

SKILL LEVEL
Experienced

SIZE
One size

FINISHED MEASUREMENTS
- 65" (165cm) square

MATERIALS
- 5 skeins Lace by Malabrigo (each approximately 1¾ oz [50g], 470 yd [430m], 100% baby merino wool), in color Damask Rose (1) super fine
- Size 4 (3.5mm) double-pointed needles (set of 5), and circular needles, 24" (61cm), 36" (91cm), and 47" (120cm) long, *or size needed to obtain gauge*
- Yarn needle
- 12 stitch markers

GAUGE
20 and 38 rows = 4" in vine pattern. *To save time, take time to check your gauge.*

SPECIAL STITCHES
(see Glossary on page 162)
cable cast-on; ring cast-on; slipknot; yo

NOTES
1. Begin with double-pointed needles; change to successively larger circular needles as needed.
2. When changing from double-pointed needles to circular needles, place markers after last twisted stitch of chart, marking the four quarters of the shawl.
3. When working two yarn overs in a row, knit into the first yarn over and purl into the second.

CHART NOTES
1. Even-numbered rows are not shown in charts unless specifically noted.
2. Unless otherwise noted, knit all stitches of even-numbered rows.
3. When working Row 44 of Right and Left Inset Leaf Charts, move the markers used to divide shawl into quarters 1 stitch to the left. Do not move any other stitch markers. Moved stitch markers will not be moved back.
4. When working Grape Chart, stitch count will increase by 2 stitches for each pattern repeat of Row 10 and decrease by 2 stitches for each pattern repeat of Rows 18, 26, 34, 42, and 50. Stitch count will return to normal in the following odd-numbered row.

INSTRUCTIONS

CENTER
Begin with a Ring Cast-On—8 stitches.

Distribute stitches evenly over 4 double-pointed needles, 2 stitches on each needle. The stitches on each double-pointed needle represent one-quarter of the shawl.

Knit 1 round.

Note: Each odd-numbered row will increase the number of stitches in the shawl by 8. From this point, instructions are given for one-quarter of the full shawl. Repeat all instructions for each quarter, which will result in a square shawl.

Work Rows 1–50 of Leaf Chart once—52 stitches per quarter.

MIDDLE
Work Rows 1–8 of Vine Chart A, Rows 3–84 of Vine Chart B, then work rows 1–70 of Vine Chart B again.

Work Row 1 of Right Inset Leaf, place marker, work Row 1 of Vine Chart C until 2 stitches are left in quarter, place marker, work Row 1 of Left Inset Leaf.

Continue working Rows 2–46 of Right Inset Leaf, Vine Chart C, and Left Inset Leaf at the same time as established.

Remove Inset Leaf markers. Continue working rows 47–76 of Vine Chart C over all stitches in quarter—231 stitches per quarter.

BORDER
Work Rows 1–12 of Grape Chart.

Work Row 1 of Right Inset Leaf, place marker, work Row 13 of Grape Chart until 2 stitches are left in quarter, work Row 1 of Left Inset Leaf.

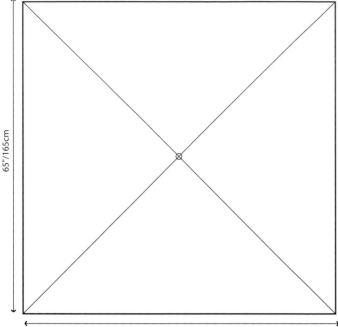

65"/165cm

65"/165cm

Note: Grape Chart has patterning on some even-numbered rows, while the Right and Left Inset Leaves do not.

Continue working Rows 2–46 of Right Inset Leaf, Rows 14–58 of Grape Chart, and Rows 2–46 of Left Inset Leaf as established.

Bind off using picot edging as follows: *Cast on 3 stitches using cable cast-on, bind off 6 stitches, slip last stitch back to left needle; repeat from * to end.

Weave in all ends.

FINISHING

Block by threading blocking wires or smooth thin thread through the picot points of the soaked shawl. Written shawl dimensions were achieved with a stringent blocking. Gentler blocking will result in a smaller shawl.

CUSTOMIZATION

For a smaller shawl, omit second repeat of Vine Chart B.

For a shawl without inset leaves in the middle vine pattern, work Leaf Chart as written, then work Vine Chart B 3 times (starting first repeat with Rows 1–8 of Vine Chart A, starting next two repeats with Row 1 of Vine Chart B). Continue pattern as written, starting with Rows 1–12 of Grape Chart.

Note: Grape Chart has patterning on some even-numbered rows, while the Right and Left Inset Leaves do not.

Leaf Chart

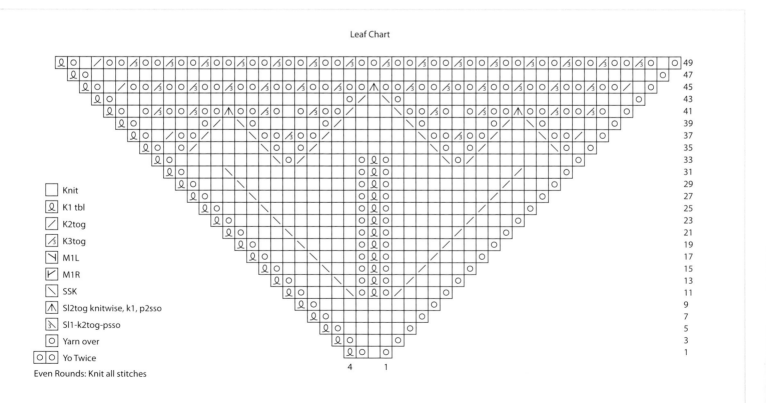

Knit
K1 tbl
K2tog
K3tog
M1L
M1R
SSK
Sl2tog knitwise, k1, p2sso
Sl1-k2tog-psso
Yarn over
Yo Twice

Even Rounds: Knit all stitches

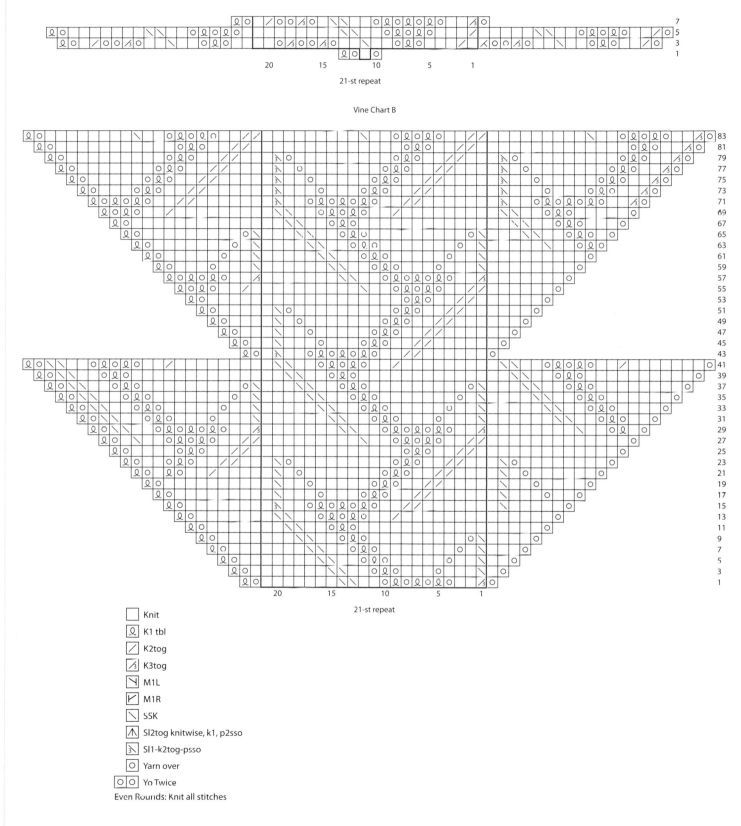

Vine Chart A

20   15   10   5   1

21-st repeat

Vine Chart B

20   15   10   5   1

21-st repeat

	Knit
Ⴍ	K1 tbl
⁄	K2tog
⫽	K3tog
⟍	M1L
⟋	M1R
＼	SSK
⅄	Sl2tog knitwise, k1, p2sso
⅔	Sl1-k2tog-psso
O	Yarn over
O O	Yo Twice

Even Rounds: Knit all stitches

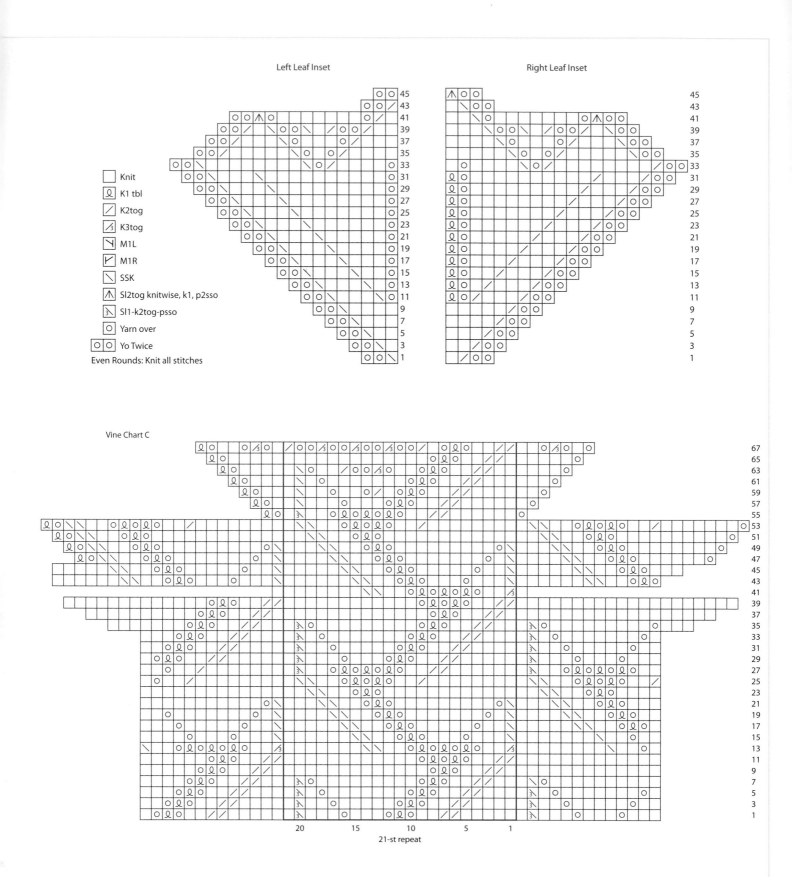

Left Leaf Inset

Right Leaf Inset

Knit
K1 tbl
K2tog
K3tog
M1L
M1R
SSK
Sl2tog knitwise, k1, p2sso
Sl1-k2tog-psso
Yarn over
Yo Twice

Even Rounds: Knit all stitches

Vine Chart C

21-st repeat

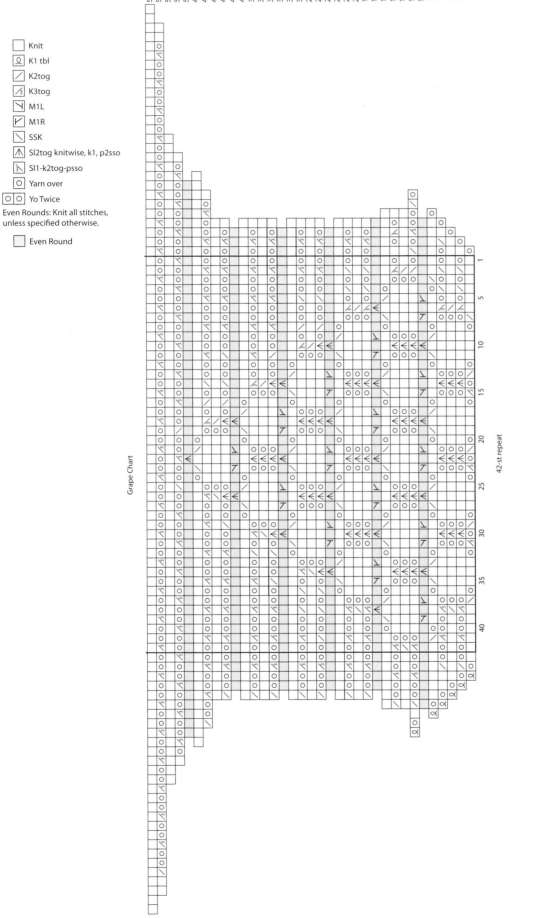

Knit

K1 tbl

K2tog

K3tog

M1L

M1R

SSK

Sl2tog knitwise, k1, p2sso

Sl1-k2tog-psso

Yarn over

Yo Twice

Even Rounds: Knit all stitches,
unless specified otherwise.

Even Round

Grape Chart

42-st repeat

MARTA TUNIC

by Melissa Matthay

SKILL LEVEL
Intermediate

SIZE
S (M, L, XL)
Directions are for smallest size, with larger sizes in parentheses.

FINISHED MEASUREMENTS
- Bust: 35 (39, 43, 47)" (89 [99, 109, 120]cm)
- Length: 29½ (31, 31½, 33)" (75 [79, 80, 84]cm)

MATERIALS
- 15 (16, 17, 17) balls Fixation by Cascade Yarns (each approximately 1¾ oz [50g], 186 yd [169m], 98.3% cotton, 1.7% elastic), in color #8176 Ecru (❸) light
- Size 7 (4.5mm) straight and circular needles, *or size needed to obtain gauge*
- Yarn needle

GAUGE
19 stitches and 24 rows = 4" (10cm) in stockinette stitch. *To save time, take time to check your gauge.*

SPECIAL STITCHES
(see Glossary on page 162)
bind off loosely; k2tog; k3tog; sl1-k1-psso; stockinette stitch; yo

NOTE
This is a pattern that will give you several style options. Because the long sleeves are done in one straight piece, converting this to short sleeves or cap sleeves is a snap. You decide the length you want. You can also change the length of the body. Marta would be in the fashion forefront as either a hip-skimming sweater or a midriff-baring cropped top.

SPECIAL PATTERN
Lace Pattern
Row 1: K1, k2tog, *k3, yo, k1, yo, k3, k3tog; repeat from * to last repeat, k3, yo, k1, yo, k3, sl1-k1-psso, k1.

Row 2 and all even rows: Purl.

Row 3: K1, k2tog, *k2, yo, k3, yo, k2, k3tog; repeat from * to last repeat, k2, yo, k3, yo, k2, sl1-k1-psso, k1.

Row 5: K1, k2tog, *k1, yo, k5, yo, k1, k3tog; repeat from * to last repeat, k1, yo, k5, yo, k1, sl1-k1-psso, k1.

Row 7: K1, k2tog, *yo, k7, yo, k3tog; repeat from * to last repeat, yo, k7, yo, sl1-k1-psso, k1.

Repeat Rows 1–8 for Lace Pattern.

INSTRUCTIONS

BACK
Cast on 83 (93, 103, 113) stitches. Begin and work in Lace Pattern until piece measures 21½ (22½, 22½, 23½)" (54.5 [57, 57, 59.5]cm).

Start Yoke Pattern: Work 30 (30, 40, 40) stitches in stockinette stitch, work center 23 (33, 23, 33) stitches in Lace Pattern, work remaining 30 (30, 40, 40) stitches in stockinette stitch, and AT THE SAME TIME shape armhole as follows: When piece measures 22 (23, 23, 24)" (56 [58.5, 58.5, 61]cm), bind off 5 stitches at beginning of next 2 rows, then decrease 1 stitch at each edge every other row 5 (6, 8, 10) times—63 (71, 77, 83) stitches. Work even until piece measures 29½ (31, 31½, 33)" (75 [79, 80, 84]cm). Bind off loosely.

FRONT
Begin and work same as back until piece measures 21½ (22½, 22½, 23½)" (54.5 [57, 57, 59.5]cm).

Start Yoke Pattern

Work 30 (30, 40, 40) stitches in stockinette stitch, work center 23 (33, 23, 33) stitches in Lace Pattern, work remaining 30 (30, 40, 40) stitches in stockinette stitch, and AT THE SAME TIME shape armhole as follows: When piece measures 22 (23, 23, 24)" (56 [58.5, 58.5, 61]cm), bind off 5 stitches at beginning of next 2 rows, then decrease 1 stitch at each edge every other row 5 (6, 8, 10) times—63 (71, 77, 83) stitches. Continue yoke pattern, and work even until piece measures 26½ (28, 28½, 30)" (67.5 [71, 72, 76]cm).

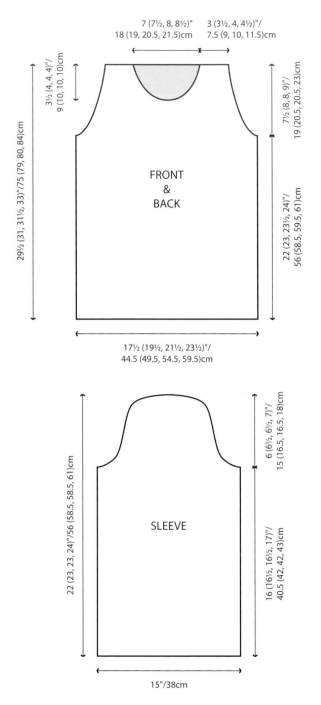

7 (7½, 8, 8½)"
18 (19, 20.5, 21.5)cm

3 (3½, 4, 4½)"/
7.5 (9, 10, 11.5)cm

3½ (4, 4, 4)"/
9 (10, 10, 10)cm

29½ (31, 31½, 33)"/75 (79, 80, 84)cm

7½ (8, 8, 9)"/
19 (20.5, 20.5, 23)cm

22 (23, 23½, 24)"/
56 (58.5, 59.5, 61)cm

FRONT
&
BACK

17½ (19½, 21½, 23½)"/
44.5 (49.5, 54.5, 59.5)cm

6 (6½, 6½, 7)"/
15 (16.5, 16.5, 18)cm

22 (23, 23, 24)"/56 (58.5, 58.5, 61)cm

SLEEVE

16 (16½, 16½, 17)"/
40.5 (42, 42, 43)cm

15"/38cm

Shape Neck

Work 21 (25, 28, 31) stitches in Lace Pattern. Join a second ball of yarn and bind off center 21 stitches and work remaining 21 (25, 28, 31) stitches in pattern. Working both sides at once, bind off at each neck edge 4 stitches once, then decrease 1 stitch every other row 4 (4, 5, 6) times—13 (17, 19, 21) stitches remaining for each shoulder. Work even until piece measures same as back. Bind off loosely.

SLEEVES

Cast on 73 (73, 73, 73) stitches. Begin and work in Lace Pattern until piece measures 16 (16½, 16½, 17)" (40.5 [42, 42, 43]cm).

Shape Cap

Bind off 5 stitches at beginning of next 2 rows, decrease 1 stitch at each edge every other row 19 (19, 20, 21) times, then bind off 2 stitches at beginning of next 4 rows. Bind off remaining 17 (17, 15, 13) stitches.

FINISHING

Sew shoulder seams. Sew on sleeves. Sew side and sleeve seams.

Neckband

With circular needles and right side facing, pick up and knit 83 stitches around neck edge. Work Rows 1–8 in Lace Pattern. Bind off all stitches loosely.

CHAPTER 3

⟨⟩ Runway Lace

HAMPTONS DRESS

by Berta Karapetyan

SKILL LEVEL
Intermediate

SIZE
XS (S, M, L)

Directions are for smallest size, with larger sizes in parentheses.

FINISHED MEASUREMENTS
- Bust: 32 (35, 38, 41)" (81 [89, 96.5, 104]cm)
- Length: 33½ (33½, 35, 35)" (85 [85, 89, 89]cm)

MATERIALS
- 10 (11, 12, 12) balls Vintage Cotton by Karabella (each approximately 1¾ oz [50g], 140 yd [130m], 100% mercerized cotton), in color #305 Khaki ❸ light
- Size 0 (2mm) circular needle, 16" (40.5cm) long
- Size 1 (2.5mm) needles, *or size needed to obtain gauge*
- Size 2 (2.75mm) needles
- Size 3 (3.25mm) needles
- Stitch holders
- Yarn needle

GAUGE
36 stitches and 36 rows = 4" (10cm) in Sunspots Pattern, using size 1 (2.5mm) needles. *To save time, take time to check your gauge.*

SPECIAL STITCHES
(see Glossary on page 162)

double increase; garter stitch; increase 1 (lifted increase); k2tog; k3tog; p2tog; p3tog; sl1-k2-psso; sl2-k1-p2sso; ssk; yo

Double increase: Work the following double increase into the next st: Knit 1 through the back loop (k1 tbl), then knit the same stitch in the front loop, then insert left-hand needle point behind the vertical strand that runs downward from between the 2 stitches just made and k1 tbl into this strand to make the 3rd stitch of the group.

SPECIAL PATTERN

Sunspots Pattern (multiple of 12 stitches + 3)

Row 1 (RS): K1, k2tog, *yo, k2tog, yo, p5, yo, ssk, yo, sl1-k2tog-psso; repeat from * to last 12 stitches, yo, k2tog, yo, p5, yo, ssk, yo, ssk, k1.

Row 2: P5, *k5, p7; repeat from * to last 10 stitches, k5, p5.

Row 3: K1, *yo, k3tog, yo, p7, yo, ssk; repeat from * to last 14 stitches, yo, k3tog, yo, p7, yo, ssk, yo, k2tog.

Rows 4, 6, and 8: P4, *k7, p5; repeat from * to last 11 stitches, k7, p4.

Row 5: Ssk, yo, *ssk, yo, p7, yo, sl2-k1-p2sso, yo; repeat from * to last 13 stitches, ssk, yo, p7, yo, sl2-k1-p2sso, yo, k1.

Row 7: K1, *yo, sl2-k1-p2sso, yo, p7, yo, k2tog; repeat from * to last 14 stitches, yo, sl2-k1-p2sso, yo, p7, yo, k2tog, yo, k2tog.

Row 9: K1, increase 1, *yo, ssk, yo, p2tog, p3tog, p2tog, yo, k2tog, yo, double increase; repeat from * to last 13 stitches, yo, ssk, yo, p2tog, p3tog, p2tog, yo, k2tog, yo, increase 1, k1.

Row 10 (Decrease Row): P6, *k3tog, p9; repeat from * to last 9 stitches, k3tog, p6.

Row 11: K1, increase 1, *[yo, ssk] twice, p1, [k2tog, yo] twice, double increase; repeat from * to last 11 stitches, [yo, ssk] twice, p1, [k2tog, yo] twice, increase 1, k1.

Row 12: P7, *k1, p11; repeat from * to last 8 stitches, k1, p7.

Row 13: K1, p3, *yo, ssk, yo, sl1-k2tog-psso, yo, k2tog, yo, p5; repeat from * to last 11 stitches, yo, ssk, yo, sl1-k2tog-psso, yo, k2tog, yo, p3, k1.

Row 14: P1, k3, *p7, k5; repeat from * to last 11 stitches, p7, k3, p1.

Row 15: K1, p4, *yo, ssk, yo, k3tog, yo, p7; repeat from * to last 10 stitches, yo, ssk, yo, k3tog, yo, p4, k1.

Rows 16, 18, and 20: P1, k4, *p5, k7; repeat from * to last 10 stitches, p5, k4, p1.

Row 17: K1, p4, *yo, sl2-k1-p2sso, yo, ssk, yo, p7; repeat from * to last 10 stitches, yo, sl2-k1-p2sso, yo, ssk, yo, p4, k1.

Row 19: K1, p4, *yo, k2tog, yo, sl2-k1-p2sso, yo, p7; repeat from * to last 10 stitches, yo, k2tog, yo, sl2-k1-p2sso, yo, p4, k1.

Row 21: K1, p2tog, *p2tog, yo, k2tog, yo, double increase, yo, ssk, yo, p2tog, p3tog; repeat from * to last 12 stitches, p2tog, yo, k2tog, yo, double increase, yo, ssk, yo, p2tog, p2tog, k1.

Row 22 (Decrease Row): P1, k2tog, *p9, k3tog; repeat from * to last 12 stitches, p9, k2tog, p1.

Row 23: K1, p1, *[k2tog, yo] twice, double increase, [yo, ssk] twice, p1; repeat from * to last 11 stitches, [k2tog, yo] twice, double increase, [yo, ssk] twice, p1, k1.

Row 24: P1, k1, *p11, k1; repeat from * to last 13 stitches, p11, k1, p1.

Repeat Rows 1–24 for Sunspots Pattern.

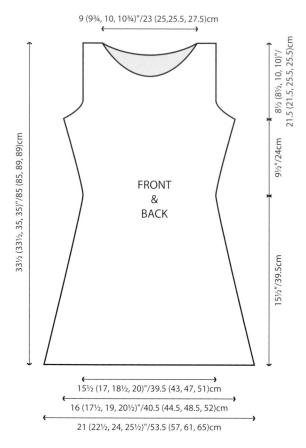

9 (9¾, 10, 10¾)"/23 (25,25.5, 27.5)cm

8½ (8½, 10, 10)"/ 21.5 (21.5, 25.5, 25.5)cm

9½"/24cm

15½"/39.5cm

33½ (33½, 35, 35)"/85 (85, 89, 89)cm

FRONT & BACK

15½ (17, 18½, 20)"/39.5 (43, 47, 51)cm

16 (17½, 19, 20½)"/40.5 (44.5, 48.5, 52)cm

21 (22½, 24, 25½)"/53.5 (57, 61, 65)cm

INSTRUCTIONS

BACK

Using size 3 needles, cast on 147 (159, 171, 183) stitches.

Work 6 rows in garter stitch (knit every row).

Work 60 rows in Sunspots Pattern.

Change to size 2 needles and continue in established Sunspots Pattern for 48 rows more.

Change to size 1 needles and continue for 36 rows more.

Change to size 0 needles and continue for 72 rows more.

Change to size 1 needles and continue for 48 rows more.

Armhole Shaping

Change to size 0 needles.

Row 1 (RS): Bind off 6 stitches, p3, yo, ssk, yo, sl1-k2tog-psso, repeat from * of Sunspots pattern Row 1 to last 12 stitches, yo, k2tog, yo, p5, yo, ssk, yo, ssk, k1—141 (153, 165, 177) stitches.

Row 2: Bind off 5 stitches, k4, p7, *k5, p7; repeat from * to last 4 stitches, k4—136 (148, 160, 172) stitches.

Row 3: Bind off 2 stitches, p2, yo, ssk, repeat from * of Sunspots Pattern Row 3 to last 9 stitches, yo, k3tog, yo, p6—134 (146, 158, 170) stitches.

Row 4: Bind off 2 stitches, k3, *p5, k7; repeat from * to last 8 stitches, p5, k3—132 (144, 156, 168) stitches.

Row 5: Bind off 2 stitches, yo, sl2-k1-p2sso, yo, repeat from * of Sunspots Pattern Row 5 to last 6 stitches, ssk, yo, p4—130 (142, 154, 166) stitches.

Row 6: Bind off 2 stitches, k1, *p5, k7; repeat from * to last 6 stitches, p6—128 (140, 152, 164) stitches.

Row 7: Bind off 2 stitches, repeat from * of Sunspots Pattern Row 7 to last 5 stitches, yo, sl2-k1-p2sso, yo, p2—126 (138, 150, 162) stitches.

Row 8: Bind off 2 stitches, p4, k7, *p5, k7; repeat from * to last 4 stitches, p4—124 (136, 148, 160) stitches).

Row 9: Bind off 1 stitch, k2, p2tog, p3tog, p2tog, yo, k2tog, yo, double increase, *yo, ssk, yo, p2tog, p3tog, p2tog, yo, k2tog, yo, double increase; repeat from * to last 14 stitches, yo, ssk, yo, p2tog, p3tog, p2tog, yo, k2tog, yo, increase 1, k2—121 (133, 145, 157) stitches.

Row 10: Bind off 2 stitches, p4, *k3tog, p9; repeat from * to last 6 stitches, k3tog, p3—114 (126, 138, 150) stitches.

Row 11: K1, yo, ssk, p1, [k2tog, yo] twice, double increase, repeat from * of Sunspots Pattern Row 11 to last 10 stitches, [yo, ssk] twice, p1, k5—117 (129, 141, 153) stitches.

Row 12: Bind off 2 stitches, p2, k1, p11, *k1, p11; repeat from * to last 3 stitches, p3—114 (126, 138, 150) stitches.

Row 13: Bind off 1 stitch, yo, sl1-k2tog-psso, yo, k2tog, yo, p5, repeat from * of Sunspots Pattern Row 13 to last 7 stitches, yo, ssk, yo, sl1-k2tog-psso, yo, k1, yo, k1—115 (127, 139, 151) stitches.

Row 14: Bind off 2 stitches, p5, *k5, p7; repeat from * to last 11 stitches, k5, p6—113 (125, 137, 149) stitches.

Row 15: Bind off 2 stitches, ssk, yo, p7, repeat from * of Sunspots Pattern Row 15 to last 5 stitches, yo, ssk, yo, k2tog, k1—111 (123, 135, 147) stitches.

Row 16: Bind off 2 stitches, p2, k7, *p5, k7; repeat from * to last 3 stitches, p3—109 (121, 133, 145) stitches.

Row 17: Bind off 2 stitches, p7, repeat from * of Sunspots Pattern Row 17 to last 3 stitches, k3—107 (119, 131, 143) stitches.

Row 18: Bind off 2 stitches, k7, *p5, k7; repeat from * to last stitch, p1—105 (117, 129, 141) stitches.

Row 19: Bind off 1 stitch, p6, repeat from * of Sunspots Pattern Row 19 to last stitch, k1—104 (116, 128, 140) stitches.

Row 20: Bind off 1 stitch, k6, *p5, k7; repeat from * to end—103 (115, 127, 139) stitches.

Row 21: Bind off 1 stitch, k1, p2tog, repeat from * of Sunspots Pattern Row 21 to last 3 stitches, p3—102 (114, 126, 138) stitches.

Row 22: Bind off 1 stitch, *k3tog, p9; repeat from * to last 4 stitches, k3tog, k1—99 (111, 123, 135) stitches.

Row 23: K1, p1, repeat from * of Sunspots Pattern Row 23 to last stitch, k1.

Row 24: P1, *k1, p11; repeat from * to last 2 stitches, k1, p1.

Work next 48 (48, 60, 60) rows in Sunspots Pattern, ending with Row (24, 24, 12, 12) of Sunspots Pattern.

Back Neck Shaping

X-Small/Small Only

Row 1 (RS): K1, k2tog, [yo, k2tog, yo, p5, yo, ssk, yo, sl1-k2tog-psso] twice, yo, k2tog, yo, p5, yo, ssk, k1; join second ball of yarn and continue the other side as follows: Bind off 25 (37) stitches, k2tog, yo, [p5, yo, ssk, yo, sl1-k2tog-psso, yo, k2tog, yo] twice, p5, [yo, ssk] twice, k1—37 stitches each side.

Row 2 (left side): P5, [k5, p7] twice, k5, p3; **(right side):** Bind off 6 stitches, k1, [p7, k5] twice, p5—31 stitches.

Row 3 (right side): K1, [yo, k3tog, yo, p7, yo, ssk] twice, yo, k3tog, yo, p3; **(left side):** Bind off 6 stitches, p2, [yo, ssk, yo, k3tog, yo, p7] twice, yo, ssk, yo, k2tog—31 stitches.

Row 4 (left side): P4, [k7, p5] twice, k7, p3; **(right side):** Bind off 6 stitches, p1, k7, p5, k7, p4—25 stitches.

Row 5 (right side): [Ssk, yo] twice, p7, yo, sl2-k1-p2sso, yo, ssk, yo, p7, k2; **(left side):** Bind off 6 stitches, k1, p7, yo, sl2-k1-p2sso, yo, ssk, yo, p7, yo, sl2-k1-p2sso, yo, k1—25 stitches.

Row 6 (left side): P4, k7, p5, k7, p2; **(right side):** Bind off 3 stitches, k5, p5, k7, p4—22 stitches.

Row 7 (right side): K1, yo, sl2-k1-p2sso, yo, p7, yo, k2tog, yo, sl2-k1-p2sso, yo, p6; **(left side):** Bind off 4 stitches, p4, yo, k2tog, yo, sl2-k1-p2sso, yo, p7, [yo, k2tog] twice—21 stitches.

Row 8 (left side): P4, k7, p5, k5; **(right side):** Bind off 3 stitches, k2, p5, k7, p4—19 stitches.

Row 9 (right side): K1, increase 1, yo, ssk, yo, p2tog, p3tog, p2tog, yo, k2tog, yo, increase 1, yo, ssk, p3; **(left side):** Bind off 3 stitches, p1, k2tog, yo, increase 1, yo, ssk, yo, p2tog, p3tog, p2tog, yo, k2tog, yo, increase 1, k1—18 stitches.

Row 10 (left side): P6, k3tog, p9; **(right side):** Bind off 2 stitches, p7, k3tog, p6—15 stitches.

Row 11 (right side): K1, increase 1, [yo, ssk] twice, p1, [k2tog, yo] twice, increase 1, yo, ssk, p1; **(left side):** Bind off 3 stitches, increase 1, [yo, ssk] twice, p1, [k2tog, yo] twice, increase 1, k1—15 stitches.

Row 12 (left side): P7, k1, p7; **(right side):** Bind off 2 stitches, p6, k1, p7—15 stitches.

Bind off 15 stitches on each side.

Medium/Large Only

Row 1 (RS): K1, p3, [yo, ssk, yo, sl1-k2tog-psso, yo, k2tog, yo, p5] 3 times, yo, ssk, k2; join second ball of yarn and continue the other side as follows: Bind off 35 (47) stitches, k2, k2tog, yo, p5, [yo, ssk, yo, sl1-k2tog-psso, yo, k2tog, yo, p5] twice, yo, ssk, yo, sl1-k2tog-psso, yo, k2tog, yo, p3, k1—44 stitches each side.

Row 2 (left side): P1, k3, [p7, k5] 3 times, p4; **(right side):** Bind off 5 stitches, k3, [p7, k5] twice, p7, k3, p1—39 stitches.

Row 3 (right side): K1, p4, [yo, ssk, yo, k3tog, yo, p7] twice, yo, ssk, yo, k3tog, yo, p5; **(left side):** Bind off 5 stitches, p4, [yo, ssk, yo, k3tog, yo, p7] twice, yo, ssk, yo, k3tog, yo, p4, k1—39 stitches.

Row 4 (left side): P1, k4, [p5, k7] twice, p5, k5; **(right side):** Bind off 5 stitches, p4, k7, p5, k7, p5, k4, p1—34 stitches.

Row 5 (right side): K1, p4, [yo, sl2-k1-p2sso, yo, ssk, yo, p7] twice, yo, sl2-k1-p2sso, yo, k2; **(left side):** Bind off 5 stitches, k2, ssk, yo, [p7, yo, sl2-k1-p2sso, yo, ssk, yo] twice, p4, k1—34 stitches.

Row 6 (left side): P1, k4, [p5, k7] twice, p5; **(right side):** Bind off 5 stitches, k6, p5, k7, p5, k4, p1—29 stitches.

Row 7 (right side): K1, p4, [yo, k2tog, yo, sl2-k1-p2sso, yo, p7] twice; **(left side):** Bind off 6 stitches, p5, yo, k2tog, yo, sl2-k1-p2sso, yo, p7, yo, k2tog, yo, sl2-k1-p2sso, yo, p4, k1—28 stitches.

Row 8 (left side): P1, k4, p5, k7, p5, k6; **(right side):** Bind off 3 stitches, k3, p5, k7, p5, k4, p1—26 stitches.

Row 9 (right side): K1, p2tog, p2tog, yo, k2tog, yo, double increase, yo, ssk, yo, p2tog, p3tog, p2tog, yo, k2tog, yo, increase 1, yo, ssk, yo, p2tog, p2; **(left side):** Bind off 4 stitches, p1, k2tog, yo, increase 1, yo, ssk, yo, p2tog, p3tog, p2tog, yo, k2tog, yo, double increase, yo, ssk, yo, p2tog, p2tog, k1—24 stitches.

Row 10 (left side): P1, k2tog, p9, k3tog, p9; **(right side):** Bind off 3 stitches, p7, k3tog, p9, k2tog, p1—20 stitches.

Row 11 (right side): K1, p1, [k2tog, yo] twice, double increase, [yo, ssk] twice, p1, [k2tog, yo] twice, increase 1, yo, ssk, k1; **(left side):** Bind off 3 stitches, increase 1, [yo, ssk] twice, p1, [k2tog, yo] twice, double increase, [yo, ssk] twice, p1, k1—21 stitches.

Row 12 (left side): P1, k1, p11, k1, p7; **(right side):** Bind off 2 stitches, p6, k1, p11, k1, p1—21 stitches.

Bind off 21 stitches on each side.

FRONT

Work as for Back until Row 24 of armhole shaping is completed.

Work next 24 (24, 36, 36) rows in Sunspots Pattern, ending with Row (24, 24, 12, 12) of Sunspots Pattern.

Front Neck Shaping

X-Small/Small Only

Row 1 (RS): K1, k2tog, [yo, k2tog, yo, p5, yo, ssk, yo, sl1-k2tog-psso] 3 times, yo, k2tog, yo, p3; join second ball of yarn and continue the other side as follows: Bind off 11 (23) stitches, p3, [yo, ssk, yo, sl1-k2tog-psso, yo, k2tog, yo, p5] 3 times, [yo, ssk] twice, k1—44 stitches each side.

Row 2 (right side): P5, [k5, p7] 3 times, k3; **(left side):** Bind off 3 stitches, p6, k5, [p7, k5] twice, p5—41 stitches.

Row 3 (left side): K1, [yo, k3tog, yo, p7, yo, ssk] 3 times, yo, ssk, yo, k2tog, k2; **(right side):** Bind off 3 stitches, [yo, ssk, yo, k3tog, yo, p7] 3 times, yo, ssk, yo, k2tog—41 stitches.

Row 4 (right side): P4, [k7, p5] 3 times, p1; **(left side):** Bind off 3 stitches, p2, [k7, p5] twice, k7, p4—38 stitches.

Row 5 (left side): [Ssk, yo] twice, [p7, yo, sl2-k1-p2sso, yo, ssk, yo] twice, p7, k3; **(right side):** Bind off 3 stitches, k2, [p7, yo, sl2-k1-p2sso, yo, ssk, yo] twice, p7, yo, sl2-k1-p2sso, yo, k1—38 stitches.

Row 6 (right side): P4, [k7, p5] twice, k7, p3; **(left side):** Bind off 2 stitches, [k7, p5] twice, k7, p4—36 stitches.

Row 7 (left side): K1, [yo, sl2-k1-p2sso, yo, p7, yo, k2tog] twice, yo, sl2-k1-p2sso, yo, p7, k1; **(right side):** Bind off 2 stitches, [p7, yo, k2tog, yo, sl2-k1-p2sso, yo] twice, p7, [yo, k2tog] twice—36 stitches.

Row 8 (right side): P4, [k7, p5] twice, k7, p1; **(left side):** Bind off 2 stitches, k5, [p5, k7] twice, p4—34 stitches.

Row 9 (left side): K1, increase 1, yo, ssk, yo, p2tog, p3tog, p2tog, yo, k2tog, yo, double increase, yo, ssk, yo, p2 tog, p3tog, p2tog, yo, k2tog, yo, increase 1, ssk, p6; **(right side):** Bind off 2 stitches, p5, k2tog, yo, increase 1, yo, ssk, yo, p2tog, p3tog, p2tog, yo, k2tog, yo, double increase, yo, ssk, yo, p2tog, p3tog, p2tog, yo, k2tog, yo, increase 1, k1—34 stitches.

Row 10 (right side): P6, k3tog, p9, k3tog, p8, k5; **(left side):** Bind off 2 stitches, k2, p8, k3tog, p9, k3tog, p6—28 stitches.

Row 11 (left side): K1, increase 1, [yo, ssk] twice, p1, [k2tog, yo] twice, double increase, [yo, ssk] twice, p1, [k2tog, yo] twice, increase 1, yo, ssk, k2, p2; **(right side):** Bind off 2 stitches, p1, k2, k2tog, yo, increase 1, [yo, ssk] twice, p1, [k2tog, yo] twice, double increase, [yo, ssk] twice, p1, [k2tog, yo] twice, increase 1, k1—32 stitches.

Row 12 (right side): P7, [k1, p11] twice, k2; **(left side):** Bind off 2 stitches, p9, k1, p11, k1, p7—30 stitches.

Row 13 (left side): K1, p3, [yo, ssk, yo, sl1-k2tog-psso, yo, k2tog, yo, p5] twice, k2; **(right side):** Bind off 2 stitches, k1, [p5, yo, ssk, yo, sl1-k2tog-psso, yo, k2tog, yo] twice, p3, k1—30 stitches.

Row 14 (right side): P1, k3, [7, k5] twice, p2; **(left side):** Bind off 2 stitches, k4, p7, k5, p7, k3, p1—28 stitches.

Row 15 (left side): K1, p4, yo, ssk, yo, k3tog, yo, p7, yo, ssk, yo, k3tog, yo, p6; **(right side):** Bind off 2 stitches, p5, yo, ssk, yo, k3tog, yo, p7, yo, ssk, yo, k3tog, yo, p4, k1—28 stitches.

Row 16 (right side): P1, k4, p5, k7, p5, k6; **(left side):** Bind off 2 stitches, k3, p5, k7, p5, k4, p1—26 stitches.

Row 17 (left side): K1, p4, yo, sl2-k1-p2sso, yo, ssk, yo, p7, yo, sl2-k1-p2sso, yo, ssk, yo, p4; **(right side):** Bind off 2 stitches, p3, yo, sl2-k1-p2sso, yo, ssk, yo, p7, yo, sl2-k1-p2sso, yo, ssk, yo, p4, k1—26 stitches.

Row 18 (right side): P1, k4, p5, k7, p5, k4; **(left side):** Bind off 2 stitches, k1, p5, k7, p5, k4, p1—24 stitches.

Row 19 (left side): K1, p4, yo, k2tog, yo, sl2-k1-p2sso, yo, p7, yo, k2tog, yo, sl2-k1-p2sso, yo, p2; **(right side):** Bind off 2 stitches, p1, yo, k2tog, yo, sl2-k1-p2sso, yo, p7, yo, k2tog, yo, sl2-k1-p2sso, yo, p4, k1—24 stitches.

Row 20 (right side): P1, k4, p5, k7, p5, k2; **(left side):** Bind off 1 stitch, p5, k7, p5, k4, p1—23 stitches.

Row 21 (left side): K1, p2tog, p2tog, yo, k2tog, yo, double increase, yo, ssk, yo, p2tog, p3tog, p2tog, yo, k2tog, yo, increase 1, k2, p1; **(right side):** Bind off 2 stitches, k1, increase 1, yo, ssk, yo, p2tog, p3tog, p2tog, yo, k2tog, yo, double increase, yo, ssk, yo, p2tog, p2tog, k1—22 stitches.

Row 22 (right side): P1, k2tog, p9, k3tog, p7; **(left side):** Bind off 1 stitch, p6, k3tog, p9, k2tog, p1—19 stitches.

Row 23 (left side): K1, p1, [k2tog, yo] twice, double increase, [yo, ssk] twice, p1, [k2tog, yo] twice, increase 1, k2; **(right side):** Bind off 1 stitch, increase 1, [yo, ssk] twice, p1, [k2tog, yo] twice, double increase, [yo, ssk] twice, p1, k1—21 stitches.

Row 24 (right side): P1, k1, p11, k1, p7; **(left side):** Bind off 2 stitches, p6, k1, p11, k1, p1—21 stitches.

Row 25 (left side): K1, [k2tog, yo] twice, p5, yo, ssk, yo, sl1-k2tog-psso, yo, k2tog, yo, p4; **(right side):** Bind off 1 stitch, p2, yo, ssk, yo, sl1-k2tog-psso, yo, k2tog, yo, p5, [yo, ssk] twice, k1—20 stitches.

Row 26 (right side): P5, k5, p7, k3; **(left side):** Bind off 1 stitch, k2, p7, k5, p5—20 stitches.

Row 27 (left side): K1, yo, k3tog, yo, p7, yo, ssk, yo, k3tog, yo, p4; **(right side):** Bind off 1 stitch, p2, yo, ssk, yo, k3tog, yo, p7, yo, ssk, yo, k2tog—19 stitches.

Row 28 (right side): P4, k7, p5, k3; **(left side):** Bind off 1 stitch, k2, p5, k7, p4—19 stitches.

Row 29 (left side): [Ssk, yo] twice, p7, yo, sl2-k1-p2sso, yo, ssk, yo, p3; **(right side):** Bind off 1 stitch, p1, yo, sl2-k1-p2sso, yo, ssk, yo, p7, yo, sl2-k1-p2sso, yo, k1—18 stitches.

Row 30 (right side): P4, k7, p5, k2; **(left side):** Bind off 1 stitch, k1, p5, k7, p4—18 stitches.

Row 31 (left side): K1, yo, sl2-k1-p2sso, yo, p7, yo, k2tog, yo, sl2-k1-p2sso, yo, p2; **(right side):** Bind off 1 stitch, yo, k2tog, yo, sl2-k1-p2sso, yo, p7, [yo, k2tog] twice—17 stitches.

Row 32 (right side): P4, k7, p5, k1; **(left side):** Bind off 1 stitch, p5, k7, p4—17 stitches.

Row 33 (left side): K1, increase 1, yo, ssk, yo, p2tog, p3tog, p2tog, yo, k2tog, yo, increase 1, k2, p1; **(right side):** Bind off 1 stitch, k1, increase 1, yo, ssk, yo, p2tog, p3tog, p2tog, yo, k2tog, yo, increase 1, k1—16 stitches.

Row 34 (right side): P6, k3tog, p7; **(left side):** Bind off 1 stitch, p6, k3tog, p6—16 stitches.

Row 35 (left side): K1, increase 1, [yo, ssk] twice, p1, [k2tog, yo] twice, increase 1, k2; **(right side):** Bind off 1 stitch, increase 1, [yo, ssk] twice, p1, [k2tog, yo] twice, increase 1, k1—15 stitches.

Row 36 (right side): P7, k1, p7; **(left side):** Bind off 1 stitch, p6, k1, p7—15 stitches.

Bind off 15 stitches on each side.

Medium/Large Only

Row 1 (RS): K1, p3, [yo, ssk, yo, sl1-k2tog-psso, yo, k2tog, yo, p5] 3 times, yo, ssk, yo, sl1-k2tog-psso, yo, k2tog, yo, p3; join second ball of yarn and continue the other side as follows: Bind off 23 (35) stitches, p3, [yo, ssk, yo, sl1-k2tog-psso, yo, k2tog, yo, p5] 3 times, yo, ssk, yo, sl1-k2tog-psso, yo, k2tog, yo, p3, k1—50 stitches each side.

Row 2 (right side): P1, k3, [p7, k5] 3 times, p7, k3; **(left side):** Bind off 3 stitches, p6, k5, [p7, k5) twice, p7, k3, p1—47 stitches.

Row 3 (left side): K1, p4, [yo, ssk, yo, k3tog, yo, p7] 3 times, yo, ssk, yo, k2tog, k2; **(right side):** Bind off 3 stitches, [yo, ssk, yo, k3tog, yo, p7] 3 times, yo, ssk, yo, k3tog, yo, p4, k1—47 stitches.

Row 4 (right side): P1, k4, [p5, k7] 3 times, p6; **(left side):** Bind off 3 stitches, p2, [k7, p5] 3 times, k4, p1—44 stitches.

Row 5 (left side): K1, p4, [yo, sl2-k1-p2sso, yo, ssk, yo, p7] 3 times, k3; **(right side):** Bind off 3 stitches, k2, [p7, yo, sl2-k1-p2sso, yo, ssk, yo,] 3 times, p4, k1—44 stitches.

Row 6 (right side): P1, k4, [p5, k7] 3 times, k3; **(left side):** Bind off 3 stitches, k6, p5, [k7, p5] twice, k4, p1—41 stitches.

Row 7 (left side): K1, p4, [yo, k2tog, yo, sl2-k1-p2sso, yo, p7] 3 times; **(right side):** Bind off 3 stitches, p6, yo, k2tog, yo, sl2-k1-p2sso, yo, [p7, yo, k2tog, yo, sl2-k1-p2sso, yo] twice, p4, k1—41 stitches.

Row 8 (right side): P1, k4, [p5, k7] 3 times; **(left side):** Bind off 2 stitches, k4, [p5, k7] twice, p5, k4, p1—39 stitches.

Row 9 (left side): K1, p2tog, p2tog, [yo, k2tog, yo, double increase, yo, ssk, yo, p2tog, p3tog, p2tog] twice, yo, k2tog, yo, increase 1, k3, p4; **(right side):** Bind off 2 stitches, p3, k3, increase 1, yo, ssk, yo, [p2tog, p3tog, p2tog, yo, k2tog, yo, double increase, yo, ssk, yo] twice, p2tog, p2tog, k1—39 stitches.

Row 10 (right side): P1, k2tog, [p9, k3tog] twice, p9, k3; **(left side):** Bind off 2 stitches, [p9, k3tog] twice, p9, k2tog, p1—32 stitches.

Row 11 (left side): K1, [p1, (k2tog, yo) twice, double increase, (yo, ssk) twice] twice, p1, [k2tog, yo] twice, increase 1, k5; **(right side):** Bind off 2 stitches, k4, increase 1, [yo, ssk] twice, [p1, (k2tog, yo) twice, double increase, (yo, ssk) twice] twice, p1, k1—37 stitches.

Row 12 (right side): P1, [k1, p11] 3 times; **(left side):** Bind off 2 stitches, p8, [k1, p11] twice, k1, p1—35 stitches.

Row 13 (left side): K1, k2tog, [yo, k2tog, yo, p5, yo, ssk, yo, sl1-k2tog-psso] twice, yo, k2tog, yo, p6; **(right side):** Bind off 2 stitches, p5, [yo, ssk, yo, sl1-k2tog-psso, yo, k2tog, yo, p5] twice, [yo, ssk] twice, k1—35 stitches.

Row 14 (right side): P5, [k5, p7] twice, k5, p1; **(left side):** Bind off 2 stitches, k3, [p7, k5] twice, p5—33 stitches.

Row 15 (left side): K1, [yo, k3tog, yo, p7, yo, ssk] twice, yo, k3tog, yo, p5; **(right side):** Bind off 2 stitches, p4, [yo, ssk, yo, k3tog, yo, p7] twice, yo, ssk, yo, k2tog—33 stitches.

Row 16 (right side): P4, [k7, p5] twice, k5; **(left side):** Bind off 2 stitches, k2, [p5, k7] twice, p4—31 stitches.

Row 17 (left side): [Ssk, yo] twice, [p7, yo, sl2-k1-p2sso, yo, ssk, yo] twice, p3; **(right side):** bind off 2 stitches, p2, [yo, sl2-k1-p2sso, yo, ssk, yo, p7] twice, yo, sl2-k1-p2sso, yo, k1—31 stitches.

Row 18 (right side): P4, [k7, p5] twice, k3; **(left side):** Bind off 1 stitch, k1, [p5, k7] twice, p4—30 stitches.

Row 19 (left side): K1, [yo, sl2-k1-p2sso, yo, p7, yo, k2tog] twice, yo, sl2-k1-p2sso, yo, p2; **(right side):** Bind off 2 stitches, [yo, k2tog, yo, sl2-k1-p2sso, yo, p7] twice, [yo, k2tog] twice—29 stitches.

Row 20 (right side): P4, [k7, p5] twice, k1; **(left side):** Bind off 1 stitch, [p5, k7] twice, p4—29 stitches.

Row 21 (left side): K1, increase 1, yo, ssk, yo, p2tog, p3tog, p2tog, yo, k2tog, yo, double increase, yo, ssk, yo, p2 tog, p3tog, p2tog, yo, k2tog, yo, increase 1, k2, p1; **(right side):** Bind off 1 stitch, k1, increase 1, yo, ssk, yo, p2tog, p3 tog, p2tog, yo, k2tog, yo, double increase, yo, ssk, yo, p2tog, p3tog, p2tog, yo, k2tog, yo, increase 1, k1—28 stitches.

Row 22 (right side): P6, k3tog, p9, k3tog, p7; **(left side):** Bind off 1 stitch, p6, k3tog, p9, k3tog, p6—24 stitches.

Row 23 (left side): K1, increase 1, [yo, ssk] twice, p1, [k2tog, yo] twice, double increase, [yo, ssk] twice, p1, [k2tog, yo] twice, increase 1, k2; **(right side):** Bind off 1 stitch, increase 1, [yo, ssk] twice, p1, [k2tog, yo] twice, double increase, [yo, ssk] twice, p1, [k2tog, yo] twice, increase 1, k1—27 stitches.

Row 24 (right side): P7, k1, p11, k7; **(left side):** Bind off 1 stitch, p6, k1, p11, k1, p7—27 stitches.

Row 25 (left side): K1, p3, yo, ssk, yo, sl1-k2tog-psso, yo, k2tog, yo, p5, yo, ssk, yo, sl1-k2tog-psso, yo, k2tog, yo, p4; **(right side):** Bind off 1 stitch, p2, yo, ssk, yo, sl1-k2tog-psso, yo, k2tog, yo, p5, yo, ssk, yo, sl1-k2tog-psso, yo, k2tog, yo, p3, k1—26 stitches.

Row 26 (right side): P1, k3, p7, k5, p7, k3; **(left side):** Bind off 1 stitch, k2, p7, k5, p7, k3, p1—26 stitches.

Row 27 (left side): K1, p4, yo, ssk, yo, k3tog, yo, p7, yo, ssk, yo, k3tog, yo, p4; **(right side):** Bind off 1 stitch, p2, yo, ssk, yo, k3tog, yo, p7, yo, ssk, yo, k3tog, yo, p4, k1—25 stitches.

Row 28 (right side): P1, k4, p5, k7, p5, k3; **(left side):** Bind off 1 stitch, k2, p5, k7, p5, k4, p1—25 stitches.

Row 29 (left side): K1, p4, yo, sl2-k1-p2sso, yo, ssk, yo, p7, yo, sl2-k1-p2sso, yo, ssk, yo, p3; **(right side):** Bind off 1 stitch, p1, yo, sl2-k1-p2sso, yo, ssk, yo, p7, yo, sl2-k1-p2sso, yo, ssk, yo, p4, k1—24 stitches.

Row 30 (right side): P1, k4, p5, k7, p5, k2; **(left side):** Bind off 1 stitch, k1, p5, k7, p5, k4, p1—24 stitches.

Row 31 (left side): K1, p4, yo, k2tog, yo, sl2-k1-p2sso, yo, p7, yo, k2tog, yo, sl2-k1-p2sso, yo, p2; **(right side):** Bind off 1 stitch, yo, k2tog, yo, sl2-k1-p2sso, yo, p7, yo, k2tog, yo, sl2-k1-p2sso, yo, p4, k1—23 stitches.

Row 32 (right side): P1, k4, p5, k7, p5, k1; **(left side):** Bind off 1 stitch, p5, k7, p5, k4, p1—23 stitches.

Row 33 (left side): K1, p2tog, p2tog, yo, k2tog, yo, double increase, yo, ssk, yo, p2tog, p3tog, p2tog, yo, k2tog, yo, increase 1, k2, p1; **(right side):** Bind off 1 stitch, k1, increase 1, yo, ssk, yo, p2tog, p3tog, p2tog, yo, k2tog, yo, double increase, yo, ssk, yo, p2tog, p2tog, k1—22 stitches.

Row 34 (right side): P1, k2tog, p9, k3tog, p7; **(left side):** Bind off 1 stitch, p6, k3tog, p9, k2tog, p1—22 stitches.

Row 35 (left side): K1, p1, [k2tog, yo] twice, double increase, [yo, ssk] twice, p1, [k2tog, yo] twice, increase 1, k2; **(right side):** Bind

off 1 stitch, increase 1, [yo, ssk] twice, p1, [k2tog, yo] twice, double increase, [yo, ssk] twice, p1, k1—21 stitches.

Row 36 (right side): P1, k1, p11, k1, p7; **(left side):** Bind off 1 stitch, p6, k1, p11, k1, p1—21 stitches.

Bind off 21 stitches on each side.

FINISHING
Sew side and shoulder seams.

Neckband
Join yarn. With size 0 circular needle and right side facing, starting from Back, pick up and knit stitches evenly around the neck (about 7 stitches per inch [2.5cm]). Join stitches in round, place marker at beginning of round and work 6 rounds in garter stitch (purl on odd rounds, knit on even rounds). K3tog at the shoulder seams in every knit round (this will help contour the neckband and create a better fit). Bind off tightly.

Armhole Finishing
Working same as neckband, starting from underarm, pick up and knit about 7 stitches per inch (2.5cm) spaced evenly around each armhole. Join stitches in round, place marker at beginning of round and work 6 rounds in garter stitch (purl on odd rounds, knit on even rounds), working k3tog at underarm in every knit round. Bind off tightly.

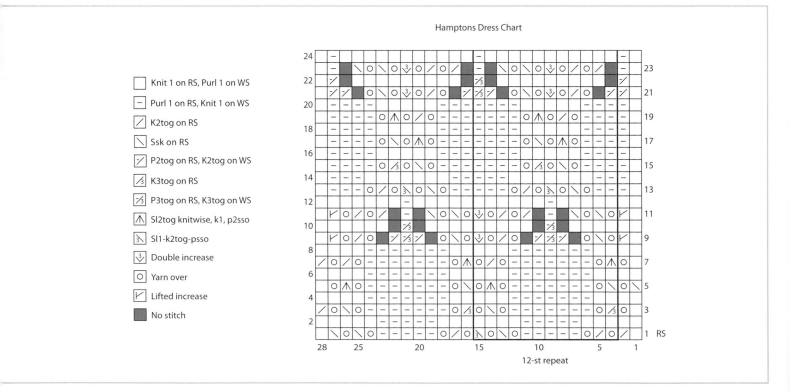

Hamptons Dress Chart

Knit 1 on RS, Purl 1 on WS
Purl 1 on RS, Knit 1 on WS
K2tog on RS
Ssk on RS
P2tog on RS, K2tog on WS
K3tog on RS
P3tog on RS, K3tog on WS
Sl2tog knitwise, k1, p2sso
Sl1-k2tog-psso
Double increase
Yarn over
Lifted increase
No stitch

12-st repeat

LACE CAP

by Phoenix Bess

SKILL LEVEL
Intermediate

SIZE
S (M, L)

Directions are for smallest size, with larger sizes in parentheses.

FINISHED MEASUREMENTS
- Head Circumference: 20 (22, 23)" (51 [56, 58.5]cm)

MATERIALS
- 1 skein Vickie Howell Love by Southwest Trading Company (each approximately 1¾ oz [50g], 99 yd [90m], 70% bamboo, 30% silk), in color #253 Shelby and Jackson (4) medium
- Size 8 (5mm) circular needle, 40" (101.5cm) long (for Magic Loop technique), *or size needed to obtain gauge*, OR
- Size 8 (5mm) set of double-pointed needles or circular needle, 16" (40.5cm) long, *or size needed to obtain gauge*
- Size 4 (3.5mm) circular needle, 16" (40.5cm) long
- Stitch marker
- Yarn needle

GAUGE
16 stitches and 26 rounds = 4" (10cm) in pattern stitch worked in the round using size 8 (5mm) needles. *To save time, take time to check your gauge.*

SPECIAL STITCHES
(see Glossary on page 162)
bind off loosely; k2tog; k2, p2 rib; kfb; magic loop; yo

NOTES
1. The Lace Cap is worked from the top down to the ribbed edge.
2. The spiral at the top of the cap begins with a small number of stitches worked in the round. These can be worked on double-pointed needles or a long circular (page 10 for Magic Loop). When there are enough stitches to go around the shorter circular needle, slip all of the stitches to the short circular needle and work in the round.

INSTRUCTIONS

CAP

Cast on 8 stitches. Divide stitches in half onto larger circular needle for the Magic Loop, or distribute stitches evenly over double-pointed needles. Join to begin working in the round, taking care not to twist stitches. Place marker at the beginning of the round.

Round 1: (Kfb) in each stitch—16 stitches.

Round 2: *Yo, k2tog; repeat from * around.

Round 3: *Kfb, k1; repeat from * around—24 stitches.

Round 4: *Yo, k2tog; repeat from * around.

Round 5: *Kfb, k2; repeat from * around—32 stitches.

Round 6: *Yo, k2tog; repeat from * around.

Round 7: *Kfb, k3; repeat from * around—40 stitches.

Round 8: *Yo, k2tog; repeat from * around.

Round 9: *Kfb, k4; repeat from * around—48 stitches.

Round 10: *Yo, k2tog; repeat from * around.

Round 11: *Kfb, k5; repeat from * around—56 stitches.

Round 12: *Yo, k2tog; repeat from * around.

Round 13: Kfb, k6; repeat from * around—64 stitches.

Round 14: *Yo, k2tog; repeat from * around.

Round 15: *Kfb, k7; repeat from * around—72 stitches.

Round 16: *Yo, k2tog; repeat from * around.

Round 17: *Kfb, k8; repeat from * around—80 stitches.

Medium Only

Round 18: *Yo, k2tog; repeat from * around.

Round 19: *Kfb, k9; repeat from * around—88 stitches

Large Only

Round 18: *Yo, k2tog; repeat from * around.

Round 19: *Kfb, k10; repeat from * around—92 stitches.

All Sizes
Repeat Round 2 for 2½" (6.5cm) more.

Ribbed Band

Change to smaller-size circular needle. Work in k2, p2 rib for
2" (5cm). Using larger needles, bind off loosely in rib pattern.

FINISHING

Weave in ends. Hand wash. Wring and blot to remove excess water,
and dry flat.

LACY SKIRT

by Kristin Omdahl

SKILL LEVEL
Intermediate

SIZE
One size

FINISHED MEASUREMENTS
- Circumference of skirt at waist: 29" (74cm)
- Circumference of skirt at hem: 54" (137cm)
- Length: 28" [71cm]

MATERIALS
- 4 skeins Sierra by Tahki Stacy Charles (each approximately 1.8oz [50g], 135 yd [123m], 62% silk, 30% linen, 8% nylon), in color #009 Light Plum 4 medium
- Size 3 (3.25mm) circular needle, *or size needed to obtain gauge*
- Size 8 (5mm) circular needle and double-pointed needles for I-cord drawstring
- Scrap cotton yarn for provisional cast-on
- Stitch markers
- Yarn needle

GAUGE
20 stitches and 32 rows = 4" (10cm) in stockinette stitch using size 3 (3.25mm) needles.

12 stitches and 16 rows = 4" (10cm) (after blocking) in lace stitch pattern using larger needles.

To save time, take time to check your gauge.

SPECIAL STITCHES
(see Glossary on page 162)
I-cord; k2tog; provisional cast-on; sl1-k2tog-psso; ssk; yo

INSTRUCTIONS

WAISTBAND

With provisional cast-on technique, cast on 156 stitches. Place marker to join in the round.

Knit even for 1" (2.5cm)

Purl the next round (leaves a garter ridge for turning the waistband later).

Knit even for ½" (1.3cm)

Next Round: Knit 72 stitches, bind off 2 stitches, knit 8 stitches, bind off 2 stitches, knit 72 stitches, slip marker.

Next Round: Knit 72 stitches, cast on 2 stitches, knit 8, cast on 2 stitches, knit 72 stitches, slip marker.

Knit even for ½" (13mm).

To join the waistband, *pick up a stitch from the provisional cast-on directly below the next stitch on left-hand needle, knit them together. Repeat from * around—156 stitches.

Knit 1 round.

SKIRT

Change to larger needles.

Round 1 and all odd-numbered rounds: Knit.

Round 2: *Yo, ssk, k1, k2tog, yo, k1; repeat from * around.

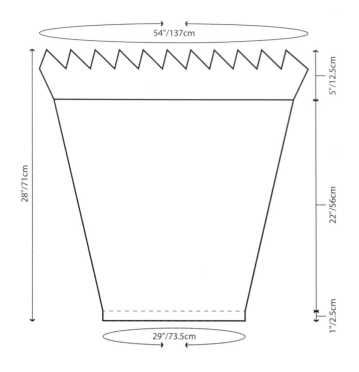

EDGING

Note: Edging is worked perpendicularly to the skirt. The last stitch of every odd row is joined to one live skirt stitch with a k2tog.

Cast on 7 stitches onto needle with skirt.

Row 1: K6, k2tog.

Row 2: K2, (yo, k2tog) twice, yo, k1.

Row 3: K7, k2tog.

Row 4: K2, (yo, k2tog) twice, yo, k2.

Row 5: K8, k2tog.

Row 6: K2, (yo, k2tog) 3 times, yo, k1.

Row 7: K9, k2tog.

Row 8: K2, (yo, k2tog) 3 times, yo, k2.

Row 9: Bind off 4 stitches, k5, k2tog.

Repeat Rows 2–9 for remainder of skirt until Row 9 of last repeat.

Row 9 of last repeat: Bind off 4 stitches, k5, k3tog.

Bind off all stitches.

Join cast-on edge to bound-off edge. Fasten off.

I-CORD DRAWSTRING

With double-pointed needles, cast on 3 stitches and knit 1 row. *Do not turn, slide the stitches back to the other side of the needle. Knit the next row, pulling the yarn snug at the beginning; repeat from * until I-cord is approximately 60" (152.5cm) long or desired length. Bind off all stitches.

FINISHING

Weave in loose ends.

Round 4: *Yo, k1, sl1-k2tog-psso, k1, yo, k1; repeat from * around.

Round 6: *K2tog, yo, k1, yo, ssk, k1; repeat from * around.

Round 8: K2tog, (yo, k1) twice, sl1-k2tog-psso, *k1, (yo, k1) twice, sl1-k2tog-psso; repeat from * until last 5 stitches, (k1, yo) twice, k2tog, k1—156 stitches.

Repeat Rounds 1–8 until skirt measures 23" (58.5cm).

Note: Make sure to determine skirt length based on blocked lace gauge.

Do not fasten off.

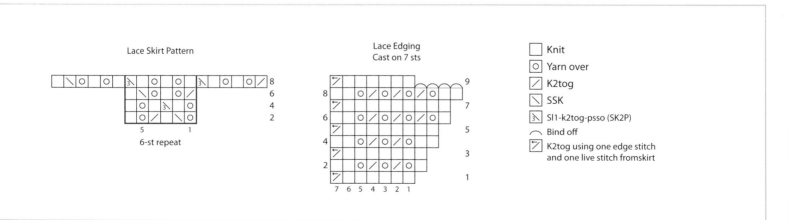

LEAF-PANELED SWEATER

by Berta Karapetyan

SKILL LEVEL
Intermediate

SIZE
XS (S, M, L)

Directions are for smallest size, with larger sizes in parentheses.

FINISHED MEASUREMENTS
- Bust: 31 (33, 35, 38)" (79 [84, 89, 96.5]cm)
- Length: 22 (22½, 22½, 22½)" (56 [57, 57, 57]cm)

MATERIALS
- 6 (6, 7, 7) balls Zodiac by Karabella (each approximately 1¾ oz [50g], 98 yd [90m], 100% mercerized cotton), in color #234 Mint Green **(4)** medium
- Size 6 (4mm) needles and circular needle, 16" (40.5cm) long, *or size needed to obtain gauge*
- Stitch markers
- Stitch holders
- Yarn needle

GAUGE
20 stitches and 24 rows = 4" (10cm) over stockinette stitch. *To save time, take time to check your gauge.*

SPECIAL STITCHES
(see Glossary on page 162)

m1; sl1-k2tog-psso; slip stitch (knit); ssk; yo

SPECIAL PATTERN(S)

Right Leaf Panel (10 stitches)
Row 1 and all other WS rows: Purl.

Row 2: K6, (ssk, return the resulting stitch to left-hand needle and with point of right-hand needle pass the next stitch on the left needle over the returned stitch and off the needle; then slip the returned stitch back to the right-hand needle—ssk and pass), yo, k1, yo.

Row 4: K4, ssk and pass, k1, [yo, k1] twice.

Row 6: K2, ssk and pass, k2, yo, k1, yo, k2.

Row 8: Ssk and pass, k3, yo, k1, yo, k3.

Repeat Rows 1–8 for pattern.

Left Leaf Panel (10 stitches)
Row 1 and all odd rows: Purl.

Row 2: Yo, k1, yo, sl1-k2tog-psso, k6.

Row 4: K1, (yo, k1) twice, sl1-k2tog-psso, k4.

Row 6: K2, yo, k1, yo, k2, sl1-k2tog-psso, k2.

Row 8: K3, yo, k1, yo, k3, sl1-k2tog-psso.

Repeat Rows 1–8 for pattern.

INSTRUCTIONS

BACK

Cast on 86 (90, 94, 100) stitches.

Row 1 (WS): K2, work Left Leaf Panel, k20 (22, 24, 27), work Right Leaf Panel, k2, work Left Leaf Panel, k20 (22, 24, 27), work Right Leaf Panel, k2.

Row 2 (RS): P2, work Left Leaf Panel, p20 (22, 24, 27), work Right Leaf Panel, p2, work Left Leaf Panel, p20 (22, 24, 27), work Right Leaf Panel, p2.

Repeat these 2 rows 14 times more.

Next Row (Decrease Row): K2, work Left Leaf Panel, place marker, k2tog, k18 (20, 22, 25), work Right Leaf Panel, k2, work Left Leaf Panel, k18 (20, 22, 25), ssk, place marker, work Right Leaf Panel, k2—84 (88, 92, 98) stitches.

Work 11 rows even in pattern, slipping markers. Repeat Decrease Row (decreasing after first marker and before last marker)—82 (86, 90, 96) stitches. Work 11 rows even.

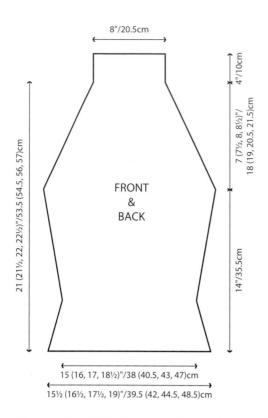

8"/20.5cm

4"/10cm

7 (7½, 8, 8½)"/
18 (19, 20.5, 21.5)cm

FRONT & BACK

21 (21½, 22, 22½)"/53.5 (54.5, 56, 57)cm

14"/35.5cm

15 (16, 17, 18½)"/38 (40.5, 43, 47)cm

15½ (16½, 17½, 19)"/39.5 (42, 44.5, 48.5)cm

Next Row (Increase Row): Work even to first marker, m1 after first marker, work in pattern between markers, m1 before last marker, work to end—84 (88, 92, 98) stitches.

Repeat this increase row every 16th row twice more—88 (92, 96, 102) stitches.

Work even until piece measures 14" (35.5cm) from cast-on.

Armhole Shaping

Note: Slip first stitch of every row for a neat edge (right-side rows as if to purl, wrong-side rows as if to knit).

X-Small and Small Only
Keeping continuity of Leaf Panels, decrease as follows:

Row 1 (WS): Slip 1, k1, work Left Leaf Panel, slip marker, k2tog, work in pattern across row to 2 stitches before next marker, ssk, slip marker, work Right Leaf Panel, k2—86 (90) stitches.

Row 2: Work even in pattern.

Row 3: Work decreases as in Row 1—84 (88) stitches.

Row 4: Work even in pattern.

Row 5: Work even in pattern.

Repeat these 5 rows until 2 stitches remain before, after, and between each of the Leaf Panels. Place remaining 50 stitches on a holder for neck.

Medium and Large Only

Row 1 (WS): Slip 1, k1, work Left Leaf Panel, slip marker, k2tog, work in pattern across row to 2 stitches before next marker, ssk, slip marker, work Right Leaf Panel, k2—(94, 100) stitches.

Row 2: Slip 1 purlwise, work even in pattern.

Repeat these 2 rows until 2 stitches remain before, after, and between each of the leaf panels.

Medium Only
Work even in pattern for 6 rows more.

Medium and Large Only
Place remaining 50 stitches on a holder for neck.

FRONT
Work same as for Back.

MOCK TURTLENECK

Note: Neck is worked in the round. When working the leaf panels, the purl stitches listed on odd-numbered rows are now worked as knit stitches. That is, Right Leaf Panel, Row 1 will now be worked as Round 1: Knit, and so forth.

Place 50 stitches from front and 50 stitches from back onto 16" (40.5cm) circular needle. With right side facing, rejoin yarn and keeping continuity of leaf panels, *p2tog, work Left Leaf Panel, p2, work Right Leaf Panel, p2, work Left Leaf Panel, P2, work Right Leaf Panel, p2tog; repeat from * once more. Join stitches in the round and work even in pattern without further decreases for 4" (10cm). Bind off.

FINISHING
Sew side seams. Weave in ends.

LACY CAP-SLEEVE BOLERO

by Phoenix Bess

SKILL LEVEL
Intermediate

SIZE
XS (S, M, L, XL)

Directions are for smallest size, with larger sizes in parentheses.

FINISHED MEASUREMENTS
- Length: 13 (15, 16½, 18, 19½)" (33 [38, 42, 45.5, 49.5]cm)
- Width from shoulder to shoulder: 17 (18, 20, 22, 23)" (43 [45.5, 51, 56, 58.5]cm)

MATERIALS
- 1 (1, 1, 1, 2) skeins Sequin Silk Disco Lights by Tilli Tomas (each approximately 3½ oz [100g], 225 yd [205m], 90% silk, 10% petite sequins), in color Rattan ⬛ medium
- Size 10½ (6.5mm) circular needle, 24" (61cm) long, *or size needed to obtain gauge*
- Size 13 (9mm) circular needle, 24" (61cm) long
- Stitch marker
- Yarn needle

GAUGE
10 stitches and 18 rows = 4" (10cm) in lace stitch worked flat using size 10½ (6.5mm) needle.

14 stitches and 24 rounds = 4" (10cm) in k2, p2 rib worked in the round using size 10½ (6.5mm) needle.

To save time, take time to check your gauge.

SPECIAL STITCHES
(see Glossary on page 162)

bind off loosely; bind off in rib; increase 1; k2, p2 rib; k2tog; pick up and knit; yo

SPECIAL PATTERN
Lace Pattern
Row 1: K1, *yo, k2tog; repeat from * to end.
Repeat this row for Lace Pattern.

NOTES
1. The Lacy Cap-Sleeve Bolero is a rectangle that is worked back and forth in rows on circular needles. It is worked from one sleeve edge to the other and then folded in half to make armholes.
2. Stitches are picked up along the long edges and worked in k2, p2 rib in the round for the neck and bottom edging.

INSTRUCTIONS

BOLERO
With smaller needle, cast on 24 (28, 32, 36, 40) stitches loosely. Work 2 rows in k2, p2 rib, decreasing 1 stitch on second row—23 (27, 31, 35, 39) stitches.

Change to Lace Pattern, and work until piece measures 16½ (17½, 19½, 21½, 22½)" (42 [44.5, 49.5, 54.5, 57]cm) from the cast-on edge.

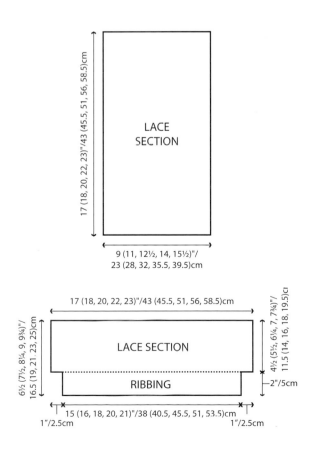

LACE SECTION

17 (18, 20, 22, 23)"/43 (45.5, 51, 56, 58.5)cm

9 (11, 12½, 14, 15½)"/
23 (28, 32, 35.5, 39.5)cm

17 (18, 20, 22, 23)"/43 (45.5, 51, 56, 58.5)cm

6½ (7½, 8¼, 9, 9¾)"/
16.5 (19, 21, 23, 25)cm

LACE SECTION

RIBBING

4½ (5½, 6¼, 7, 7¾)"/
11.5 (14, 16, 18, 19.5)cm

2"/5cm

15 (16, 18, 20, 21)"/38 (40.5, 45.5, 51, 53.5)cm

1"/2.5cm   1"/2.5cm

Work 2 rows in k2, p2 rib, increasing 1 stitch on first row—24 (28, 32, 36, 40) stitches. Bind off in rib.

Fold the lace rectangle in half lengthwise. Using a yarn needle and matching yarn, sew together 1" (2.5cm) at either end of long edges for armholes.

Edging

With right side facing and smaller needle, pick up and knit 108 (112, 128, 140, 148) stitches evenly around the remaining long edges of folded rectangle for neck and back edging.

Place stitch marker, and join for working in the round, being careful not to twist stitches.

Work in k2, p2 rib for 2" (5cm). Work 1 round very loosely to prepare for switching to the larger needle (otherwise, the larger needle will not fit in the stitches). Change to the larger needle for the last round, and knit very loosely to make sure the last row will have some give. Bind off loosely in rib.

FINISHING

Weave in ends.

TRELLIS SHAWL

by Berta Karapetyan

SKILL LEVEL
Easy

SIZE
S/M (L/XL)

Directions are for smallest size, with larger sizes in parentheses.

FINISHED MEASUREMENTS
- Length: 20" (51cm)
- Width: 70 (75)" (178 [191]cm)

MATERIALS
- 5 (6) balls Margrite by Karabella (each approximately 1¾ oz [50g], 154 yd [140m], 80% extra-fine merino wool, 20% cashmere), in color #4 Grey **(3)** light
- 3 (4) balls Mirage by Karabella (each approximately 1¾ oz [50g] balls, 245 yd [225m], 72% kid mohair, 28% polyamide), in color #50211 Beige **(4)** medium
- Size 8 (5mm) needles, *or size needed to obtain gauge*
- Yarn needle

GAUGE
12½ stitches and 22 rows = 4" (10cm) in trellis pattern with 1 strand of each yarn held together.
To save time, take time to check your gauge.

SPECIAL STITCHES
(see Glossary on page 162)
k2tog; slip stitch (knit); ssk

SPECIAL PATTERN
Vertical Lace Trellis (odd number of stitches)
Row 1: (RS) Slip 1, k1, *yo, k2tog; repeat from * to last stitch, k1.
Rows 2 and 4: Slip 1, purl to end.
Row 3: Slip 1, *ssk, yo; repeat from * to last 2 stitches, k2.
Repeat these 4 rows for pattern.

INSTRUCTIONS

BODY
With 1 strand of each yarn held together, cast on 63 stitches and work in trellis pattern for 70 (75)" [178 (191)cm]. Bind off.

SLEEVES
With 1 strand of each yarn held together, cast on 51 stitches and work in trellis pattern for 7" (18cm). Bind off.

FINISHING
With wrong side facing, fold both ends of the Body to the center. Sew Sleeves to each end of folded Body as shown on schematic. Leave the rest of the Body unsewn. Sew Sleeve seams together.

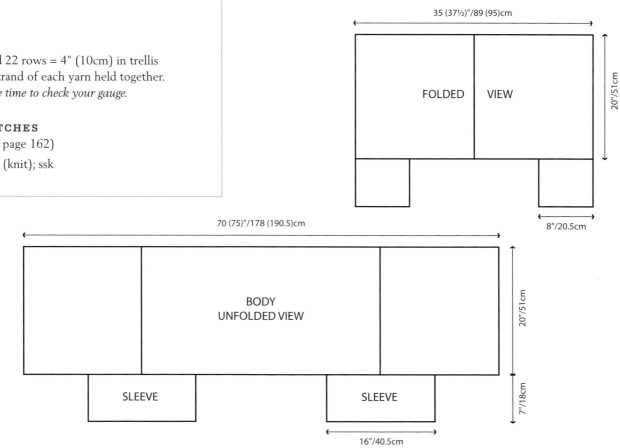

GIVERNY WRAP

by Cheryl Niamath

SKILL LEVEL
Easy

SIZE
One size

FINISHED MEASUREMENTS
- Width: 17" (43cm)
- Length: 64" (163cm)

MATERIALS
- 3 balls Kidsilk Haze by Rowan (each approximately 25g, 229yd [210m], 70% kid mohair, 30% silk), in color #600 Dewberry (Purple) **(3)** light
- For optional knot closures: Approximately 50 yards (46m) smooth sportweight yarn, preferably in a wool-silk or cotton-silk blend
- Size 8 (5mm) circular needles, 26" (66cm) long, *or size needed to obtain gauge*
- Two size 6 (4mm) double-pointed needles to make knot closures (optional)
- Yarn needle

GAUGE
16 stitches and 22 rows = 4" (10cm) in lace pattern using size 8 (5mm) needle. *To save time, take time to check your gauge.*

SPECIAL STITCHES
(see Glossary on page 162)

cable cast-on; I-cord; k2tog; yo

NOTE
This project is not worked in the round, but a circular needle is helpful to hold all the stitches.

INSTRUCTIONS

WRAP

Cast on 255 stitches using the cable cast-on method. This will give the long edge some extra stability.

Note: For a longer wrap, cast on additional stitches, making sure to have an odd number.

Knit 1 row.

Row 1: *K1, p1; repeat from * to last stitch, k1.

Row 2: *K1, p1; repeat from * to last stitch, k1.

Row 3: K2, *yo k2tog; repeat from * to last stitch, k1.

Row 4: K1, *yo k2tog; repeat from * to last 2 stitches, k2.

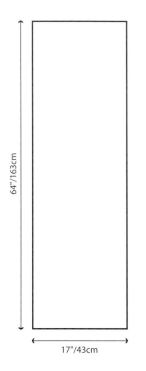

64"/163cm

17"/43cm

Make 7 more I-cords 5" (12.5cm) long, and one more 8" (20cm) long. Using tapestry needle, carefully thread tails back through the I-cord to hide the ends. Tie an overhand knot close to the end of each 5" (12.5cm) I-cord, ensuring that there is approximately ¼" (6mm) of space (but no more) between the two knots. Double the 8" (20.5cm) I-cord and tie a slipknot close to the ends.

To use shorter knot closures:
Slip both knots through adjacent eyelets in the lace. Overlap another section of lace, and slip the buttons through corresponding eyelets. The open lace pattern gives you lots of options for fastening the wrap together.

Here are some examples of ways the wrap can be worn, but don't let these limit your imagination:

To wear wrap as a shrug, use 8 short closures (4 per side). Fold wrap lengthwise and fasten along outside edges, leaving center third open (see Fig. 1).

To wear wrap as a capelet, use 5 short closures. Overlap one long end of the wrap so that it is at a right angle to the other long end (see Fig. 2) and fasten along top edge.

Use the longer closure to fasten the wrap together at one shoulder: Slip the loop end through eyelets on either side of the wrap, then slip loop over knot to secure.

Row 5: K2, *yo k2tog; repeat from * to last stitch, k1.

Row 6: *K1, p1; repeat from * to last stitch, k1.

Row 7: *K1, p1; repeat from * to last stitch, k1.

Row 8: K2, *yo k2tog; repeat from * to last stitch, k1.

Row 9: K1, *yo k2tog; repeat from * to last 2 stitches, k2.

Row 10: K2, *yo k2tog; repeat from * to last stitch, k1.

Row 11: K1, *yo k2tog; repeat from * to last 2 stitches, k2.

Row 12: K2, *yo k2tog; repeat from * to last stitch, k1.

Repeat Rows 1–12, the lace pattern, 6 more times.

Work Rows 1–7 once more.

Knit 1 row.

Bind off loosely to match cast-on tension.

FINISHING
Block to finished measurements.

Optional I-cord Knot Closures
Using sportweight yarn and double-pointed needle, leaving a 4" (10cm) tail, cast on 4 stitches. Knit all stitches. Without turning, slide stitches to the end of the needle, carry working yarn behind work, and knit again. Continue in this manner until the I-cord is 5" (12.5cm) long. Bind off and break yarn, leaving a 4" (10cm) tail.

Figure 1

Figure 2

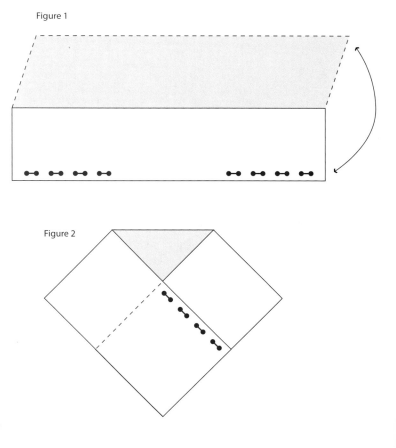

Knit on RS, Purl on WS

– Purl on RS, Knit on WS

O Yarn over

／ K2tog on RS

／ K2tog on WS

SILKY TURTLENECK

by Berta Karapetyan

SKILL LEVEL
Experienced

SIZE
S (M, L)

Directions are for smallest size, with larger sizes in parentheses.

FINISHED MEASUREMENTS
- Bust: 33 (35, 39)" (84 [89, 99]cm)
- Length: 22 (22½, 23)" (56 [57, 58.5]cm)

MATERIALS
- 9 (11, 13) balls Empire Silk by Karabella (each approximately 1¾ oz [50g], 90 yd [85m], 100% Italian silk), in color #509 Taupe (**4**) medium
- Size 5 (3.75mm) needles and circular needle, 16" (40.5cm) long, *or size needed to obtain gauge*
- Stitch holders
- Yarn needle

GAUGE
30 stitches and 24 rows = 4" (10cm) in Lace Pattern.
To save time, take time to check your gauge.

SPECIAL STITCHES
(see Glossary on page 162)

k1 tbl; k1, p1 rib; k2tog; m1; p1 tbl; p2tog; p2tog tbl; reverse stockinette stitch; stockinette stitch; ssk; yo

SPECIAL PATTERN

Lace Pattern (multiple of 23 stitches)

Row 1 (RS): *K1 tbl, yo, [k1 tbl, p1] twice, ssk, [k1 tbl, p1] 4 times, k1 tbl, k2tog, [p1, k1 tbl] twice, yo, k1 tbl; repeat from * to end.

Row 2 (WS): *P1 tbl, k1, yo, [p1 tbl, k1] twice, p2tog, [k1, p1 tbl] 3 times, k1, p2tog tbl, [k1, p1 tbl] twice, yo, k1, p1 tbl; repeat from * to end.

Row 3: *K1 tbl, p1, k1 tbl, yo, [k1 tbl, p1] twice, ssk, [k1 tbl, p1] twice, k1 tbl, k2tog, [p1, k1 tbl] twice, yo, k1 tbl, p1, k1 tbl; repeat from * to end.

Row 4: *[P1 tbl, k1] twice, yo, [p1 tbl, k1] twice, p2tog, k1, p1 tbl, k1, p2tog tbl, [k1, p1 tbl] twice, yo, [k1, p1 tbl] twice; repeat from * to end.

Row 5: *[K1 tbl, p1] twice, k1 tbl, yo, [k1 tbl, p1] twice, ssk, k1 tbl, k2tog, [p1, k1 tbl] twice, yo, [k1 tbl, p1] twice, k1 tbl; repeat from * to end.

Row 6: *Yo, [p1 tbl, k1] 5 times, p3tog, [k1, p1 tbl] 5 times, yo.

Note: In working repeats of Row 6, 2 yarn-over stitches will be next to each other. To do this, wrap yarn around needle twice. On the next row, drop one wrap and knit in the front and the back of the remaining large yarn over.

Repeat Rows 1–6 for Lace Pattern.

INSTRUCTIONS

BACK
Cast on 117 (125, 141) stitches.

Small Only

Row 1 (RS): K1, starting with Row 1, repeat 23 stitches of Lace Pattern 5 times, k1.

Row 2 (WS): P1, working Row 2, repeat 23 stitches of Lace Pattern 5 times, p1.

Medium Only

Row 1 (RS): K1, [k1, p1] twice (rib established), starting with Row 1 of Lace Pattern, repeat 23 stitches of Lace Pattern 5 times, [p1, k1] twice (rib established), k1.

Row 2 (WS): P1, [p1, k1] twice, working Row 2, repeat 23 stitches of Lace Pattern 5 times, [k1, p1] twice, p1.

Large Only

Row 1 (RS): K1, k1 tbl, [p1, k1 tbl] twice, k2tog, [p1, k1 tbl] twice, yo, k1 tbl, starting with Row 1, repeat 23 stitches of Lace Pattern 5 times, k1 tbl, yo, [k1 tbl, p1] twice, ssk, [k1 tbl, p1] twice, k1 tbl, k1.

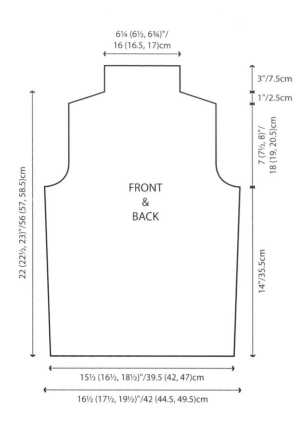

6¼ (6½, 6¾)"/
16 (16.5, 17)cm

3"/7.5cm

1"/2.5cm

7 (7½, 8)"/
18 (19, 20.5)cm

FRONT
&
BACK

22 (22½, 23)"/56 (57, 58.5)cm

14"/35.5cm

15½ (16½, 18½)"/39.5 (42, 47)cm

16½ (17½, 19½)"/42 (44.5, 49.5)cm

Row 2 (WS): P1, [p1 tbl, k1] twice, p2tog tbl, [k1, p1 tbl] twice, yo, k1, p1 tbl, working Row 2, repeat 23 stitches of Lace Pattern 5 times, p1 tbl, k1, yo, [p1 tbl, k1] twice, p2tog, [k1, p1 tbl] twice, p1.

Row 3: K1, k1 tbl, p1, k1 tbl, k2tog, [p1, k1 tbl] twice, yo, k1 tbl, p1, k1 tbl, working Row 3 of Lace Pattern, repeat 23 stitches of Lace Pattern 5 times, k1 tbl, p1, k1 tbl, yo, [k1 tbl, p1] twice, ssk, k1 tbl, p1, k1 tbl, k1.

Row 4: P1, p1 tbl, k1, p2tog tbl, [k1, p1 tbl] twice, yo, [k1, p1 tbl] twice, working Row 4, repeat 23 stitches of Lace Pattern 5 times, [p1 tbl, k1] twice, yo, [p1 tbl, k1] twice, p2tog, k1, p1 tbl, p1.

Row 5: K1, k1 tbl, k2tog, [p1, k1 tbl] twice, yo, [k1 tbl, p1] twice, k1 tbl, working Row 5, repeat 23 stitches of Lace Pattern 5 times, [k1 tbl, p1] twice, k1 tbl, yo, [k1 tbl, p1] twice, ssk, k1 tbl, k1.

Row 6: P1, p2tog tbl, [k1, p1 tbl] 5 times, yo, working Row 6, repeat 23 stitches of Lace Pattern 5 times, yo, [p1 tbl, k1] 5 times, p2tog, p1.

All Sizes
Continuing as established, repeat 6 rows of Lace Pattern for 30 rows. Increase 1 stitch after the first and before the last stitch on Row 31—119 (127, 143) stitches. Work new stitches in reverse stockinette stitch.

Continue as established, increasing 1 stitch after the first and before the last stitch of row 51—121 (129, 145) stitches. Work new stitches in stockinette stitch.

Continue as established, increasing 1 stitch after the first and before the last stitch of row 71—123 (131, 147) stitches. Work new stitches in reverse stockinette stitch.

Continue as established for 84 rows total (piece measures about 14" [35.5cm] from beginning), ending with Row 6 of Lace Pattern.

Armhole Shaping

Row 1 (RS): Bind off 5 (7, 11) stitches, k1, [p1, k1] 0 (1, 3) times, p1, k1 tbl, p1, ssk, [k1 tbl, p1] 4 times, k1 tbl, k2tog, [p1, k1 tbl] twice, yo, k1 tbl, working Row 1, repeat 23 stitches of Lace Pattern 4 times, [p1, k1] 2 (4, 8) times—117 (123, 135) stitches.

Row 2 (WS): Bind off 6 (8, 12) stitches, [p1, k1] 0 (1, 3) times, [p1 tbl, k1] twice, p2tog, [k1, p1 tbl] 3 times, k1, p2tog tbl, [k1, p1 tbl] twice, yo, k1, p1 tbl, working Row 2, repeat 23 stitches of Lace Pattern 3 times, p1 tbl, k1, yo, [p1 tbl, k1] twice, p2tog, [k1, p1 tbl] 3 times, k1, p2tog tbl, k1, p1 tbl, k1, [p1, k1] 0 (1, 3) times, p1—109 (113, 121) stitches.

Row 3: Slip 1, [p1, k1] 0 (1, 3) times, p1, k1 tbl, p1, ssk, [k1 tbl, p1] twice, k1 tbl, k2tog, [p1, k1 tbl] twice, yo, k1 tbl, p1, k1 tbl, working Row 3, repeat 23 stitches of Lace Pattern 3 times, k1 tbl, p1, k1 tbl, yo, [k1 tbl, p1] twice, ssk, [k1 tbl, p1] twice, k1 tbl, k2tog, p1, k1 tbl, p1, [k1, p1] 0 (1, 3) times, k1—107 (111, 119) stitches.

Row 4: Slip 1, [k1, p1] 0 (1, 3) times, k1, p1 tbl, k1, p2tog, k1, p1 tbl, k1, p2tog tbl, [k1, p1 tbl] twice, yo, [k1, p1 tbl] twice, working Row 4; repeat 23 stitches of Lace Pattern 3 times, [p1 tbl, k1] twice, yo, [p1 tbl, k1] twice, p2tog, k1, p1 tbl, k1, p2tog tbl, k1, p1 tbl, k1, [p1, k1] 0 (1, 3) times, p1—105 (109, 117) stitches.

Row 5: Slip 1, [p1, k1] 0 (1, 3) times, p1, k1 tbl, p1, ssk, k1 tbl, k2tog, [p1, k1 tbl] twice, yo, [k1 tbl, p1] twice, k1 tbl, working Row 5, repeat 23 stitches of Lace Pattern 3 times, [k1 tbl, p1] twice, k1 tbl, yo, [k1 tbl, p1] twice, ssk, k1 tbl, k2tog, p1, k1 tbl, p1, [k1, p1] 0 (1, 3) times, k1—103 (107, 115) stitches.

Row 6: Slip 1, [k1, p1] 0 (1, 3) times, k1, p1 tbl, k1, p3tog, [k1, p1 tbl] 5 times, yo, working Row 6, repeat 23 stitches of Lace Pattern 3 times, yo, [p1 tbl, k1] 5 times, p3tog, k1, p1 tbl, k1, [p1, k1] 0 (1, 3) times, p1—101 (105, 113) stitches.

Row 7: Slip 1, [k1, p1] 0 (1, 3) times, ssk, [p1, k1 tbl] 3 times, k2tog, [p1, k1 tbl] twice, yo, k1 tbl, working Row 1, repeat 23 stitches of Lace Pattern 3 times, k1 tbl, yo, [k1 tbl, p1] twice, ssk, [k1 tbl, p1] 3 times, k2tog, [k1, p1] 0 (1, 3) times, k1—99 (103, 111) stitches.

Row 8: Slip 1, [k1, p1] 0 (1, 3) times, p2tog, [p1 tbl, k1] twice, p2tog tbl, [k1, p1 tbl] twice, yo, k1, p1 tbl, working Row 2, repeat 23 stitches of Lace Pattern 3 times, p1 tbl, k1, yo, [p1 tbl, k1] twice, p2tog, [k1, p1 tbl] twice, p2tog tbl, [p1, k1] 0 (1, 3) times, p1—97 (101, 109) stitches.

Row 9: Slip 1, [p1, k1] 0 (1, 3) times, ssk, p1, k1 tbl, k2tog, [p1, k1 tbl] twice, yo, k1 tbl, p1, k1 tbl, working Row 3, repeat 23 stitches of Lace Pattern 3 times, k1 tbl, p1, k1 tbl, yo, [k1 tbl, p1] twice, ssk, k1 tbl, p1, k2tog, [k1, p1] 0 (1, 3) times, k1—95 (99, 107) stitches.

Row 10: Slip 1, [k1, p1] 0 (1, 3) times, p1 tbl, k1, p2tog tbl, [k1, p1 tbl] twice, yo, [k1, p1 tbl] twice, working Row 4, repeat 23 stitches of Lace Pattern 3 times, [p1 tbl, k1] twice, yo, [p1 tbl, k1] twice, p2tog, k1, p1 tbl, [p1, k1] 0 (1, 3) times, p1—95 (99, 107) stitches.

Row 11: Slip 1, [p1, k1] 0 (1, 3) times, k1 tbl, k2tog, [p1, k1 tbl] twice, yo, [k1 tbl, p1] twice, k1 tbl, working Row 5, repeat 23 stitches of Lace Pattern 3 times, [k1 tbl, p1] twice, k1 tbl, yo, [k1 tbl, p1] twice, ssk, k1 tbl, [k1, p1] 0 (1, 3) times, k1.

Row 12: Slip 1, [k1, p1] 0 (1, 3) times, p2tog tbl, [k1, p1 tbl] 5 times, yo, working Row 6, repeat 23 stitches of Lace Pattern 3 times, yo, [p1 tbl, k1] 5 times, p2tog, [p1, k1] 0 (1, 3) times, p1.

Row 13: Slip 1, [k1, p1] 0 (1, 3) times, k1 tbl, [p1, k1 tbl] twice, k2tog, [p1, k1 tbl] twice, yo, k1 tbl, working Row 1, repeat 23 stitches of Lace Pattern 3 times, k1 tbl, yo, [k1 tbl, p1] twice, ssk, [k1 tbl, p1] twice, k1 tbl, [k1, p1] 0 (1, 3) times, k1.

Row 14: Slip 1, [k1, p1] 0 (1, 3) times, [p1 tbl, k1] twice, p2tog tbl, [k1, p1 tbl] twice, yo, k1, p1 tbl, working Row 2, repeat 23 stitches of Lace Pattern 3 times, p1 tbl, k1, yo, [p1 tbl, k1] twice, p2tog, [k1, p1 tbl] twice, [p1, k1] 0 (1, 3) times, p1. Repeat Rows 9–14 until armhole measures 7 (7½, 8)" (18 [19, 20.5]cm), ending with wrong-side row and Row 6 (4, 6) of Lace Pattern.

Shoulder Shaping

Bind off 7 (8, 10) stitches at the beginning of the next 2 rows—81 (83, 87) stitches.

Bind off 8 (8, 10) stitches at the beginning of the next 2 rows—65 (67, 67) stitches.

Bind off 8 (9, 9) stitches at the beginning of the next 2 rows—49 stitches.

Place remaining 49 stitches onto stitch holder for back neck.

FRONT

Work the same as for Back.

NECK

Sew shoulder seams. Place 49 stitches from back neck stitch holder and 49 stitches from front neck stitch holder onto the circular needle—98 stitches. With right side facing, join yarn at one shoulder. **Note:** Circular needle is used for ease in working around neckline, but neck is worked back and forth in rows.

Small Only

Row 1 (RS): K1, *k1 tbl, [p1, k1 tbl] twice, k2tog, [p1, k1 tbl] twice, yo, k1 tbl, working row 1, repeat 23 stitches of Lace pattern, k1 tbl, yo, [k1 tbl, p1] twice, ssk, [k1 tbl, p1] twice, k1 tbl*, k2tog; repeat from * to * to last stitch, k1—97 stitches.

Row 2 (WS): P1, p1 tbl, *k1, p1tbl, k1, p2tog tbl, [k1, p1 tbl] twice, yo, k1, p1 tbl, working Row 2, repeat 23 stitches of Lace Pattern, p1 tbl, k1, yo, [p1 tbl, k1] twice, p2tog, k1, p1 tbl, k1*, p3tog; repeat from * to * to last 2 stitches, p1 tbl, p1—95 stitches.

Row 3: K1, k1 tbl, p1, k1 tbl, k2tog, [p1, k1 tbl] twice, yo, k1 tbl, p1, k1 tbl, working Row 3, repeat 23 stitches for Lace Pattern 3 times, k1 tbl, p1, k1 tbl, yo, [k1 tbl, p1] twice, ssk, k1 tbl, p1, k1 tbl, k1.

Row 4: P1, p1 tbl, k1, p2tog tbl, [k1, p1 tbl] twice, yo, [k1, p1 tbl] twice, working Row 4, repeat 23 stitches for Lace Pattern 3 times, [p1 tbl, k1] twice, yo, [p1 tbl, k1] twice, p2tog, k1, p1 tbl, p1.

Row 5: K1, k1 tbl, k2tog, [p1, k1 tbl] twice, yo, [k1 tbl, p1] twice, k1 tbl, working Row 5, repeat 23 stitches of Lace Pattern 3 times, [k1 tbl, p1] twice, k1 tbl, yo, [k1 tbl, p1] twice, ssk, k1 tbl, k1.

Row 6: P1, p2tog tbl, [k1, p1 tbl] 5 times, yo, working Row 6, repeat 23 stitches of Lace Pattern 3 times, yo, [p1 tbl, k1] 5 times, p2tog, p1.

Row 7: K1, k1 tbl, [p1, k1 tbl] twice, k2tog, [p1, k1 tbl] twice, yo, k1 tbl, working Row 2, repeat 23 stitches of Lace Pattern 3 times, k1 tbl, yo, [k1 tbl, p1] twice, ssk, [k1 tbl, p1] twice, k1 tbl, k1.

Row 8: P1, [p1 tbl, k1] twice, p2tog tbl, [k1, p1 tbl] twice, yo, k1, p1 tbl, working Row 3, repeat 23 stitches for Lace Pattern 3 times, p1 tbl, k1, yo, [p1 tbl, k1] twice, p2tog, [k1, p1 tbl] twice, p1.

Repeat Rows 3–8 until neck measures 3" (7.5cm). Bind off.

Medium Only

Row 1: K1, *k1 tbl, k2tog, [p1, k1 tbl] twice, yo, [k1 tbl, p1] twice, k1 tbl, working Row 5, repeat 23 stitches of Lace Pattern, [k1 tbl, p1] twice, k1 tbl, yo, [k1 tbl, p1] twice, ssk, k1 tbl*, k2tog; repeat from * to *, k1—97 stitches.

Row 2: P1, *p2tog tbl, [k1, p1 tbl] 5 times, yo, working Row 6, repeat 23 stitches of Lace Pattern, yo, [p1 tbl, k1] 5 times, p2tog, p1; repeat from * to end—97 stitches.

Row 3: K1, *k1 tbl, [p1, k1 tbl] twice, k2tog, [p1, k1 tbl] twice, yo, k1 tbl, working Row 1, repeat 23 stitches for Lace Pattern, k1 tbl, yo, [k1 tbl, p1] twice, ssk, [k1 tbl, p1] twice, k1 tbl, k1; repeat from * to end.

Row 4: P1, *[p1 tbl, k1] twice, p2tog tbl, [k1, p1 tbl] twice, yo, k1, p1 tbl, working Row 2, repeat 23 stitches for Lace Pattern, p1 tbl, k1, yo, [p1 tbl, k1] twice, p2tog, [k1, p1 tbl] twice, p1; repeat from * to end.

Row 5: K1, *k1 tbl, p1, k1 tbl, k2tog, [p1, k1 tbl] twice, yo, k1 tbl, p1, k1 tbl, working Row 3, repeat 23 stitches of Lace Pattern, k1 tbl, p1, k1 tbl, yo, [k1 tbl, p1] twice, ssk, k1 tbl, p1, k1 tbl, k1*; repeat from * to end.

Row 6: P1, *p1 tbl, k1, p2tog tbl, [k1, p1 tbl] twice, yo, [k1, p1 tbl] twice, working Row 4, repeat 23 stitches of Lace pattern, [p1 tbl, k1] twice, yo, [p1 tbl, k1] twice, p2tog, k1, p1 tbl, p1; repeat from * to end.

Row 7: K1, *k1 tbl, k2tog, [p1, k1 tbl] twice, yo, [k1 tbl, p1] twice, k1 tbl, working row 5, repeat 23 stitches of Lace pattern, [k1 tbl, p1] twice, k1 tbl, yo, [k1 tbl, p1] twice, ssk, k1 tbl, k1; repeat from * to end.

Repeat Rows 2–7 until neck measures 3" (7.5cm). Bind off.

Large Only

Row 1 (RS): K1, m1, *k1 tbl, [p1, k1 tbl] twice, k2tog, [p1, k1 tbl] twice, yo, k1 tbl, working Row 1, repeat 23 stitches of Lace Pattern, k1 tbl, yo, [k1 tbl, p1] twice, ssk, [k1 tbl, p1] twice, k1 tbl*, k1, m1, k1; repeat from * to *, m1, k1—101 stitches.

Row 2 (WS): P1, k1, *[p1 tbl, k1] twice, p2tog tbl, [k1, p1 tbl] twice, yo, k1, p1 tbl, working Row 2, repeat 23 stitches of Lace Pattern, p1 tbl, k1, yo, [p1 tbl, k1] twice, p2tog, [k1, p1 tbl] twice*, p1, k1, p1; repeat from * to *, k1, p1—101 stitches.

Row 3: K1, p1 *k1 tbl, p1, k1 tbl, k2tog, [p1, k1 tbl] twice, yo, k1 tbl, p1, k1 tbl, working Row 3, repeat 23 stitches of Lace Pattern, k1 tbl, p1, k1 tbl, yo, [k1 tbl, p1] twice, ssk, k1 tbl, p1, k1 tbl*, k1, p1, k1; repeat from * to *, p1, k1.

Row 4: P1, k1, *p1 tbl, k1, p2tog tbl, [k1, p1 tbl] twice, yo, [k1, p1 tbl] twice, working Row 4, repeat 23 stitches of Lace Pattern, [p1 tbl, k1] twice, yo, [p1 tbl, k1] twice, p2tog, k1, p1 tbl*, p1, k1, p1; repeat from * to *, k1, p1.

Row 5: K1, p1, *k1 tbl, k2tog, [p1, k1 tbl] twice, yo, p1] twice, k1 tbl, working Row 5, repeat 23 stitches of Lace Pattern, [k1 tbl, p1] twice, k1 tbl, yo, [k1 tbl, p1] twice, ssk, k1 tbl*, k1, p1, k1; repeat from * to *, p1, k1.

Row 6: P1, k1, *p2tog tbl, [k1, p1 tbl] 5 times, yo, working Row 6, repeat 23 stitches of Lace Pattern, yo, [p1 tbl, k1] 5 times, p2tog*, p1, k1, p1; repeat from * to *, k1, p1.

Row 7: K1, p1, *k1 tbl, [p1, k1 tbl] twice, k2tog, [p1, k1 tbl] twice, yo, k1 tbl, working Row 1, repeat 23 stitches of Lace Pattern, k1 tbl, yo, [k1 tbl, p1] twice, ssk, [k1 tbl, p1] twice, k1 tbl*, k1, p1, k1; repeat from * to *, p1, k1.

Repeat Rows 2–7 until neck measures 3" (7.5cm). Bind off.

FINISHING

Sew side and neck seam. Weave in loose ends.

INGENUE HAT & SCARF SET

by Berta Karapetyan

SKILL LEVEL
Easy

SIZE
One size

FINISHED MEASUREMENTS

Scarf
- Length: 88" (223.5cm)
- Width: 8" (20.5cm)

Hat
- To fit 20 (22)" (51 [56]cm) head

MATERIALS

Scarf
- 10 balls Aurora Bulky by Karabella (each approximately 1¾ oz [50g], 54 yd [50m], 100% extra-fine merino wool), in color #3 White **(5)** bulky

Hat
- 2 balls Aurora Bulky by Karabella (each approximately 1¾ oz [50g], 54 yd [50m], 100% extra-fine merino wool), in color #3 White **(5)** bulky
- Size 10½ (6.5mm) double-pointed needles and straight needles, *or size needed to obtain gauge*
- Cable needle
- Stitch markers
- Yarn needle

GAUGE
19 stitches and 20 rows = 4" (10cm) over lace cable pattern. *To save time, take time to check your gauge.*

SPECIAL STITCHES
(see Glossary on page 162)

8-st LC; k2tog; pick up stitches; slip stitch (knit); ssk; yo

INSTRUCTIONS

SCARF
Cast on 38 stitches.

Rows 1, 5, and 9 (RS): Slip 1, p1, k1, p1, *k2tog, yo, p2, k3, k2tog, yo, k3, p2; repeat from * once more, k2tog, yo, [p1, k1] twice.

Row 2 and all WS rows: Slip 1, work stitches as they appear (knit the knit stitches, purl the purl stitches, purl all yo stitches).

Rows 3, 7, and 11: Slip 1, p1, k1, p1, *yo, ssk, p2, k3, yo, ssk, k3, p2; repeat from * once more, yo, ssk, [p1, k1] twice.

Row 13: Slip 1, p1, k1, p1, *k2tog, yo, p2, k8, p2; repeat from * once more, k2tog, yo, [p1, k1] twice.

Row 15: Slip 1, p1, k1, p1, *yo, ssk, p2, slip 4 stitches to cable needle and hold to front, k4, k4 from cable needle, p2; repeat from * once more, yo, ssk, [p1, k1] twice.

Rows 17–28: Repeat Rows 1–12.

Repeat these 28 rows 14 times more or to desired length. Bind off. Weave in loose ends.

If making a longer scarf, you will need more yarn.

HAT
Cast on 30 stitches.

Rows 1, 5, and 9 (RS): Slip 1, k3, k2tog, yo, k3, p2, k2tog, yo, p2, k3, k2tog, yo, k3, p2, k2tog, yo, p1, k2.

Row 2 and all wrong-side rows: Slip 1, work stitches as they appear (knit the knit stitches, purl the purl stitches—purl all yo stitches).

Rows 3, 7, and 11: Slip 1, k3, yo, ssk, k3, p2, yo, ssk, p2, k3, ssk, yo, k3, p2, yo, ssk, p1, k2.

Row 13: Slip 1, k8, p2, k2tog, yo, p2, k8, p2, k2tog, yo, p1, k2.

Row 15: Slip 1, slip 4 stitches to cable needle and hold to front, k4, k4 from cable needle, p2, yo, ssk, p2, slip 4 stitches to cable needle and hold to front, k4, k4 from cable needle, p2, yo, ssk, p1, k2.

Rows 17–28: Repeat Rows 1–12.

Repeat these 28 rows twice more.

Bind off.

Sew cast-on edge to bind-off edge.

Crown

With right side facing, pick up 66 stitches evenly along top edge (the beginning of the right-side row) using double-pointed needles. Place marker at beginning of round.

Round 1: *K2tog, k9; repeat from * to end of round—60 stitches.

Round 2: *K2tog, k8; repeat from * to end of round—54 stitches.

Round 3: *K2tog, k7; repeat from * to end of round—48 stitches.

Round 4: *K2tog, k6; repeat from * to end of round—42 stitches.

Round 5: *K2tog, k5; repeat from * to end of round—36 stitches.

Round 6: *K2tog, k4; repeat from * to end of round—30 stitches.

Round 7: *K2tog, k3; repeat from * to end of round—24 stitches.

Round 8: *K2tog, k2; repeat from * to end of round—18 stitches.

Round 9: *K2tog, k1; repeat from * to end of round—12 stitches.

Round 10: *K2tog; repeat from * to end of round—6 stitches remain.

Cut yarn, leaving 4" (10cm) tail. Draw yarn through remaining 6 stitches and pull them together to close top of hat. Weave in loose ends to wrong side.

LAURA'S LACE CARDIGAN

by Kristin Omdahl

SKILL LEVEL
Intermediate

SIZE
XS (S, M, L, XL, 2X)
Directions are for smallest size, with larger sizes in parentheses.

FINISHED MEASUREMENTS
- Bust: 34 (38, 42, 46, 50, 54)" (86 [96.5, 106.5, 117, 127, 137]cm)

MATERIALS
- 4 (4, 4, 4, 4, 5) skeins Tilli Tomas Demi Plie (each approximately 1 3/4 oz [50g], 290 yd [265m], 100% silk) in Natural (1) super fine
- Size 7 (4.5mm) needles
- Size G/6 (4mm) crochet hook
- Stitch markers
- Yarn needle

GAUGE
16 stitches and 20 rows = 4" (10cm) in blocked lace stitch pattern. *To save time, take time to check your gauge.*

SPECIAL STITCHES
(See Glossary on page 162)
I-cord; k2tog; pick up and knit; p2tog; s2kp; single crochet; ssk; yo

INSTRUCTIONS

BACK
Cast on 69 (77, 85, 93, 101, 109) stitches (multiple of 8 + 5).

Row 1 and all odd rows: Purl.

Row 2: K2, *k2, yo, ssk, k1, k2tog, yo, k1*, end k3.

Row 4: K2, *yo, k2kp, yo, k3, yo, k2tog*, end yo, ssk, k1.

Row 6: K1, yo, *s2kp, yo, k2tog, yo, k1, yo, ssk, yo*, end s2kp, yo, k1.

Row 8: K2, *k1, k2tog, yo, k3, yo, ssk*, end k3.

Row 10: K2, *k2, yo, k2tog, yo, s2kp, yo, k1*, end k3.

Row 12: K2tog, yo, *k1, yo, ssk, yo, s2kp, yo, k2tog, yo*, end k1, yo, ssk.

Row 13–80: Repeat Rows 1–12 5 more times, then rows 1–8 once more.

Note: Place markers for underarms.

Row 81–126: Repeat Rows 9–12 once, then Rows 1–12 3 times, then Rows 1–6 once more.

Bind off all stitches.

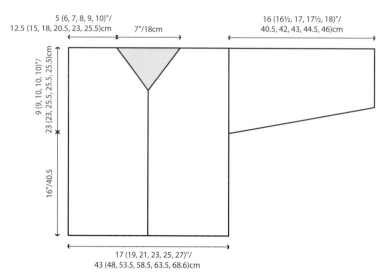

**5 (6, 7, 8, 9, 10)"/
12.5 (15, 18, 20.5, 23, 25.5)cm** · **7"/18cm** · **16 (16½, 17, 17½, 18)"/
40.5 (42, 43, 44.5, 46)cm**

**9 (9, 10, 10, 10)"/
23 (23, 25.5, 25.5, 25.5)cm**

16"/40.5

**17 (19, 21, 23, 25, 27)"/
43 (48, 53.5, 58.5, 63.5, 68.6)cm**

LEFT FRONT

Cast on 37 (45, 53, 61, 69, 77) stitches (multiple of 8 + 5).

Rows 1–80: Repeat Rows 1–80 of back.

Note: Place markers for underarms.

Armhole Shaping

Follow Lace Chart for row and Left Front Chart for last repeat at armhole edge.

Note: You may want to place a stitch marker between the body and the last repeat (armhole decreasing section).

Rows 109–120: Repeat Rows 1–12 of Left Front Chart.

Sizes S and M

Rows 120–126: Repeat Rows 1–6 of Left Front Chart.

Sizes L, XL, and 2X

Row 120–132: Repeat Rows 1–12 of Left Front Chart.
Bind off.

RIGHT FRONT

Cast on 37 (45, 53, 61, 69, 77) stitches (multiple of 8 + 5).

Rows 1–80: Work as Left Front.

Note: Place markers for underarms.

Armhole Shaping

Rows 109–120: Repeat Rows 1–12 of Right Front Chart.

Sizes S and M:

Row 120–126: Repeat Rows 1–6 of Right Front Chart.

Sizes L, XL, and 2X

Rows 120–132: Repeat Rows 1–12 of Right Front Chart.
Bind off.

SLEEVES (MAKE 2)

Cast on 69 (69, 69, 77, 77, 77) stitches (multiple of 8 + 5).

Follow lace chart for 16½ (17, 17½, 18, 18½)" (42, [43, 44.5, 45.5, 47]cm).

WHILE AT THE SAME TIME, decrease on each side of every 4th row 16 (17, 18, 17, 17, 16) times—37 (35, 33, 43, 43, 45, stitches). Then, decrease on each side of every other row 2 (2, 0, 2, 5, 5) times—33 (31, 33, 39, 33, 35 stitches). Work even for the rest of the sleeves.

Note: Maintain a stockinette stitch (knit on the right side, purl on the wrong side) edge to compensate the decreases. Use stitch markers to separate these stitches from the lace pattern. Start with enough stitches for an 8-stitch pattern repeat, and when the decreases have consumed these stitches, slip the marker over another 8 stitches on each side.
Bind off.

I-CORD TIES:

Create two 3-stitch I-cords, 12" (30.5cm) in length, and sew to front edges approximately 10" (25.5cm) below shoulder.

Assembly:

Sew shoulder seams, side seams, and sleeves to arm openings. Weave in all loose ends.

BAND:

With right side facing, pick up and knit 36 (44, 52, 68, 76) stitches along Right Front, 36 (36, 40 40, 40) stitches along right neck, 28 stitches along back neck, 36 (36, 40, 40, 40) stitches along left neck, and 36 (44, 52, 68, 76) stitches along Left Front. Knit for 1" (2.5cm), ending on a wrong-side row. Bind off on right side. With crochet hook, single crochet around entire perimeter of sweater, along entire band, and along bottom edge.
Single crochet around perimeter of sleeve cuffs.

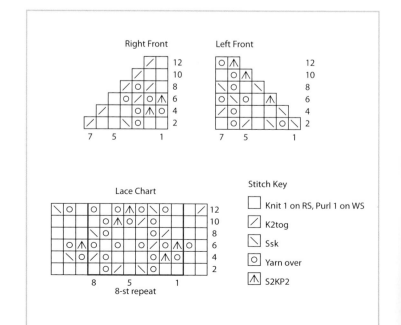

SEA-FOAM TOP

by Berta Karapetyan

SKILL LEVEL
Intermediate

SIZE
S (M, L, XL)
Directions are for smallest size, with larger sizes in parentheses.

FINISHED MEASUREMENTS
- Bust: 32 (35, 38, 41)" (81 [89, 96.5, 104]cm)
- Length: 22½ (22¾, 23¼, 23½)" (57 [58, 59, 59.5]cm)

MATERIALS
- 6 (7, 7, 8) balls Zodiac by Karabella (each approximately 1¾ oz [50g], 98 yd [90m], 100% mercerized cotton), in color #405 Sea Foam ④ medium
- Size 5 (3.75mm) circular needles, 24" [61cm] long, *or size needed to obtain gauge*
- Size 4 (3.5mm) needles
- Stitch markers
- Yarn needle

GAUGE
20 stitches and 30 rows = 4" (10cm) in Easy Eyelet Lace Pattern, using size 5 (3.75mm) needles. *To save time, take time to check your gauge.*

SPECIAL STITCHES
(see Glossary on page 162)
k2tog; m1; pick up and knit; slip stitch (knit); ssk; stockinette stitch; yo

SPECIAL PATTERN
Easy Eyelet Lace Pattern (multiple of 8 stitches)
Row 1 (RS): Knit.
Row 2 and all other WS rows: Purl.
Row 3: *K6, yo, k2tog; repeat from * to end.
Row 5: Knit.
Row 7: K2, *yo, k2tog, k6; repeat from * to last 6 stitches, end last repeat yo, k2tog, k4.
Row 8: Purl.
Repeat Rows 1–8 for pattern.

INSTRUCTIONS

BACK
With size 4 (3.5mm) needles, cast on 80 (88, 96, 104) stitches.

Eyelet Hem
Row 1: Knit.

Row 2: Purl.

Row 3 (Eyelet Row): K1, *k2tog, yo; repeat from * to last stitch, k1.

Main Body
Change to size 5 (3.75mm) needles.

Row 4 and all other WS rows: Purl.

Row 5: Knit.

Row 7 (Row 3 of Easy Eyelet Lace Pattern): *K6, yo, k2tog; repeat from * to end of row.

Row 9: (Row 5 of Easy Eyelet Lace Pattern): Knit.

Row 11 (Row 7 of Easy Eyelet Lace Pattern): K2, *yo, k2tog, k6; repeat from * to last 6 stitches, end last repeat yo, k2tog, k4.

Row 13 (Row 1 of Easy Eyelet Lace Pattern): Knit.

Row 14 (Row 2 of Easy Eyelet Lace Pattern): Purl.

Work even in Easy Eyelet Lace Pattern until work measures 2" (5cm) from eyelet hem Row 3, ending with wrong-side row.

Next RS Row: Decrease 1 stitch at beginning and end of next row (work decreases after the first and before the last stitch)—78 (86, 94, 102) stitches.

Repeat this decrease row every 1½" (3.8cm) twice more—74 (82, 90, 98) stitches.

Work even in established pattern for 2" (5cm), ending with a wrong-side row.

Increase 1 stitch at beginning and end of next row (work increases after the first and before the last stitch)—76 (84, 92, 100) stitches.

Repeat this increase every 3" (7.5cm) twice more—80 (88, 96, 104) stitches.

Work even in established pattern until piece measures 14½" (37cm) from Eyelet Hem Row 3, ending with wrong-side row.

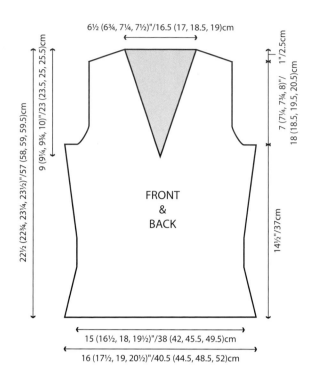

6½ (6¾, 7¼, 7½)"/16.5 (17, 18.5, 19)cm

1"/2.5cm

7 (7¼, 7¾, 8)"/18 (18.5, 19.5, 20.5)cm

9 (9¼, 9¾, 10)"/23 (23.5, 25, 25.5)cm

22½ (22¾, 23¾, 23½)"/57 (58, 59, 59.5)cm

FRONT
&
BACK

14½"/37cm

15 (16½, 18, 19½)"/38 (42, 45.5, 49.5)cm

16 (17½, 19, 20½)"/40.5 (44.5, 48.5, 52)cm

Armhole Shaping

Bind off 5 (6, 7, 8) stitches at beginning of next 2 rows—70 (76, 82, 88) stitches.

Next Row: Slip 1, knit1, k2tog, work in pattern to last 4 stitches, ssk, k2—68 (74, 80, 86) stitches.

Next Row: Slip 1, purl to end.

Repeat these 2 rows 4 (5, 6, 7) times more—60 (64, 68, 72) stitches.

Continue in established pattern until armhole measures 7 (7¼, 7¾, 8)" (18 [18.5, 19.5, 20.5]cm).

Shoulder Shaping

Bind off 5 (5, 5, 6) stitches at beginning of next 2 rows—50 (54, 58, 60) stitches.

Bind off 5 (5, 5, 6) stitches at beginning of next 2 rows—40 (44, 48, 48) stitches.

Bind off 4 (5, 6, 5) stitches at beginning of next 2 rows—32 (34, 36, 38) stitches.

Bind off 32 (34, 36, 38) stitches for back neck.

FRONT

Work as for Back until piece measures 13½" (34.5cm) from eyelet hem Row 3, ending with a wrong-side row. Divide Front into two parts, place marker in the center for V-neck.

Next Row: Work in pattern to last 4 stitches before marker, k2tog, k2, join second ball of yarn, slip 1, k1, ssk, work in pattern to end—39 (43, 47, 51) stitches on each side of neck.

Note: Slip first stitch at beginning of each row on right and left side of the garment for a neat edge.

Next Row: Purl.

Working both sides at the same time, repeat the decrease row every 4 rows 15 (16, 17, 18) times more—68 (70, 72, 76) rows total, 24 (27, 30, 33) stitches on each side of neck. AT THE SAME TIME, when piece measures 14½" (37cm), begin shaping armholes as for Back.

When armhole measures 7 (7¼, 7¾, 8)" (18 [18.5, 19.5, 20.5]cm), shape shoulders as for Back.

NECK RUFFLE

Sew shoulder seams. With wrong side facing and starting at left shoulder seam, pick up and knit 2 stitches (from the back and front of each stitch) of bind-off row across the back neck, 2 stitches of each edge stitch down the right front and up the left front—ensure you have an even number. Join in the round.

Round 1: *K2tog, yo; repeat from * to end of round.

Round 2: Knit.

Repeat last 2 rows 7 times more.

Bind off.

SLEEVE RUFFLE

With right side facing, place 2 markers 3½ (4, 4½, 5)" (9 [10, 11.5, 12.5]cm) down on both sides from shoulder seam. Pick up and knit 2 stitches from each edge stitch between markers—ensure you have an even number.

Row 1 (WS): *P2, m1; repeat from * to end of picked-up stitches.

Row 2 (RS): *K2tog, yo; repeat from * to end of row, then pick up and knit 2 additional stitches from sleeve edge.

Row 3: Purl to end of row, pick up and purl 2 additional stitches from sleeve edge.

Repeat last 2 rows 4 (4, 5, 5) times more.

Bind off.

FINISHING

Sew side seams. Fold the hem at the lower edge to wrong side at Eyelet Hem row and sew in place, carefully matching knitting tension. Do not allow the sewing stitches to become tighter than the knitting.

CHAPTER 4
Casual Lace

TWILIGHT SCARVES

by Lisa Lloyd

SKILL LEVEL
Easy

SIZE
One size

FINISHED MEASUREMENTS

Scarf
- Width: 10" (25.5cm)
- Length: 60" (152.5cm)

Stole
- Width: 22" (56cm)
- Length: 65" (165cm)

MATERIALS

Scarf
- Handspun Border Leicester (100%) with trace amounts of Angelina® by Foxfire Fiber and Designs, 400–600 yd (366–549m) laceweight to fingering weight, in colors Winter Sky and Lupine (contrast) (1) super fine
- 1 cone Zephyr 218 Wool-Silk by JaggerSpun (each approximately 1 lb [.45kg], 5,040 yd [4609m], 50% merino wool, 50% Chinese tussah silk), in color Marine Blue (1) super fine
- Handspun Corriedale (100%) and Mohair (contrast, 100%), 400–600 yd (366–549m) laceweight to fingering weight, in color natural gray (1) super fine

Stole
- 1 skein Heaven by Lorna's Laces (each approximately 7 oz [199g], 975 yd [892m], 90% kid mohair, 10% nylon), in color Happy Valley (1) super fine
- Size 5 (3.75mm) needles for scarf, *or size needed to obtain gauge*
- Size 8 (5mm) needles for stole, *or size needed to obtain gauge*
- Yarn needle

GAUGE

Scarf
20 stitches = 4" (10cm) in chart pattern using size 5 (3.75mm) needles.
To save time, take time to check your gauge.

Stole
16 stitches = 4" (10cm) in chart pattern using size 8 (5mm) needles.
To save time, take time to check your gauge.

SPECIAL STITCHES
(see Glossary on page 162)

garter stitch; k2tog; reverse stockinette stitch; sl1-k2tog-psso; ssk; stockinette stitch; yo

NOTE
The garter ridge dividing the repeats of the lace can be worked in a contrasting yarn, by way of a contrast color or even in a contrasting weight, as shown in the handspun scarf version here. The choice of yarns greatly affects gauge with this pattern. Swatch to get a feel for how open you want your lace to appear.

INSTRUCTIONS

SCARF

Note: For a two-color scarf or stole, work all garter rows, eyelet rows, and Rows 11–14 of chart with a contrast yarn.

Cast on 46 stitches.

Knit 4 rows (2 garter ridges on the right side).

Eyelet Row (RS): K2, *yo, k2tog; repeat from * to the last 2 stitches, k2.

Work 4 rows in garter stitch, increasing 1 stitch on the last row—47 stitches.

Set Up for Twilight Chart (RS): K2, begin where indicated and work 15 stitches of chart once, then repeat the 14-stitch repeat twice, k2.

Continue and work chart as established, keeping first 2 and last 2 stitches in garter stitch, until scarf measures approximately 59" (150cm) or 1" (2.5cm) less than desired length, stretching slightly, ending with Row 12 of chart and decreasing 1 stitch by k2tog anywhere on the last wrong-side row. Work Eyelet Row, then 3 rows of garter stitch. Bind off very loosely on the right side purlwise.

SCARF FINISHING

Hand wash and pin out carefully to measurements. Allow to dry completely before removing pins.

STOLE

Cast on 88 stitches.

Knit 4 rows (2 garter ridges on right side).

Eyelet Row (RS): K2, *yo, k2tog; repeat from * to the last 2 stitches, k2.

Work 4 rows in garter stitch, increasing one stitch on the last row—89 stitches.

Set Up for Twilight Chart (RS): K2, begin where indicated and work 15 stitches of chart once, then repeat the 14-stitch repeat twice, k2.

Continue and work chart as established keeping first 2 and last 2 stitches in garter stitch until stole measures 64" (162.5cm) or 1" (2.5cm) less than desired length, stretching slightly, ending with Row 12 of chart and decreasing 1 stitch by k2tog anywhere on the last wrong-side row. Work Eyelet Row, then 3 rows of garter stitch. Bind off very loosely on the right side purlwise.

STOLE FINISHING

Hand wash and pin out carefully to measurements. Allow to dry completely before removing pins.

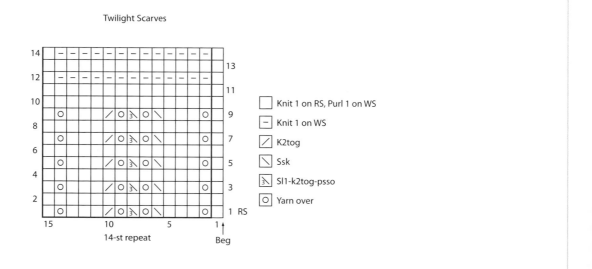

Twilight Scarves

	Knit 1 on RS, Purl 1 on WS
-	Knit 1 on WS
/	K2tog
\	Ssk
⅄	Sl1-k2tog-psso
O	Yarn over

RAVENSONG SWEATER

by Lisa Lloyd

SKILL LEVEL
Intermediate

SIZE
S (M, L, XL, 2X)

Directions are for smallest size, with larger sizes in parentheses.

FINISHED MEASUREMENTS
- Chest: 36 (39½, 43, 46, 50)" (91 [100.5, 109, 117, 127]cm)
- Length: 21 (21, 22, 22½, 23)" (53.5 [53.5, 56, 57, 58.5]cm)

MATERIALS
- 5 (5, 6, 7, 7) skeins Ultra Alpaca by Berroco, (each approximately 3½ oz [100g], 215 yd [198m], 50% super fine alpaca, 50% wool), in color #6282 Cranberry Mix (④) medium
- 100% Handspun Cotswold, 1,000 (1,100, 1,200, 1,350, 1,450) yd (914 [1,006, 1,097, 1,234, 1,326]m) sportweight or worsted weight, in colors natural black and gray (④) medium
- Size 8 (5mm) needles, *or size needed to obtain gauge*
- Size 11 (8mm) needles and circular needle, 24" (61cm) long (see Note on Sleeves and collar)
- Stitch markers
- Yarn needle

GAUGE
16 stitches and 24 rows = 4" (10cm) in Chart A pattern using size 8 (5mm) needles. *To save time, take time to check your gauge.*

SPECIAL STITCHES
(see Glossary on page 162)

join; k2tog; m1; p2tog; p2tog tbl; pick up and knit; selvedge; ssk; stockinette stich

NOTE
One stitch at each edge is worked in stockinette stitch for selvedge stitches throughout.

INSTRUCTIONS

BACK
With smaller needles, cast on 72 (79, 86, 93, 100) stitches.

Work 4 rows in stockinette stitch, ending with a wrong-side row.

Set Up Main Pattern: K1 (selvedge stitch), work Chart A to last stitch, k1 (selvedge stitch). Continue working Chart A as established for 8 rows.

Shape Waist

Decrease Row (RS): K1 (selvedge stitch), ssk, work across to last 3 stitches, k2tog, k1 (selvedge stitch).

Work Decrease Row every 8 (8, 10, 10, 10) rows 3 more times—64 (71, 78, 85, 92) stitches.

Increase Row (RS): K1 (selvedge stitch), m1 right, work across row until 1 stitch remains, m1 left, k1 (selvedge stitch).

Work Increase Row every 8 (8, 10, 10, 10) rows 3 more times—72 (79, 86, 93, 100) stitches.

Continue until Back measures 13 (13, 13½, 13½, 13½)" (33 [33, 34.5, 34.5, 34.5]cm) from the beginning, ending with a wrong-side row.

Shape Armhole
Bind off 6 (7, 8, 8, 9) stitches at the beginning of the next 2 rows—60 (65, 70, 77, 82) stitches.

Decrease Row (RS): K1 (selvedge stitch), ssk, work across to last 3 stitches, k2tog, k1 (selvedge stitch)—58 (63, 68, 75, 80) stitches.

Continue to work Decrease Row every other row 4 (6, 6, 6, 8) more times—50 (51, 56, 63, 64) stitches.

Work even until the armhole measures 7 (7, 7½, 8, 8½)" (18 [18, 19, 20.5, 21.5]cm).

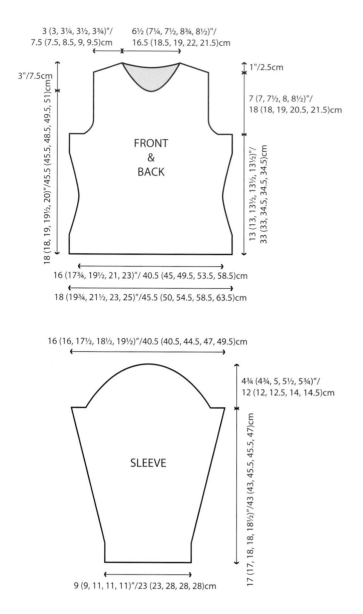

3 (3, 3¼, 3½, 3¾)"/
7.5 (7.5, 8.5, 9, 9.5)cm

6½ (7¼, 7½, 8¾, 8½)"/
16.5 (18.5, 19, 22, 21.5)cm

1"/2.5cm

3"/7.5cm

7 (7, 7½, 8, 8½)"/
18 (18, 19, 20.5, 21.5)cm

FRONT
&
BACK

18 (18, 19, 19½, 20)"/45.5 (45.5, 48.5, 49.5, 51)cm

13 (13, 13½, 13½, 13½)"/
33 (33, 34.5, 34.5, 34.5)cm

16 (17¾, 19½, 21, 23)"/ 40.5 (45, 49.5, 53.5, 58.5)cm

18 (19¾, 21½, 23, 25)"/45.5 (50, 54.5, 58.5, 63.5)cm

16 (16, 17½, 18½, 19½)"/40.5 (40.5, 44.5, 47, 49.5)cm

4¾ (4¾, 5, 5½, 5¾)"/
12 (12, 12.5, 14, 14.5)cm

SLEEVE

17 (17, 18, 18, 18½)"/43 (43, 45.5, 45.5, 47)cm

9 (9, 11, 11, 11)"/23 (23, 28, 28, 28)cm

Shape Shoulders and Back Neck

Row 1: Bind off 4 (4, 5, 5, 5) stitches at the beginning of the row—46 (47, 51, 58, 59) stitches.

Row 2: Bind off 4 (4, 5, 5, 5) stitches at the beginning of the row, work across 8 (8, 9, 10, 10) stitches, join a second ball of yarn and bind off 24 (27, 28, 33, 32) stitches for back neck, work to the end of the row. Work both shoulders at same time with separate balls of yarn.

Row 3: Bind off 4 (4, 4, 5, 5) stitches at the beginning of the row and decrease 1 stitch at each neck edge as follows: Work across first shoulder until 3 stitches remain, k2tog, k1 (for neck selvedge). For second shoulder, k1 (for neck selvedge), ssk, work to end.

Row 4: Bind off 4 (4, 4, 5, 5) stitches at the beginning of the row.

Rows 5 and 6: Bind off 4 (3, 4, 4, 5) stitches at the beginning of each row.

FRONT

Work as for Back until Front measures 18 (18, 19, 19½, 20)" (45.5 [45.5, 48.5, 49.5, 51]cm) from the beginning.

Shape Front Neck

Work across 19 (18, 20, 23, 24) stitches, join a second ball of yarn and bind off center 12 (15, 16, 17, 16) stitches, work to the end of the row. Decrease 1 stitch at each neck edge on every right-side row 7 (7, 7, 9, 9) times as follows: Work across first shoulder until 3 stitches remain, k2tog, k1 (for neck selvedge). For second shoulder, k1 (for neck selvedge), ssk, work to end—12 (11, 13, 14, 15) stitches remain for each shoulder. AT THE SAME TIME, when armhole measures 7 (7, 7½, 8, 8½)" (18 [18, 19, 20.5, 21.5]cm), shape shoulders as for Back.

SLEEVES (MAKE 2)

Note: A larger needle is used for a flared and lacier cuff. Choose a needle that is 3 sizes larger than the main body needle, or a needle size that makes lace that is appealing to you. For a straight sleeve, use the same size needle as used for the body for the entire sleeve.

With larger needles, cast on 37 (37, 44, 44, 44) stitches. Work 4 rows in stockinette stitch, ending with a wrong-side row.

Set Up Main Pattern: K1 (selvedge stitch) work Chart A to last stitch, k1 (selvedge stitch). Continue until Sleeve measures 2½" (6.5cm).

Shape Sleeve

Note: Work new stitches into chart pattern, being sure to work lace decreases only when there are enough stitches to work accompanying yarn overs within a repeat, otherwise keep new stitches at outside edges in stockinette stitch as stitches are increased. Change to smaller needle once sleeve measures 4" (10cm).

Increase 1 stitch at each edge, inside selvedge stitches, every 4 (4, 6, 4, 4) rows 1 (1, 8, 1, 6) times, then every 6 (6, 8, 6, 6) rows 13 (13, 5, 14, 11) times, using m1 left and right accordingly—65 (65, 70, 74, 78) stitches. Work even until Sleeve measures 17 (17, 18, 18, 18½)" (43 [43, 45.5, 45.5, 47]cm) from the beginning, ending with a wrong-side row.

Sleeve Cap

Bind off 5 (6, 7, 8, 9) stitches at the beginning of the next 2 rows—55 (53, 56, 58, 60).

Note: Work decreases on right-side rows as follows: K1 (selvedge stitch), ssk, work across row as established to last 3 stitches, k2tog, k1 (selvedge stitch). Work decreases on wrong-side rows as follows: P1 (selvedge stitch), p2tog, work across row as established to last 3 stitches, p2tog tbl, p1 (selvedge stitch).

Decrease 1 stitch at each edge every other row 5 (6, 7, 7, 8) times—45 (41, 42, 44, 44) stitches.

Decrease 1 stitch at each edge every row 11 (9, 7, 3, 3) times—23 (23, 28, 38, 38) stitches.

Decrease 1 stitch at each edge every other row 2 (2, 3, 6, 6) times—19 (19, 22, 26, 26) stitches.

Bind off 2 (2, 2, 3, 3) stitches at the beginning of the next 4 rows—11 (11, 14, 14, 14) stitches.

Bind off remaining 11 (11, 14, 14, 14) stitches.

FINISHING

Sew shoulder and side seams. Sew sleeve seams and with right sides together, set sleeves into armholes.

Collar

With larger circular needle and wrong side facing, join yarn at right shoulder seam, pick up and knit 78 (84, 84, 90, 90) stitches evenly around neck edge, place a stitch marker for the beginning of round. Work Chart B over all stitches. Work until collar measures 8" (20.5cm) or desired length, ending with Row 10 or 20 of Chart B. Bind off very loosely.

Weave in all loose ends and block flat.

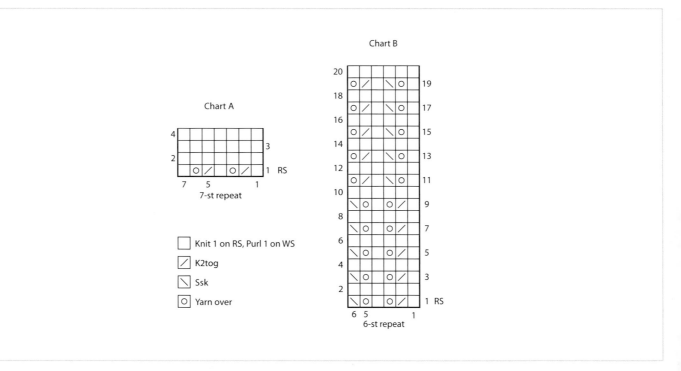

Chart A

7-st repeat

Knit 1 on RS, Purl 1 on WS

K2tog

Ssk

Yarn over

Chart B

6-st repeat

GUERNSEY SOCKS

by Amy King

SKILL LEVEL
Intermediate

SIZE
Women's size Medium (Knit the foot shorter or longer to fit your specific size.)

FINISHED MEASUREMENTS
- Cuff Length: 7¼" (18.5cm)
- Foot Length: 9" (23cm)

MATERIALS
Sock A (left)
- 2 skeins Cormo Wool by Elsa Sheep and Wool Company (each approximately 2½ oz [70g], 213 yd [195m], 100% wool), in color White ② fine

Sock B (right)
- 1 skein Sock Yarn by Tongue River Farm (each approximately 8 oz [226g], 600 yd [549m], 100% Icelandic wool), in color Creamy White (undyed), or 330 yd (302m) of worsted-spun 2-ply sport weight yarn ② fine
- Size 3 (3.25mm) double-pointed needles, *or size needed to obtain gauge*
- Stitch marker
- Stitch holder
- Yarn needle

GAUGE
28 stitches and 40 rows = 4" (10cm) in stockinette stitch using size 3 (3.25mm) needles. *To save time, take time to check your gauge.*

SPECIAL STITCHES
(see Glossary on page 162)

2-st LC; 2-st RC; 4-st LC; 4-st RC; garter stitch; join in the round; k2tog; kitchener stitch; p2tog; slip stitch (knit); ssk; stockinette stitch; yo

INSTRUCTIONS

CUFF

Cast on 60 stitches and join in the round, making sure not to twist the stitches. Place a stitch marker to indicate the beginning of the round. Work Rows 1–4 of the Rib Pattern Chart 4 times. After the ribbing is complete, knit 1 full round and purl 1 full round.

Next Round: Begin the Guernsey Cable Cuff Chart. Work 7 full repeats of the 8-row chart.

START HEEL

Row 1 (RS): K28, turn.

Row 2 (WS): P2tog, p29, turn—30 working stitches. Place the remaining 29 stitches on a holder for the top of the foot.

Row 3: *Slip 1, k1; repeat from * across, turn.

Row 4: Slip 1, purl across, turn.

Work Rows 3–4 until your heel flap measures 2½" (6.5cm), and the next facing row is a right-side row.

TURN HEEL

Row 1 (RS): K17, ssk, k1, turn.

Row 2: Slip 1, p5, p2tog, p1, turn.

Row 3: Knit to 1 stitch before the gap from the previous row's decreases, ssk, k1, turn.

Row 4: Purl to 1 stitch before the gap, p2tog, p1, turn.

Continue in this manner until you have 18 heel stitches remaining.

The needle that holds your heel flap stitches will be needle 1. Knit all stitches on needle 1. Pick up and knit 18 stitches along the left edge of the heel flap. Using needles 2 and 3, take 29 stitches from the stitch holder and work the first row of the Guernsey Cable Foot Chart. Using needle 4, pick up and knit 18 stitches along the right edge of the heel flap, then knit the first 9 stitches from needle 1. This is now the beginning of your round—83 stitches.

GUSSET

Round 1: Knit all stitches on needle 1. Work across needles 2 and 3 in the corresponding row of Guernsey Cable Foot Chart. Knit all stitches on needle 4.

Round 2: Needle 1: Knit to the last 3 stitches, k2tog, k1. Work across needles 2 and 3 in the corresponding row of Guernsey Cable Foot Chart. Needle 4: K1, ssk, knit to end.

Repeat Rounds 1–2 until you have 59 stitches.

Next Round: Needle 1: Knit to the last 3 stitches, k2tog, k1. Work across needles 2 and 3 in the corresponding row of Guernsey Cable Foot Chart. Needle 4: Knit to the end of the round—58 stitches.

Work even, keeping needles 1 and 4 in stockinette stitch and needles 2 and 3 in the Guernsey Cable Foot until the foot of your sock measures 1½" (3.8cm) less than the overall desired length.

Next 2 Rounds: Work all needles in stockinette stitch.

SHAPE TOE

Round 1: Needle 1: Work to the last 3 stitches, k2tog, k1. Needle 2: K1, ssk, knit to the end of the needle. Needle 3: Work to the last 3 stitches, k2tog, k1. Needle 4: K1, ssk, knit to the end of the needle.

Round 2: Knit all stitches.

Repeat Rounds 1–2 until 30 stitches remain. Finish by knitting all stitches on needle 1. Fasten off yarn, leaving about 12" (30.5cm) of length. Work Kitchener stitch to stitch the toe together. Weave in all ends.

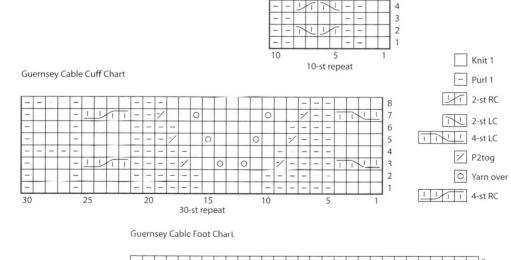

Rib Pattern Chart

10-st repeat

Guernsey Cable Cuff Chart

30-st repeat

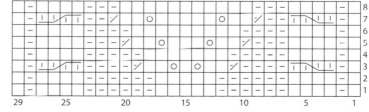

Knit 1

Purl 1

2-st RC

2-st LC

4-st LC

P2tog

Yarn over

4-st RC

Guernsey Cable Foot Chart

DIAMONDS AND PEARLS SHAWL

by Shelia January

SKILL LEVEL
Intermediate

SIZE
One size

FINISHED MEASUREMENTS
- Width: 56" (142cm)
- Length: 19" (48.5cm)

MATERIALS
- 1 skein Silk Rhapsody by Artyarns (each approximately 3½ oz [100g], 260 yd [238m], 80% silk, 20% mohair), in color #RH123, or 260 yd [238m] of 2-ply worsted-weight yarn, preferably a yarn with shimmer and drape (4) medium
- Size 9 (5.5mm) circular needle, 29" (74cm) long, *or size needed to obtain gauge*
- 4 stitch markers
- Yarn needle

GAUGE
16 stitches and 20 rows = 4" (10cm) over stockinette stitch (blocked). *To save time, take time to check gauge.*

SPECIAL STITCHES
(see Glossary on page 162)
k2tog; knitted cast-on; sl1-k2tog-psso; slip stitch (knit); ssk; yo

NOTES
1. The stitch count jumps in Rows 31, 39, and 41 to create shoulder shaping.
2. The bind-off chosen for this pattern may seem difficult, but it's easy to complete and creates a wonderful airy edge that's very open to blocking.

INSTRUCTIONS

SHAWL
Cast on 5 stitches using the knitted cast-on or your preferred method.

Row 1: K1, yo, place marker, k1, place marker, yo, k1, place marker, yo, k1, place marker, yo, k1—9 stitches.

Row 2 and all even rows: Purl all stitches.

Note: In remaining rows, slip stitch markers as the row is worked. The markers will help you keep track of your place in the each row.

Row 3: [K1, yo, k3, yo] twice, k1—13 stitches.

Row 5: [K1, yo, k5, yo] twice, k1—17 stitches.

Row 7: [K1, yo, k7, yo] twice, k1—21 stitches.

Row 9: K1, yo, k4, yo, k5, yo, k1, yo, k5, yo, k4, yo, k1—27 stitches.

Row 11: K1, yo, k3, k2tog, yo, k1, yo, ssk, k4, yo, k1, yo, k4, k2tog, yo, k1, yo, ssk, k3, yo, k1—31 stitches.

Row 13: K1, yo, k3, k2tog, yo, k3, yo, ssk, k4, yo, k1, yo, k4, k2tog, yo, k3, yo, ssk, k3, yo, k1—35 stitches.

Row 15: K1, yo, k6, yo, sl1-k2tog-psso, yo, k7, yo, k1, yo, k7, yo, sl1-k2tog-psso, yo, k6, yo, k1—39 stitches.

Row 17: K1, yo, k8, yo, ssk, k8, yo, k1, yo, k8, k2tog, yo, k8, yo, k1—43 stitches.

Row 19: [K1, yo, k20, yo] twice, k1—47 stitches.

Row 21: [K1, yo, k22, yo] twice, k1—51 stitches.

Row 23: K1, yo, k1, *yo, k1, k2tog; repeat from * 7 times, k2, yo, k1, yo, k2, *ssk, k1, yo, repeat from * 7 times, k1, yo, k1—55 stitches.

Row 25: K1, yo, k2, *yo, k1, k2tog, repeat from * 8 times, yo, k1, yo, *ssk, k1, yo; repeat from * 8 times, k2, yo, k1—59 stitches.

Row 27: K1, yo, k3, *yo, k1, k2tog; repeat from * 8 times, [k1, yo] twice, k1, *ssk, k1, yo; repeat from * 8 times, k3, yo, k1—63 stitches.

Row 29: [K1, yo, k30, yo] twice, k1—67 stitches.

Row 31: [K1, yo, k32, yo] twice, k1—71 stitches.

Row 33: [K1, yo, k8, yo, (k9, yo) twice, k8, yo] twice, k1—81 stitches.

Row 35: [K1, yo, k7, k2tog, yo, k1, yo, ssk, k5, k2tog, yo, k1, yo, ssk, k5, k2tog, yo, k1, yo, ssk, k7, yo] twice, k1—85 stitches.

Row 37: [K1, yo, k7, k2tog, yo, k3, yo, ssk, k3, k2tog, yo, k3, yo, ssk, k3, k2tog, yo, k3, yo, ssk, k7, yo] twice, k1—89 stitches.

Row 39: [K1, yo, k10, yo, sl1-k2tog-psso, yo, k7, yo, sl1-k2tog-psso, yo, k7, yo, sl1-k2tog-psso, yo, k10, yo] twice, k1—93 stitches.

Row 41: [K1, yo, k12, yo, k2tog, k8, yo, k2tog, k8, yo, k2tog, k11, yo] twice, k1—97 stitches.

Row 43: [K1, yo, k47, yo] twice, k1—101 stitches.

Row 45: [K1, yo, k49, yo] twice, k1—105 stitches.

Row 47: K1, yo, k1, *yo, k1, k2tog; repeat from * 16 times, k2, yo, k1, yo, k2, *ssk, k1, yo; repeat from * 16 times, k1, yo, k1—109 stitches.

Row 49: K1, yo, k2, *yo, k1, k2tog; repeat from * 16 times, k3, yo, k1, yo, k3, *ssk, k1, yo; repeat from * 16 times, k2, yo, k1—113 stitches.

Row 51: K1, yo, k3, *yo, k1, k2tog; repeat from * 17 times, k1, yo, k1, yo, k1, *ssk, k1, yo; repeat from * 17 times, k3, yo, k1—117 stitches.

Row 53: K1, yo, k1, *yo, k1, k2tog; repeat from * 18 times, k2, yo, k1, yo, k2, *ssk, k1, yo; repeat from * 18 times, k1, yo, k1—121 stitches.

Row 55: K1, yo, k2, *yo, k1, k2tog; repeat from * 18 times, k3, yo, k1, yo, k3, *ssk, k1, yo; repeat from * 18 times, k2, yo, k1—125 stitches.

Row 57: K1, yo, k3, *yo, k1, k2tog; repeat from * 19 times, k1, yo, k1, yo, k1, *ssk, k1, yo; repeat from * 19 times, k3, yo, k1—129 stitches.

Row 59: K1, yo, k1, *yo, k1, k2tog; repeat from * 20 times, k2, yo, k1, yo, k2, *ssk, k1, yo; repeat from * 20 times, k1, yo, k1—133 stitches.

Row 61: K1, yo, k2, *yo, k1, k2tog; repeat from * 20 times, k3, yo, k1, yo, k3, *ssk, k1, yo; repeat from * 20 times, k2, yo, k1—137 stitches.

Row 63: K1, yo, k3, *yo, k1, k2tog; repeat from * 21 times, k1, yo, k1, yo, k1, *ssk, k1, yo; repeat from * 21 times, k3, yo, k1—141 stitches.

Row 65: K1, yo, k1, *yo, k1, k2tog; repeat from * 22 times, k2, yo, k1, yo, k2, *ssk, k1, yo; repeat from * 22 times, k1, yo, k1—145 stitches.

Row 67: K1, yo, k2, *yo, k1, k2tog; repeat from * 22 times, k3, yo, k1, yo, k3, *ssk, k1, yo; repeat from * 22 times, k2, yo, k1—149 stitches.

Row 69: K1, yo, k3, *yo, k1, k2tog; repeat from * 23 times, k1, yo, k1, yo, k1, *ssk, k1, yo; repeat from * 23 times, k3, yo, k1—153 stitches.

Row 71: K1, yo, k1, *yo, k1, k2tog; repeat from * 24 times, k2, yo, k1, yo, k2, *ssk, k1, yo; repeat from * 24 times, k1, yo, k1—157 stitches.

Row 73: K1, yo, k2, *yo, k1, k2tog; repeat from * 24 times, k3, yo, k1, yo, k3, *ssk, k1, yo; repeat from * 24 times, k2, yo, k1—161 stitches.

Row 75: K1, yo, k3, *yo, k1, k2tog; repeat from * 25 times, k1, yo, k1, yo, k1, *ssk, k1, yo; repeat from * 25 times, k3, yo, k1—165 stitches.

Row 77: K1, yo, k1, *yo, k1, k2tog; repeat from * 26 times, k2, yo, k1, yo, k2, *ssk, k1, yo; repeat from * 26 times, k1, yo, k1—169 stitches.

Edging

Row 79: K1, *k1, (slip 1 stitch back to left-hand needle, k1) 6 times, slip 1 stitch back to left-hand needle, k3tog, bind off first stitch on the right-hand needle by passing over the second stitch. Repeat from * across row until the center stitch is the next stitch. Slip and knit the stitch before the center stitch 6 times, then slip 1 back to left-hand needle and k2tog with the center stitch, bind off first stitch on the right-hand needle afterward. Continue from * until second half is completed, then fasten off yarn, pulling tight.

FINISHING

Weave in all ends. Silk blocks well with heat blocking, as it retains the softness, drape, and shine. Since this shawl is a manageable size, you can pin it out on a heatproof blocking surface (especially pinning out all the edge loops) and then iron it flat with a dry iron on a silk setting.

HARRIET SWEATER

by Lisa Lloyd

SKILL LEVEL
Intermediate

SIZE
S (M, L, XL)

Directions are for smallest size, with larger sizes in parentheses.

FINISHED MEASUREMENTS
- Chest: 41 (45, 49, 53)" (104 [114, 124.5, 134.5]cm)
- Length: 23½ (23½, 26½, 26½)" (59.5 [59.5, 67.5, 67.5]cm)
- **Note:** The finished length can be adjusted by 3" (7.5cm) by working more or less repeats of Chart B. Allow extra yardage for additional length.

MATERIALS
- 100% Handspun Shetland, 1,200 (1,300, 1,500, 1,600) yd (1,097 [1,189, 1,372, 1,463]m) DK to worsted weight, in color natural black (4) medium
- 10 (11, 12, 13) skeins Scottish Tweed DK by Rowan Yarns (each approximately 1¾ oz [50g], 123 yd [113m], 100% pure new wool, in color #018 Thatch (4) medium
- Size 6 (4mm) needles and circular needles, 16" (40.5cm) and 29" (74cm) long, *or size needed to obtain gauge*
- Stitch holders
- Yarn needle
- 7 buttons, ¾" (2cm) in diameter

GAUGE
16 stitches and 24 rows = 4" (10cm) in stockinette stitch. *To save time, take time to check your gauge.*

SPECIAL STITCHES
(see Glossary on page 162)

3-needle bind-off; bind off loosely; garter stitch; k2tog; m1; pick up and knit; selvedge stitch; sl1-k2tog-psso ; ssk; stockinette stitch; yo

INSTRUCTIONS

BACK
Cast on 83 (91, 99, 107) stitches.

Work in garter stitch for 4 rows (2 ridges on the right side). Keeping the first and last stitches of every row in stockinette stitch for selvedge stitches, work Chart A for 5" (12.5cm), ending with a wrong-side row, increasing 1 stitch on the last row using the m1 method—84 (92, 100, 108) stitches.

Eyelet Ridge: Work 4 rows in garter stitch.

Eyelet Row (RS): K1 (selvedge stitch), k2, *yo, k2tog; repeat from *, end k2, k1 (selvedge stitch).

Work 3 rows in garter stitch, decreasing 2 stitches evenly on the last row using k2tog—82 (90, 98, 106) stitches.

Main Body Pattern

Set-Up Row (RS): Work stockinette stitch over 8 (12, 16, 20) stitches, work Chart B over 29 stitches, work stockinette stitch over center 8 stitches, work Chart B over 29 stitches, work stockinette stitch over 8 (12, 16, 20) stitches.

Continue working as established until the piece measures 14 (13½, 16, 15½)" (35.5 [34.5, 40.5, 39.5]cm) from the beginning, ending with a wrong-side row.

Shape Armhole
Bind off 5 (7, 7, 7) stitches at the beginning of the next 2 rows for armhole—72 (76, 84, 92) stitches.

Continue until the armhole measures 9½ (10, 10½, 11)" (24 [25.5, 26.5, 28]cm), ending with Row 18 of Chart B. Place remaining stitches on a holder.

LEFT FRONT
Cast on 43 (43, 51, 51) stitches.

Work in garter stitch for 4 rows (2 ridges on right side). Keeping the first and last stitches of every row in stockinette stitch for selvedge stitches, work Chart A for 5" (12.5cm), ending with a wrong-side row, increasing 1 (5, 1, 5) stitches evenly on last row using the m1 method—44 (48, 52, 56) stitches.

Eyelet Ridge: Work 4 rows in garter stitch.

Eyelet Row (RS): K1 (selvedge stitch), k2, *yo, k2tog; repeat from *, end k2, k1 (selvedge stitch). Work 3 rows in garter stitch, decreasing 3 stitches evenly on last row using k2tog—41 (45, 49, 53) stitches.

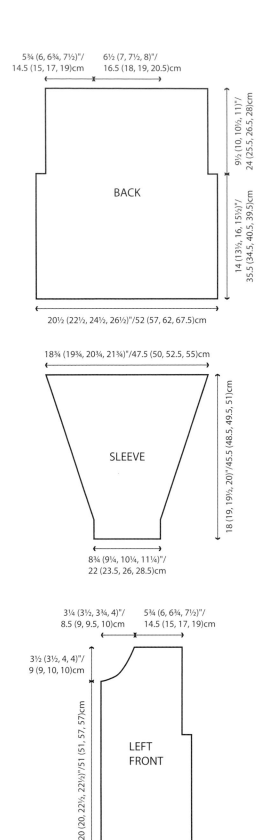

5¾ (6, 6¾, 7½)"/ 14.5 (15, 17, 19)cm   6½ (7, 7½, 8)"/ 16.5 (18, 19, 20.5)cm

9½ (10, 10½, 11)"/ 24 (25.5, 26.5, 28)cm

14 (13½, 16, 15½)"/ 35.5 (34.5, 40.5, 39.5)cm

BACK

20½ (22½, 24½, 26½)"/52 (57, 62, 67.5)cm

18¾ (19¾, 20¾, 21¾)"/47.5 (50, 52.5, 55)cm

18 (19, 19½, 20)"/45.5 (48.5, 49.5, 51)cm

SLEEVE

8¾ (9¼, 10¼, 11¼)"/ 22 (23.5, 26, 28.5)cm

3¼ (3½, 3¾, 4)"/ 8.5 (9, 9.5, 10)cm   5¾ (6, 6¾, 7½)"/ 14.5 (15, 17, 19)cm

3½ (3½, 4, 4)"/ 9 (9, 10, 10)cm

20 (20, 22½, 22½)"/51 (51, 57, 57)cm

LEFT FRONT

10¼ (11¼, 12¼, 13¼)"/ 26 (28.5, 31, 33.5)cm

Main Body Pattern

Set-Up Row (RS): Work stockinette stitch over 8 (12, 16, 20) stitches, work Chart B over 29 stitches, work stockinette stitch over 4 stitches. Continue until the piece measures 14 (13½, 16, 15½)" (35.5 [34.5, 40.5, 39.5]cm) from the beginning, ending with a wrong-side row.

Shape Armhole

Bind off 5 (7, 7, 7) stitches at the beginning of the next row—36 (38, 42, 46) stitches. Continue as established until the armhole measures 6 (6½, 6½, 7)" (15 [16.5, 16.5, 18]cm), ending with a right-side row.

Shape Front Neck

At neck edge, bind off 6 (7, 7, 8) stitches, work to the end of the row.

Decrease Row (RS): Work across to last 3 stitches, k2tog, k1 (selvedge stitch). Continue to work Decrease Row every right-side row 6 (6, 7, 7) more times—23 (24, 27, 30) stitches. Work even until Front armhole measures 9½ (10, 10½, 11)" (24 [25.5, 26.5, 28]cm), or same length as Back to shoulders. Place remaining stitches on a holder.

RIGHT FRONT

Cast on 43 (43, 51, 51) stitches. Work in garter stitch for 4 rows (2 ridges on right side). Keeping the first and last stitches of every row in stockinette stitch for selvedge stitches, work Chart A for 5" (12.5cm), ending with a wrong-side row, increasing 1 (5, 1, 5) stitches evenly on the last row using the m1 method—44 (48, 52, 56) stitches.

Eyelet Ridge: Work 4 rows in garter stitch.

Eyelet Row (RS): K1 (selvedge stitch), k2, *yo, k2tog; repeat from *, end k2, k1 (selvedge stitch).

Work 3 rows in garter stitch, decreasing 3 stitches evenly on the last row using k2tog—41 (45, 49, 53) stitches.

Main Body Pattern

Set-Up Row (RS): Work stockinette stitch over 4 stitches, work Chart B over 29 stitches, work stockinette stitch over 8 (12, 16, 20) stitches. Continue working until the piece measures 14 (13½, 16, 15½)" (35.5 [34.5, 40.5, 39.5]cm) from the beginning, ending with a right-side row.

Shape Armhole

Bind off 5 (7, 7, 7) stitches at the beginning of the next row—36 (38, 42, 46) stitches. Continue working until armhole measures 6 (6½, 6½, 7)" (15 [16.5, 16.5, 18]cm), ending with a wrong-side row.

Shape Front Neck

At neck edge, bind off 6 (7, 7, 8) stitches, work to the end of the row.

Decrease Row (RS): K1, ssk, work across row as established.

Continue to work Decrease Row every right-side row 6 (6, 7, 7) more times—23 (24, 27, 30) stitches. Work even until Front armhole measures 9½ (10, 10½, 11)" (24 [25.5, 26.5, 28]cm), or same length as Back to shoulders.

JOIN SHOULDERS

Join the shoulders using a 3-needle bind-off.

SLEEVES (MAKE 2)

Cast on 34 (36, 40, 44) stitches.

Eyelet Ridge: Work 4 rows in garter stitch.

Eyelet Row (RS): K2, *yo, k2tog; repeat from *, end k2. Work 3 rows in garter stitch, increasing 1 stitch on last row using the m1 method—35 (37, 41, 45) stitches.

Main Sleeve Pattern

Set-Up Row (RS): Work stockinette stitch over 3 (4, 6, 8) stitches, work Chart B over center 29 stitches, work stockinette stitch over 3 (4, 6, 8) stitches.

Shape Sleeve

Increase 1 stitch on each edge, using m1 left and m1 right accordingly, every 4 rows 11 (12, 11, 9) times, then every 6 rows 9 (9, 10, 12) times, working new stitches in stockinette stitch—75 (79, 83, 87) stitches. Continue until Sleeve measures 18 (19, 19½, 20)" (45.5 [48.5, 49.5, 51]cm) from the beginning, ending with Row 12 (18, 4, 6) of Chart B. Bind off all stitches.

FINISHING

Sew Sleeves into armholes. Sew sleeve and side seams.

Neckband

With 16" (40.5cm) circular needle and right side facing, pick up and knit 68 (72, 80, 84) stitches evenly around the neck edge. Working back and forth in rows, work 3 rows in garter stitch.

Eyelet Row (RS): K2, *yo, k2tog; repeat from *, end k2.

Work 3 rows in garter stitch. Bind off loosely purlwise on the right side.

Button Band (Left Front)

With 29" (74cm) circular needle and right side facing, pick up and knit 86 (86, 94, 94) stitches along the front edge. Work in garter stitch for 7 rows. Bind off loosely purlwise on the right side.

Buttonhole Band (Right Front)

With 29" (74cm) circular needle and right side facing, pick up and knit 86 (86, 94, 94) stitches along the front edge. Work in garter stitch for 2 rows.

Buttonhole Row: Work 2 stitches, bind off the next 2 stitches, *work 9 (9, 11, 11) stitches, bind off 2 stitches; repeat from * 6 times, work the last 16 (16, 12, 12) stitches.

Next Row: Work across row, casting on 2 stitches over bound-off stitches. Work 3 more rows in garter stitch. Bind off loosely purlwise on the right side.

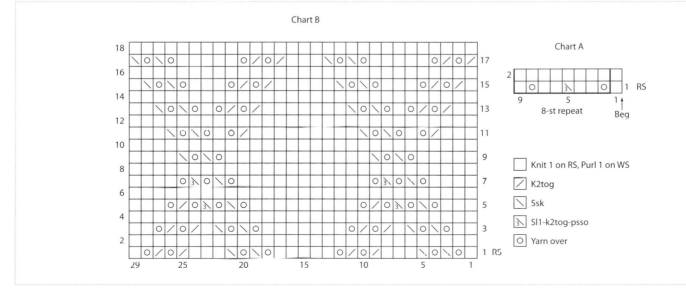

ROAD NOT TAKEN SCARVES

by Lisa Lloyd

SKILL LEVEL
Easy

SIZE
One size

FINISHED MEASUREMENTS
- Width: 8" (20.5cm)
- Length: 60" (152.5cm)

MATERIALS
- 1 skein Helen's Lace by Lorna's Laces (each approximately 4 oz [114g], 1,250 yd [1,143m], 50% silk, 50% wool), in color Tuscany  super fine
- Handspun Romney (100%), 400 yd (366m) lace-weight or fingering weight, hand dyed super fine
- Handspun Merino (100%), 400 yd (366m) lace-weight or fingering weight, natural moorit super fine
- Size 6 (4mm) needles, *or size needed to obtain gauge*
- Yarn needle

GAUGE
20 stitches = 4" (10cm) in chart lace pattern. *To save time, take time to check your gauge.*

SPECIAL STITCHES
(see Glossary on page 162)

garter stitch; k2tog; ssk; stockinette stitch; yo

NOTE
"Choose your own road" by working all 20 rows of the chart or just working rows 1–10 for main pattern.

INSTRUCTIONS

SCARF
Cast on 38 stitches.

Work garter stitch (knit every row) for 4 rows.

Next Row: K2, begin where indicated and work 12 stitches of Chart once, then work 11-stitch repeat of Chart twice, k2.

Continue working Chart, repeating either Rows 1–20 or Rows 1–10 and keeping the first 2 and the last 2 stitches in garter stitch, until scarf measures 60" (152cm) or desired length, stretching slightly, and ending with a wrong-side row. Work garter stitch over all stitches for 4 rows. Bind off very loosely purlwise on the right side.

FINISHING
Weave in all loose ends. Hand wash and pin out carefully to finished measurements, allowing to dry completely before removing pins.

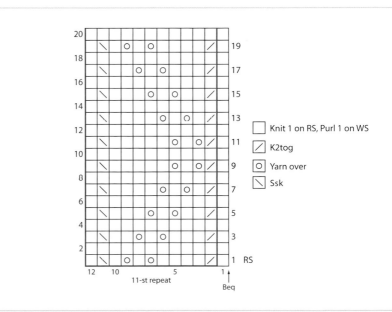

☐	Knit 1 on RS, Purl 1 on WS
◿	K2tog
⊙	Yarn over
◹	Ssk

11-st repeat

Beg

RUBY VEST

By Lisa Lloyd

SKILL LEVEL
Intermediate

SIZE
XS (S, M, L, XL, 2X)

Directions are for smallest size, with larger sizes in parentheses.

FINISHED MEASUREMENTS
- Chest: 37½ (40, 42, 45½, 48, 50)" (95 [101.5, 106.5, 115.5, 122, 127]cm)
- Length: 18½ (20, 20½, 21½, 22, 22½)" (47 [51, 52, 54.5, 56, 57]cm)

MATERIALS
- Handspun Border Leicester (100%) with Angelina®, 750 (850, 950, 1,050, 1,150, 1,250) yd (686 [777, 869, 960, 1,052, 1,143]m) sportweight, hand-dyed ruby red (**2**) fine
- 6 (7, 8, 9, 9, 10) skeins Frog Tree Yarns Alpaca Sport (each approximately 1¾ oz [50g], 130 yd [119m], 100% alpaca), in color 13 Bronze (**2**) fine
- Size 3 (3.25mm) needles, *or size needed to obtain gauge*
- Size 2 (2.75mm) needles, and circular needles, 24" (61cm) and 29" (74cm) long
- Stitch holders
- Stitch markers
- Yarn needle
- 5 buttons, ⅝" (16mm) in diameter

GAUGE
24 stitches and 32 rows = 4" (10cm) over Chart A or B patterns using size 3 (3.25mm) needles. *To save time, take time to check your gauge.*

SPECIAL STITCHES
(see Glossary on page 162)

bind off loosely; k2tog; m1; psso; selvedge stitch; sl1-k2-psso; slip stitch (knit); ssk; yo

NOTE
The first and last stitch of every row is worked in stockinette stitch for a selvedge stitch at the front edges.

INSTRUCTIONS

BACK
With smaller needles, cast on 111 (119, 127, 135, 143, 151) stitches.

Ribbing Pattern
Note: The stitch count does not remain constant and changes every row.

Row 1 (RS): K1 (selvedge stitch), p1, * sl1-k2-psso, p2, k1, p2; repeat from *, end sl1-k2-psso, p1, k1 (selvedge stitch).

Row 2: P1, k1, *p1, yo, p1, k2, p1, k2; repeat from *, end p1, yo, p1, k1, p1.

Row 3: K1, p1, *k3, p2, k1, p2; repeat from *, end k3, p1, k1.

Row 4: P1, k1, *p3, k2, p1, k2; repeat from *, end p3, k1, p1.

Continue until piece measures 2½" (6.5cm), ending with Row 4 of Ribbing Pattern.

Main Body Pattern
Change to larger needles.

Row 1 (RS): K1 (selvedge stitch), work Chart A over 109 (117, 125, 133, 141, 149) stitches, k1 (selvedge stitch). Continue working Chart A and AT THE SAME TIME shape waist, beginning with the next right-side row.

Shape Waist
Decrease Row (RS): K1 (selvedge stitch), ssk, knit to last 3 stitches, k2tog, k1 (selvedge stitch).

Repeat Decrease Row on right-side rows every 4 (2, 4, 4, 4, 6) rows 6 (0, 0, 2, 4, 4) more times, then every 0 (4, 6, 6, 6, 8) rows 0 (7, 5, 4, 3, 1) times—97 (103, 115, 121, 127, 139) stitches, ending with a wrong-side row.

Increase Row (RS): K1 (selvedge stitch), m1 right, knit across the row until 1 stitch remains, m1 left, k1 (selvedge stitch). Repeat Increase Row on right-side rows every 0 (4, 6, 6, 6, 8) rows 0 (6, 4, 3, 2, 0) more times, then every 4 (2, 4, 4, 4, 6) rows 7 (1, 1, 3, 5, 5) times—111 (119, 127, 135, 143, 151) stitches.

Continue until Back measures 10¼ (11¼, 11¼, 12¼, 12¼, 12¾)" (26 [28.5, 28.5, 31, 31, 32.5]cm) from the beginning, ending with a wrong-side row.

Shape Armhole
Bind off 9 (11, 12, 13, 14, 16) stitches at the beginning of the next 2 rows.

Decrease Row (RS): K1 (selvedge stitch), ssk, work across to last 3 stitches, k2tog, k1 (selvedge stitch). Continue to work Decrease Row every other

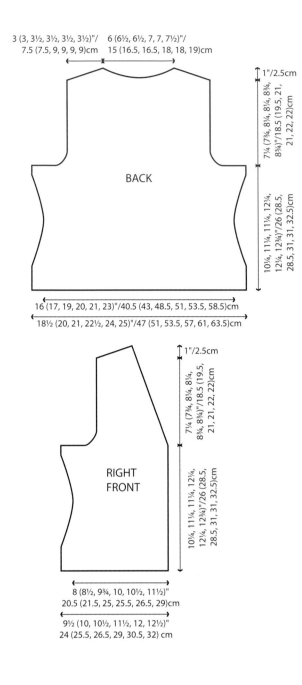

BACK

3 (3, 3½, 3½, 3½, 3½)"/ 7.5 (7.5, 9, 9, 9, 9)cm

6 (6½, 6½, 7, 7, 7½)"/ 15 (16.5, 16.5, 18, 18, 19)cm

1"/2.5cm

7¼ (7¾, 8¼, 8¼, 8¾, 8¾)"/18.5 (19.5, 21, 21, 22, 22)cm

10¼, 11¼, 11¼, 12¼, 12¼, 12¾)"/26 (28.5, 28.5, 31, 31, 32.5)cm

16 (17, 19, 20, 21, 23)"/40.5 (43, 48.5, 51, 53.5, 58.5)cm

18½ (20, 21, 22½, 24, 25)"/47 (51, 53.5, 57, 61, 63.5)cm

RIGHT FRONT

1"/2.5cm

7¼ (7¾, 8¼, 8¼, 8¾, 8¾)"/18.5 (19.5, 21, 21, 22, 22)cm

10¼, 11¼, 11¼, 12¼, 12¼, 12¾)"/26 (28.5, 28.5, 31, 31, 32.5)cm

8 (8½, 9¾, 10, 10½, 11½)" 20.5 (21.5, 25, 25.5, 26.5, 29)cm

9½ (10, 10½, 11½, 12, 12½)" 24 (25.5, 26.5, 29, 30.5, 32) cm

row 8 (9, 10, 11, 13, 14) more times—75 (77, 81, 85, 87, 89) stitches. Work even until the armhole measures 7¼ (7¾, 8¼, 8¼, 8¾, 8¾)" (18.5 [19.5, 21, 21, 22, 22]cm), ending with Row 6 or 12 of Chart A.

Shape Shoulders and Back Neck

Rows 1 and 2: Bind off 7 (7, 7, 7, 8, 8) stitches at the beginning of each row.

Row 3: Bind off 6 (6, 7, 7, 7, 7) stitches, work 10 (10, 11, 11, 11, 11) stitches, join a second ball of yarn and bind off center 35 (37, 38, 42, 42, 44) stitches for back neck, work to the end of the row.

Row 4: Using two balls of yarn and working both sides at the same time, bind off 6 (6, 6, 6, 6, 6) stitches at the beginning of the row, work to end, work across second shoulder stitches.

Row 5: Bind off 6 (6, 7, 7, 7, 7) stitches at the beginning of the row, decrease 1 stitch at each neck edge as follows: Work until 3 stitches remain for first shoulder, k2tog, k1 (selvedge). For second shoulder, k1 (for neck selvedge), ssk, work to end.

Row 6: Bind off 6 (6, 7, 7, 7, 7) stitches.

RIGHT FRONT

With smaller needles, cast on 56 (60, 64, 68, 72, 76) stitches.

Ribbing Pattern

Note: The stitch count does not remain constant and changes every row.

Sizes XS, M, and XL Only

Row 1 (RS): K1 (selvedge stitch), k1, p2, k1, p2, * sl1-k2-psso, p2, k1, p2; repeat from *, end k1 (selvedge stitch).

Row 2: P1, k2, p1, k2, *p1, yo, p1, k2, p1, k2; repeat from *, end p2.

Row 3: K2, p2, k1, p2, *k3, p2, k1, p2; repeat from *, end k1.

Row 4: P1, k2, p1, k2, *p3, k2, p1, k2; repeat from *, end p2.

Sizes S, L, and 2X Only

Row 1: K1 (selvedge stitch), p2, * sl1-k2-psso, p2, k1, p2; repeat from *, end k1 (selvedge stitch).

Row 2: P1, k2, p1, k2, *p1, yo, p1, k2, p1, k2; repeat from *, end p1, yo, p1, k2, p1.

Row 3: K1, p2, *k3, p2, k1, p2; repeat from *, end k1.

Row 4: P1, k2, p1, k2, *p3, k2, p1, k2; repeat from *, end p1, yo, p1, k2, p1.

All Sizes

Continue until the piece measures 2½" (6.5cm), ending with Row 4 of Ribbing Pattern.

Main Body Pattern

Change to larger needles.

Row 1 (RS): K1 (selvedge stitch), k1, beginning with stitch 1 (5, 1, 5, 1, 5) of the 8-stitch repeat, work Chart B over 53 (57, 61, 65, 69, 73) stitches, end k1 (selvedge stitch).

Continue working Chart B and AT THE SAME TIME shape waist beginning with the next right-side row.

Decrease Row (RS): K1 (selvedge stitch), work as established to last 3 stitches, k2tog, k1 (selvedge stitch).

Repeat Decrease Row every 4 (2, 4, 4, 4, 6) rows 6 (0, 0, 2, 4, 4) more times, then every 0 (4, 6, 6, 6, 8) rows 0 (7, 5, 4, 3, 1) times—49 (52, 58, 61, 64, 70) stitches, ending with a wrong-side row.

Increase Row (RS): K1 (selvedge stitch), work across until 1 stitch remains, m1 left, k1 (selvedge stitch).

Repeat Increase Row every 0 (4, 6, 6, 6, 8) rows 0 (6, 4, 3, 2, 0) more times, then every 4 (2, 4, 4, 4, 6) rows 7 (1, 1, 3, 5, 5) times—56 (60, 64, 68, 72, 76) stitches.

Continue until Right Front measures 10¼ (11¼, 11¼, 12¼, 12¼, 12¾)" (26 [28.5, 28.5, 31, 31, 32.5]cm) from the beginning, ending with a right-side row.

Shape Armhole and V-Neck

Bind off 9 (11, 12, 13, 14, 16) stitches at the beginning of the next wrong-side row for armhole.

Next Row (RS): K1, ssk, work as established to last 3 stitches, k2tog, k1.

Continue to decrease 1 stitch at the beginning of every right-side row using ssk 9 (10, 8, 10, 10, 10) more times, then every fourth right-side row 9 (9, 11, 11, 11, 12) times for neck.

AT THE SAME TIME, decrease 1 stitch at the end of every right-side row using k2tog 8 (9, 10, 11, 13, 14) more times for armhole—19 (19, 21, 21, 22, 22) stitches remain for shoulder.

Work even until the armhole measures 7¼ (7¾, 8¼, 8¼, 8¾, 8¾)" (18.5 [19.5, 21, 21, 22, 22]cm), or same length as Back to shoulders, ending with Row 6 or 12 of Chart B.

Shape Shoulder

Rows 1, 3, and 5 (RS): Work even.

Row 2: Bind off 7 (7, 7, 7, 8, 8) stitches at the beginning of the row.

Row 4: Bind off 6 (6, 7, 7, 7, 7) stitches at the beginning of the row.

Row 6: Bind off 6 (6, 7, 7, 7, 7) stitches.

LEFT FRONT

With smaller needle, cast on 56 (60, 64, 68, 72, 76) stitches.

Ribbing Pattern

Note: The stitch count does not remain constant and changes every row.

Sizes XS, M, and XL Only

Row 1: K1 (selvedge stitch), p2, k1, p2, *sl1-k2-psso, p2, k1, p2 * repeat from *, end, k1, k1 (selvedge stitch).

Row 2: P2, k2, p1, k2, *p1, yo, p1, k2, p1, k2; repeat from *, end p1.

Row 3: K1, p2, k1, p2, *k3, p2, k1, p2; repeat from *, end k1.

Row 4: P2, k2, p1, k2, *p3, k2, p1, k2; repeat from *, end p1.

Sizes S, L, and 2X Only

Row 1: K1 (selvedge stitch), p2, k1, p2, * sl1-k2-psso, p2, k1, p2; repeat from *, end sl1-k2-psso, p2, k1 (selvedge stitch).

Row 2: P1, k2, *p1, yo, p1, k2, p1, k2; repeat from *, end p1.

Row 3: K1, p2, k1, p2, *k3, p2, k1, p2; repeat from *, end k3, p2, k1.

Row 4: P1, k2, *p3, k2, p1, k2; repeat from *, end p1.

All Sizes

Continue until the piece measures 2½" (6.5cm), ending with Row 4 of Ribbing Pattern.

Main Body Pattern

Row 1 (RS): Change to larger needles. K1 (selvedge stitch), work the 8-stitch repeat of Chart B over 53 (57, 61, 65, 69, 73) stitches ending with stitch 13 (8, 13, 8, 13, 8), end k1, k1 (selvedge stitch).

Continue working Chart B and *AT THE SAME TIME*, shape waist beginning with the next right-side row.

Decrease Row (RS): K1 (selvedge stitch), ssk, work as established across row.

Repeat Decrease Row every 4 (2, 4, 4, 4, 6) rows 6 (0, 0, 2, 4, 4) more times, then every 0 (4, 6, 6, 6, 8) rows 0 (7, 5, 4, 3, 1) times—49 (52, 58, 61, 64, 70) stitches, ending with a wrong-side row.

Increase Row (RS): K1 (selvedge stitch), m1 right, work as established across row.

Repeat Increase Row every 0 (4, 6, 6, 6, 8) rows 0 (6, 4, 3, 2, 0) more times, then every 4 (2, 4, 4, 4, 6) rows 7 (1, 1, 3, 5, 5) times—56 (60, 64, 68, 72, 76) stitches.

Continue until Left Front measures 10¼ (11¼, 11¼, 12¼, 12¼, 12¾)" (26 [28.5, 28.5, 31, 31, 32.5]cm) from the beginning, ending with a wrong-side row.

Shape Armhole and V-Neck

Bind off 9 (11, 12, 13, 14, 16) stitches at the beginning of the next right-side row for armhole.

Next Row (RS): K1, ssk, work as established to last 3 stitches, k2tog, k1.

Continue to decrease 1 stitch at the end of every right-side row using k2tog 9 (10, 8, 10, 10, 10) more times, then every fourth right-side row 9 (9, 11, 11, 11, 12) times for neck. At the same time, decrease 1 stitch at the beginning of every right-side row using ssk 8 (9, 10, 11, 13, 14) more times for armhole—19 (19, 21, 21, 22, 22) stitches remain for shoulder.

Work even until the armhole measures 7¼ (7¾, 8¼, 8¼, 8¾, 8¾)" (18.5 [19.5, 21, 21, 22, 22]cm), or same length as Back to shoulders, ending with Row 5 or 11 of Chart B.

Shape Shoulders

Rows 1 (RS): Bind off 7 (7, 7, 7, 8, 8) stitches at the beginning of the row.

Rows 2, 4, and 6: Work even.

Row 3: Bind off 6 (6, 7, 7, 7, 7) stitches at the beginning of the row.

Row 5: Bind off 6 (6, 7, 7, 7, 7) stitches.

FINISHING

Sew shoulder and side seams.

Armhole Edging

With 24" (61cm) circular needle and right side facing, pick up and knit 112 (126, 133, 133, 140, 147) stitches evenly around armhole beginning at the underarm. Place marker for the beginning of round.

Ribbing Pattern: *K2, p2, k1, p2; repeat from * around. Work until the edging measures 1" (2.5cm). Bind off loosely in pattern. Repeat for the second armhole.

Front Bands

With 29" (74cm) circular needle and right side facing, begin at the lower right edge, pick up and knit 74 (74, 80, 85, 86, 86) stitches along the right front edge to the first neck decrease, place marker, pick up and knit 49 (52, 56, 56, 59, 59) stitches along the right side of the V-neck edge, 43 (44, 45, 49, 48, 48) stitches along the back neck, 49 (52, 56, 56, 59, 59) stitches along the left side of the V-neck edge, place marker, pick up and knit 74 (74, 80, 85, 86, 86) stitches along the left front edge—289 (296, 317, 331, 338, 338) stitches.

Ribbing Pattern (WS): * P2, k2, p1, k2; repeat from *, end p2.

Next Row: Knit the knit stitches and purl the purl stitches as they appear.

Work 1 more row.

Buttonhole Row (RS): Work 8 (8, 7, 8, 8, 8) stitches, *bind off 2 stitches, work 13 (13, 15, 16, 16, 16) stitches; repeat from * 3 more times, bind off 2 stitches, end k4 (4, 3, 3, 4, 4) stitches before marker, work to the end of row.

Next Row (WS): Work across row in established ribbing, casting on 2 stitches over bound-off stitches. Work 2 more rows then bind off loosely in pattern on the right side.

Sew buttons opposite buttonholes. Weave in all loose ends. Hand wash and block gently to measurements.

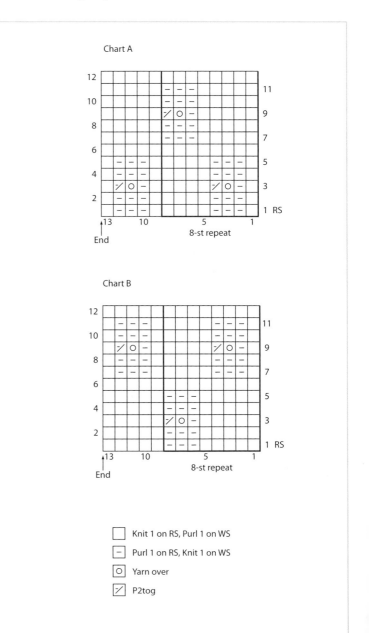

Chart A

Chart B

Knit 1 on RS, Purl 1 on WS

Purl 1 on RS, Knit 1 on WS

Yarn over

P2tog

LITTLE SHELL SOCKS

by Shelia January

SKILL LEVEL
Experienced

SIZE
Women's M (L)

Directions are for smallest size, with larger sizes in parentheses.

FINISHED MEASUREMENTS
- Cuff Length: 7½ (8½)" (19 [21.5]cm)
- Foot Length: 8 (9)" (20.5 [23]cm)

MATERIALS
- 2 skeins Satakieli Yarn by Wooly West (each approximately 3½ oz [100g], 360 yd [329m], 100% wool) in color #441 Rose, or 440 yd (402m) fingering-weight yarn ❶ super fine
- Size 1 (2.25mm) double-pointed needles, *or size needed to obtain gauge*
- Size 3 (3.25mm) needle
- Stitch marker
- Stitch holder (optional)
- Yarn needle

GAUGE
32 stitches and 44 rows = 4" (10cm) in stockinette stitch. *To save time, take time to check your gauge.*

SPECIAL STITCHES
(see Glossary on page 162)

bind off in rib; k1, p1 rib; k3tog; long-tail cast-on; m1; p3tog; pick up and knit; short rows; ssk; stockinette stitch; yo

SPECIAL PATTERN

Little Shells Lace Pattern
Rounds 1–2: Knit all stitches.

Round 3: *K1, yo, p1, p3tog, p1, yo, k1; repeat from * to end of round.

Round 4: Knit all stitches.

INSTRUCTIONS

TOE
Cast on 10 stitches using the long-tail cast-on method.

Work in stockinette stitch for ½" (13mm), ending with a right-side row. Do not turn work.

Place stitch marker to indicate the beginning of the round. Using the second needle, pick up and knit 4 stitches, working counterclockwise along the edge immediately to the left of the last stitch knitted. Do not turn work.

Continue counterclockwise to the cast-on edge, and pick up and knit 10 stitches along this edge.

Continue to the last side, and pick up and knit 4 stitches.

You now have a small rectangle, with a needle on each of the four sides—28 stitches. The working yarn is back to the marker, indicating the beginning of the round.

Round 1: Knit.

Round 2: Needle 1: Knit. Needles 2 and 4: K1, m1, k2, m1, k1. Needle 3: Knit—32 stitches.

Round 3: Knit.

Round 4: Needles 1 and 3: Knit. Needles 2 and 4: K2, m1, k2, m1, k2—36 stitches.

Round 5: Knit.

Round 6: Needles 1 and 3: Knit all stitches. Needles 2 and 4: K3, m1, k2, m1, k3.

Round 7: Knit, rearranging stitches on the needles so that the 2 middle stitches of needles 2 and 4 become the last stitches on needles 1 and 3. Move the stitch marker to the new beginning point of needle 1—40 stitches.

Round 8: Needles 1 and 3: Knit to last stitch, m1, k1. Needles 2 and 4: K1, m1, knit to end—44 stitches.

Round 9: Knit.

Repeat Rounds 8–9 until you have 56 (64) stitches total. The toe is now complete.

INSTEP

Continue knitting in the round in stockinette stitch until the foot measures 5½ (6½)" (14 [16.5]cm), including the toe, or approximately 2½" (6.5cm) shorter than desired foot length.

HEEL

In preparation, remove the stitch marker. Position the stitches so they are evenly distributed across the needles. The stitches on needles 1 and 4 will be the heel/sole stitches, and those on needles 2 and 3 will be the instep. Move 3 stitches from each of the instep needles to the adjacent heel needles. There will now be 17 (19) stitches on needles 1 and 4 and 11 (13) stitches on needles 2 and 3. Combine the stitches from needles 1 and 4 onto one needle. These are all of the working stitches for the heel. The stitches on needles 2 and 3 can be put on a stitch holder if desired until the heel is completed.

Short Row Heel

Note: Work heel stitches only.

Row 1: Knit 33 (37) stitches, turn, and bring yarn over your working needle from back to front. (This will create a yarn-over loop at the beginning of the next row.)

Row 2: Purl 32 (36) stitches, turn, and bring yarn from back to front.

Row 3: Knit 31 (35) stitches, turn, and bring yarn from back to front.

Row 4: Purl 30 (34) stitches, turn, and bring yarn from back to front.

Continue in this manner, working 1 less stitch each row and bringing yarn from back to front each time until 10 stitches remain unworked.

Next Row: K10. Do not knit the yarn-over loop, but turn and bring yarn from back to front. (This will create a second yarn-over loop next to the first.)

Next Row: P10. Do not purl the yarn-over loop, but turn and bring yarn from back to front. (This will create a second yarn-over loop next to the first.)

Heel Decrease Rows

Note: Make sure to correct the mount of your yarn-over loops so that the right leg of the stitch is on the front of the left needle when you work the stitches.

Row 1: Knit until the next 2 stitches are yarn-over loops, k3tog (the 2 loops with the next stitch). Turn work and bring yarn from back to front.

Row 2: Purl across stitches until the next 2 stitches are yarn-over loops, p3tog (the 2 loops with the next stitch). Turn work and bring yarn from back to front.

Repeat Rows 1–2, working in the yarn-over loops and bringing yarn from back to front each time until you have 2 rows left with double yarn-over loops.

Next Row: K32 (36), k3tog (last 3 stitches on the needle), turn.

Last Heel Row: Yo, p33 (37), p2tog (last 3 stitches on the needle), turn.

You will now begin knitting in the round again, including the instep stitches that have been sitting idle while the heel was worked.

Next Round: Yo, k17 (19), place stitch marker, which will mark the back of the heel, k17 (19) stitches. Knit the yarn-over loop together with the first stitch of the instep needle, which resumes the round. If there is a hole forming at the intersection of the heel and the instep stitches, pick up and knit an additional stitch, which can be decreased away in the next round. K21 (25) stitches, to 1 stitch before the end of the instep stitches. Ssk the last instep stitch with the yarn-over loop on the next needle. Another stitch can be picked up and knit if a hole is noted, again to be decreased away in the next round. Knit to marker—55 (63) stitches.

CUFF

Knit 4 rounds. (For size Medium, increase 1 stitch in the fourth round for a total of 56 stitches.)

Begin Little Shells Lace Pattern (page 149) and work for 5 (6)" (12.5 [15]cm), or until the desired cuff length less 2½" (6.5cm) is reached, ending with Round 4 of Little Shells Lace Pattern. (For size Large, increase 1 stitch in the fourth round for a total of 64 stitches.)

Change to k1, p1 rib for the next 2½" (6.5cm). Bind off in rib very loosely using a needle two sizes larger to achieve a stretchy cuff.

FINISHING

Weave in the loose ends.

CAT'S EYE SCARF

by Lisa Lloyd

SKILL LEVEL
Easy

SIZE
One size

FINISHED MEASUREMENTS
- Width: 9" (23cm)
- Length: 60" (152.5cm)

MATERIALS
- Handspun Rambouillet Crossbred with Angelina® from Foxfire Fiber and Designs 430 yd [393m] fingering weight, in color Forest **①** super fine
- 2 skeins Alpaca Fingering by Frog Tree (each approximately 1¾ oz [50g], 215 yd [197m], 100% alpaca), in color #000 Natural White **①** super fine
- Size 6 (4mm) needles, *or size needed to obtain gauge*
- Stitch markers
- Yarn needle

GAUGE
20 stitches = 4" (10cm) in Chart patterns. *To save time, take time to check your gauge.*

SPECIAL STITCHES
(see Glossary on page 162)

garter stich; m1; k2tog; reverse stockinette stitch; ssk; stockinette stitch; yo

INSTRUCTIONS

SCARF
Cast on 42 stitches.

Work in garter stitch for 4 rows.

First Border

Set-Up Row: K2, begin where indicated and work Chart A across center 38 stitches, ending where indicated, k2. Continue working Chart A, keeping the first and last 2 stitches in garter stitch, until Scarf measures 2½" (6.5cm) from the beginning, ending with a wrong-side row.

Main Scarf Pattern

Set-Up Row (RS): K2, work Chart A over 11 stitches, place stitch marker, beginning where indicated, repeat the 6-stitch repeat of Chart B over center 18 stitches, increasing 4 stitches evenly spaced using the m1 method, ending where indicated, place stitch marker, work Chart A over 11 stitches, k2—46 stitches.

Continue until scarf measures 57½" (146cm) or 2½" (6.5cm) less than desired length, decreasing 4 stitches evenly between markers using k2tog on the last wrong-side row—42 stitches.

Second Border

Set-Up Row: K2, work Chart A as for first border, ending k2, removing markers. Continue until the second border measures 2½" (6.5cm), then work garter stitch over all stitches for 4 rows. Bind off very loosely purlwise on the right side.

FINISHING
Weave in all loose ends and block to final measurements.

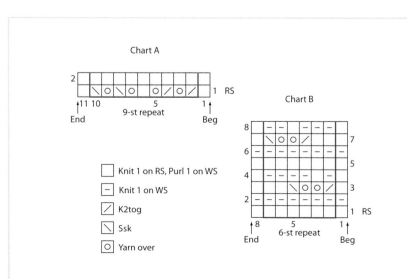

RASPBERRY RHAPSODY SCARF

by Jackie Erickson-Schweitzer

SKILL LEVEL
Intermediate

SIZE
One size

FINISHED MEASUREMENTS

Before Washing and Blocking
- Width: 8" (20.5cm)
- Length: 50" (127cm)

After Washing and Blocking
- Width: 9" (23cm)
- Length: 52" (132cm)

MATERIALS
- 1 skein Helen's Lace by Lorna's Laces (each approximately 4 oz [113.5g], 1,250 yd [1,143m], 50% silk, 50% wool) in color Pink Blossom, or 300 yd (274m) of 2-ply laceweight yarn (**1**) super fine
- Size 5 (3.75mm) straight or circular needles, *or size needed to obtain gauge*
- Yarn needle

GAUGE

Before Blocking
24 stitches and 24 rows = 4" (10cm) in Raspberry Lace Pattern

After Blocking under Moderate Tension
20½ stitches and 21¼ rows = 4" (10cm) in Raspberry Lace Pattern

To save time, take time to check your gauge.

NOTE
Because this isn't a form-fitting garment, your gauge doesn't need to be 100 percent exact. But be aware that major changes in gauge may require more (or less) yarn than specified. Too dense of a gauge will not retain the open, airy look of the lace. Too loose of a gauge can cause the texture of the raspberries to be lost.

SPECIAL STITCHES
(see Glossary on page 162)
CDD; k1 tbl; k1 tbl-yo-k1; k2tog-k3tog-pso; k3tog; m1; slip; ssk; wyif; yo

SPECIAL PATTERN

Raspberry Lace Pattern (multiple of 6 stitches + 1)

Row 1 (RS): P3, k1 tbl, *p5, k1 tbl; repeat from * to last 3 stitches, p3.

Row 2: K3tog, *yo, k1 tbl-yo-k1, yo, k2tog-k3tog-pso; repeat from * to last 4 stitches, yo, k1 tbl-yo-k1, yo, k3togtbl.

Row 3: K1 tbl, *p5, k1 tbl; repeat from * to end.

Row 4: *P1, k5; repeat from * to last stitch, p1.

Row 5: Repeat Row 3.

Row 6: K1, m1, yo, *k2tog-k3tog-pso, yo, k1 tbl-yo-k1, yo; repeat from * to last 6 stitches, k2tog-k3tog-pso, yo, m1, k1.

Row 7: Repeat Row 1.

Row 8: K3, *p1, k5; repeat from * to last 4 stitches, p1, k3.

Repeat Rows 1–8 for pattern.

INSTRUCTIONS

BEGINNING BORDER
Cast on 49 stitches loosely.

Row 1 (RS of outer border): Slip 1 purlwise wyif, k1, (yo, ssk) 11 times, k1, (k2tog, yo) 11 times, k2.

Row 2: Slip 1 purlwise wyif, purl to last stitch, k1.

Row 3: Slip 1 purlwise wyif, yo, (ssk, yo) 11 times, CDD, (yo, k2tog) 11 times, yo, k1.

Row 4: Repeat Row 2.

Rows 5–8: Repeat Rows 1–4.

Row 9: Repeat Row 1.

Row 10: Establish inner border pattern while maintaining 7 stitches at each edge of scarf in the established outer border pattern: Slip 1 purlwise wyif, p6, k35, p6, k1.

Row 11: Slip 1 purlwise wyif, yo, (ssk, yo) twice, ssk, k35, k2tog, (yo, k2tog) twice, yo, k1.

Row 12: Repeat Row 10.

MAIN AREA

Row 1 (RS): Establish main pattern while maintaining 9 stitches at each edge of scarf in the established border patterns: Slip 1 purlwise wyif, k1, (yo, ssk) twice, k3, p3, k1 tbl, (p5, k1 tbl) 4 times, p3, k3, (k2tog, yo) twice, k2.

Row 2: Slip 1 purlwise wyif, p6, k2, k3tog, (yo, k1 tbl-yo-k1, yo, k2tog-k3tog-pso) 4 times, yo, k1 tbl-yo-k1, yo, k3tog tbl, k2, p6, k1.

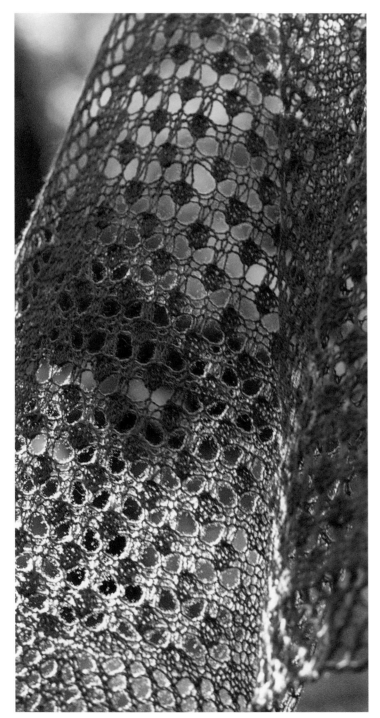

Row 3: Slip 1 purlwise wyif, yo, (ssk, yo) twice, ssk, k2, k1 tbl, (p5, k1 tbl) 5 times, k2, k2tog, (yo, k2tog) twice, yo, k1.

Row 4: Slip 1 purlwise wyif, p6, k2, (p1, k5) 5 times, p1, k2, p6, k1.

Row 5: Slip 1 purlwise wyif, k1, (yo, ssk) twice, k3, k1 tbl, (p5, k1 tbl) 5 times, k3, (k2tog, yo) twice, k2.

Row 6: Slip 1 purlwise wyif, p6, k2, m1, k1, yo, (k2tog-k3tog-pso, yo, k1 tbl-yo-k1, yo) 4 times, k2tog-k3tog-pso, yo, k1, m1, k2, p6, k1.

Row 7: Slip 1 purlwise wyif, yo, (ssk, yo) twice, ssk, k2, p3, k1 tbl, (p5, k1 tbl) 4 times, p3, k2, k2tog, (yo, k2tog) twice, yo, k1.

Row 8: Slip 1 purlwise wyif, p6, k2, k3, (p1, k5) 4 times, p1, k5, p6, k1.

Repeat Rows 1–8 until scarf measures approximately 40" (101.5cm) in a relaxed state, or about 50" (127cm) stretched to simulate blocking, and completing Row 7. If adjusting length, work until stretched length is 2" (5cm) less than desired finished blocked size.

ENDING BORDER

Row 1 (WS): Slip 1 purlwise wyif, p6, k35, p6, k1.

Row 2: Slip 1 purlwise wyif, k1, (yo, ssk) twice, k1, k35, k1, (k2tog, yo) twice, k2.

Row 3: Repeat Row 1.

Work Rows 3–4 of Beginning Border, then Rows 1–4 of Beginning Border, then Rows 1–3 of Beginning Border again.

Bind off all stitches loosely.

FINISHING

Weave in ends invisibly, either before blocking or afterward. If before, be sure to leave enough tail to allow for stretching and then trim any remaining ends after blocking has been completed.

Wet-block under tension by pinning the still-damp scarf on a flat surface while gently stretching it into shape and opening up the lace pattern. Use as many pins as it takes to keep the edges as straight as possible. Let it dry thoroughly before removing the blocking pins.

ENDPAPERS SHAWL

by Elanor Lynn

SKILL LEVEL
Experienced

SIZE
One size

FINISHED MEASUREMENTS
- Width: 64" (163cm)
- Depth: 41" (104cm)

MATERIALS

Yarn A
- 3 skeins Painter's Palette Premium Merino Yarn by Koigu (each approximately 1¾ [50g], 175 yd [160m], 100% merino wool), in color #P621 (multicolored with fuchsia and red tones), or 525 yd (480m) multicolor 2-ply fingering-weight yarn **(1)** super fine

Yarn B
- 1 skein Premium Merino Solid Yarn by Koigu (each approximately 1¾ oz [50g], 175 yd [160m], 100% merino), in colors #2233 medium rose pink (light), #1170 fuchsia (medium), and #2120 cherry red (dark), or 175 yd (160m) each of three solid colors in 2-ply fingering-weight yarn **(1)** super fine
- Size 11 (8mm) circular needles, 24" (61cm) long
- Size 10½ (6.5mm) circular needles, 24" (61cm) long
- Size 9 (5.5mm) circular needles, 24" (61cm) long
- Size 7 (4.5mm) circular needles, 24" (61cm) long, *or size needed to obtain gauge*
- Different-colored stitch markers
- Yarn needle

GAUGE
20 stitches and 30 rows = 4" (10cm) in stockinette stitch using size 7 (4.5mm) needles. *To save time, take time to check your gauge.*

SPECIAL STITCHES
(see Glossary on page 162)

cdd; garter stitch; k2tog; p2tog; reverse stockinette stitch; short rows; sl2-k1-psso; ssk; stockinette stitch; yarn over (double); yo

NOTE
Pay attention on Row 5 of the border. On this row you will work decreases to form unit shaping at the edges of units B and C only. On all other right-side rows, you will be working both the unit shaping and the stitch pattern decreases.

INSTRUCTIONS

BORDER

Note: Use a different-colored marker to set off repeats within the units. For example, use a red marker between units and green markers within the repeats. This will help you keep track of where to work the garment decreases.

With size 11 (8mm) needles and yarn A, cast on 315 stitches. Change to size 10½ needles and knit 2 rows. These will be your foundation.

Begin stitch pattern on next row as follows: K3, work Chart B once over 21 stitches, work Chart A 11 times over 111 stitches, work Chart C once over 21 stitches, yo, CDD, work Chart B once over 21 stitches, work Chart A 11 times over 111 stitches, work Chart C once over 21 stitches, k3 (each right-side row will decrease your stitch count by 4 stitches) and, AT THE SAME TIME, after the first 12 pattern rows, change to size 9 (5.5mm) needles and work the next 12 pattern rows. Change to size 7 (4.5mm) needles for the final 18 rows—44 rows total, including 2 foundations rows—235 stitches.

MIDDLE

With right side facing, size 7 (4.5mm) needles, and the darkest solid in
yarn B group, begin working short rows, incorporating 1 border stitch at
the end of every row.

Slip stitches so that you have 5 stitches before the CDD on the border (between units B and C). Using short rows, work the next 10 rows as follows, adding 1 stitch at each end by working 1 additional stitch from border (in stockinette stitch).

Row 1: K2tog, k3, yo, k1, yo, k3, ssk.

Row 2 and all even rows: Purl.

Row 3: K1, k2tog, k3, yo, k1, yo, k3, ssk, k1.

Row 5: K2, k2tog, k3, yo, k1, yo, k3, ssk, k2.

Row 7: CDD, (k2tog) twice, k1, yo, k1, yo, k1, (ssk) twice, CDD.

Row 9: K1, CDD, k3, yo, k1, yo, k3, CDD, k1.

Row 10: Purl—14 stitches now being worked in this row.

Work the Fir Cone Chart, beginning on Row 11. Continue to add 1 stitch at the end of each row, working the newly incorporated stitches in stockinette stitch until there are enough stitches to start a new repeat. In this way, you will gradually use up all the border stitches. The pattern shift of the Fir Cone will cause the number of stitches being worked to increase only every other row. The stitch count will increase by 15 stitches in the next 10-row pattern repeat and by 20 stitches every 2 pattern repeats or 20 rows and, AT THE SAME TIME, after working 100 rows, change to the second-darkest solid in yarn B group (medium color) and work the entire skein, then change to the lightest solid in yarn B group to work the remainder of the middle of the shawl. If needed, change back to yarn A for the remainder of the middle. When there are no more border stitches remaining, change to size 10½ (6.5mm) needles to bind off. This is to ensure that your cast-off edge is not too tight, which would draw your shawl into a horseshoe shape.

TOP EDGE

With right side facing and using size 9 (5.5mm) needles and yarn A, work (k1, yo, k1) in the very first stitch of the Chart B edge. Then work another (k1, yo, k1) as close as possible to the next garter ridge. Continuing across the Chart B edge, work (k1, yo, k1) in or next to each garter ridge, for a total of 7 times—21 stitches. Work the last of the seven repeats at the intersection of the border and middle sections. Continue picking up over the Fir Cone middle section by working (k1, yo, k1) in the center stitch of the Chart A motifs, and in the last yo between motifs, across the entire middle section—144 stitches. Work the final Chart B Border section as you did for the beginning of row, repeat the (k1, yo, k1) 7 times, with the last repeat in the last stitch—21 stitches. This gives you a total of 187 stitches for the top border.

Knit 3 rows, ending with wrong-side row.

Next Row (RS): K21, then work eyelet row as follows: *Double yarn over (wrap yarn twice around needle), k3; repeat from * across to the last 21 stitches, double yarn over, k21.

Next Row (WS): Knit the next row, working each double yarn over from the previous row as follows: Knit into the first loop, purl into the second.

Knit 2 rows, ending with a wrong-side row. Bind off all stitches with size 11 (8mm) needles.

Weave in all ends.

FINISHING

Note: Lace looks best stretched to emphasize the eyelets, but merino will only take so much blocking before bouncing back to its original crimpy shape. Lay flat to dry, stretching to finished measurements. If you find that the shawl stretched too much with washing, you can always put it in the dryer on a low setting for a few minutes before blocking.

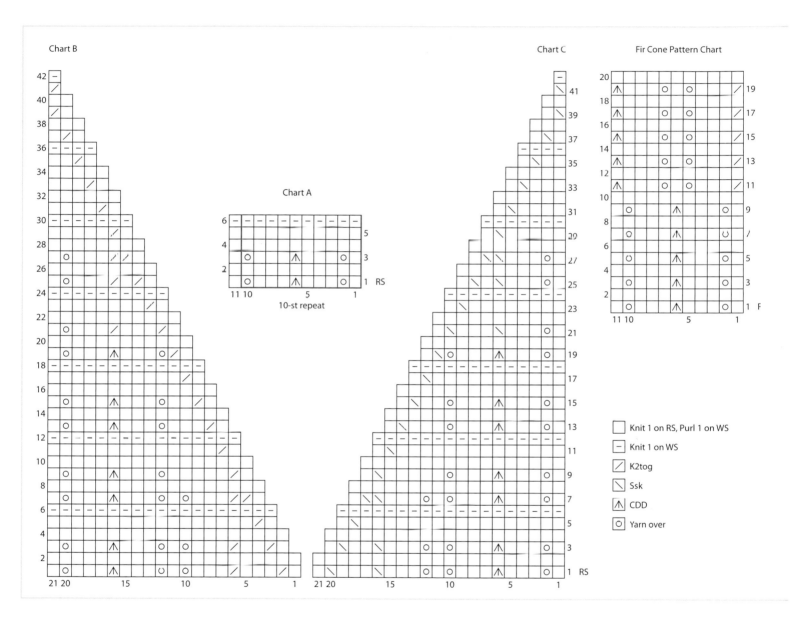

Chart B

Chart A

Chart C

Fir Cone Pattern Chart

			Knit 1 on RS, Purl 1 on WS
			Knit 1 on WS
			K2tog
			Ssk
			CDD
			Yarn over

10-st repeat

GLOSSARY

( ) PARENTHESES: Work instructions within parentheses in place directed. Also used to indicate collective stitch groups worked as one procedure in the same place; for additional or clarifying information, indicated in italic text; to enclose instructions that should be worked the exact number of times specified immediately following the parentheses, i.e., (k1, p1) twice; or to list the garment sizes and to provide additional information to clarify instructions.

[ ] BRACKETS: Repeat instructions within brackets as directed; used to indicate additional or clarifying information; used in the same way as parentheses, but are usually used in combination with them to further clarify instructions.

* ASTERISK: Repeat instructions following the single asterisk as directed.

** DOUBLE ASTERISKS: Repeat instructions between asterisks, as directed.

2-ST LC (TWO-STITCH LEFT CABLE): This is a left-twisting cable. Slip next stitch purlwise onto cable needle and hold in front, knit 1 stitch, knit 1 stitch from cable needle.

2-ST RC (TWO-STITCH RIGHT CABLE): This is a right-twisting cable. Slip next stitch purlwise onto cable needle and hold in back, knit 1 stitch, knit 1 stitch from cable needle.

3-NEEDLE BIND OFF: The 3-needle bind off is a great way to both bind off and seam at the same time. It is often used for the shoulder seams of sweaters. Step 1: With the right side of the two pieces facing each other, and the needles parallel, insert a third needle knitwise into the first stitch of each needle, wrap the yarn around the needle as if to knit. Knit these two stitches together and slip them off the needles. Step 2: Knit the next two stitches together from each needle in the same way as in Step 1. Step 3: Slip the first stitch on the third needle over the second stitch and off the needle. Repeat steps 2 and 3 across the row until all the stitches are bound off.

4-ST LC (FOUR-STITCH LEFT CABLE): This is a left-twisting cable. Slip two stitches purlwise onto cable needle and hold in front, knit 2 stitches, knit 2 stitches from cable needle.

4-ST RC (FOUR-STITCH RIGHT CABLE): This is a right-twisting cable. Slip two stitches purlwise onto cable needle and hold in back, knit 2 stitches, knit 2 stitches from cable needle.

8-ST LC (EIGHT-STITCH LEFT CABLE): This is a left-twisting cable. Slip four stitches purlwise onto cable needle, knit next four stitches, and then knit four stitches from cable needle.

AS ESTABLISHED: The instructions or pattern introduced and set up previously.

AS IF TO KNIT: Also known as KNITWISE or K-WISE. Put the needle into the stitch as if you were going to knit it.

AS IF TO PURL: Also known as PURLWISE or P-WISE. Put the needle into the stitch as if you were going to purl it.

AT THE SAME TIME: Do what the new instructions tell you to do, but at the same time keep following the instructions that came just before.

ATTACH: Join a new strand of yarn.

BAR INCREASE (KFB): This is a single increase that is visible. On a knit row, knit first into the front of the stitch normally, then, before slipping it off the needle, knit again into the back of the same stitch, and slip the stitch off. The same method is applied to a purl row; in this case, you purl into the front then the back of the stitch.

BEING CAREFUL NOT TO TWIST STITCHES: In circular knitting, before making your join, make sure that all the stitches are facing the same direction.

BIND OFF/BIND-OFF (BO): The basic last step to get the stitches of your project off the needles by making a finished edge.

BIND OFF IN RIB: Knit the knit stitches and purl the purl stitches as you bind them off.

BIND OFF LOOSELY: Be careful not to pull the yarn too tight when binding off. It is helpful to use a needle one or two size bigger.

BLOCKING: The process of wetting, steaming, or spraying (misting) to stretch and shape a finished knitted piece to reach the dimensions suggested in the pattern, to make two pieces that need to match the same size, or to make your stitches look nicer and more even. The decisions about how to block your pieces depends on the content of the yarn and the type of stitch pattern. Understanding the properties of the yarns used will help decide on how to block. Always read the yarn's ball band carefully before proceeding to know the important information about the care of the yarn.

CDD (CENTER DOUBLE DECREASE): Also known as Sl2-K1-P2SSO (S2KP2) and VDD (VERTICAL DOUBLE DECREASE). This is a centered, double decrease when used on the right side of the work. Slip two stitches together knitwise, knit one stitch, and then pass the two slipped stitches together over the knitted stitch and off the right hand needle.

CM: Centimeter(s)

CABLE CAST-ON: Useful when you need to cast on stitches at the end of a row or to cast them on over stitches that you have bound off (such as a buttonhole). It has a very nice decorative edge that looks like a cable. Step 1: Start with a slipknot on the left needle. Insert the right needle as if to knit, wrap the yarn around the right needle just as if you were going to knit it and pull this loop through the loop on the needle. Place this new loop or stitch on the left needle. Step 2: Insert right needle between the last two stitches on the left needle. Wrap the yarn around the right needle just as if you were going to knit it. Pull the loop through and place this new stitch on the left needle. Repeat Step 2 until you have cast on the number of stitches you need.

CABLE NEEDLE (CN): Short knitting needle, used as an aid in the twisting of a cable.

CAST ON/CAST-ON: Also known as BINDING ON. The method by which stitches are formed that you then knit or purl to form your knitted item. There are many different methods for casting on, and different ones are more appropriate for different projects. The most basic types of casting on are the long-tail cast-on and the knitted cast-on.

CHANGE TO SMALLER OR LARGER NEEDLES: Sometimes different-sized needles are used in different parts of a project. The pattern will tell you when to use the different sizes.

CONTINUE IN PATTERN: Keep working in the same pattern stitch.

CROCHET CAST-ON: Make a slipknot in the contrast color yarn and place it on the crochet hook. Step 1: Hold the needle and yarn in the left hand, and the crochet hook with the slipknot in the right hand as though to crochet. Step 2: Place the needle on top of the yarn held in the left hand. Step 3: Holding the hook over the needle, crochet a chain stitch over the top of the knitting needle. Step 4: Move the yarn under the knitting needle and back toward the left. Repeat Steps one to four for required number of stitches. Cut the yarn and fasten off. Tie a knot in the end of this tail to remember from which end to remove the chain.

CROCHET CHAIN BIND-OFF: With crochet hook, insert hook into the next 4 stitches, yarn over hook, pull through all stitches, chain 8. Repeat to last 4 stitches. Insert hook into last four stitches, yarn over hook, and pull through all stitches. Fasten off. This technique gives you a very stretchy edge as well as a delicate scalloped edge. This technique works very well for an edge that will be fringed as each scallop is shaped well for spacing out sections of fringe evenly.

DECREASE OR INCREASE EVENLY: Sometimes a pattern will tell you specifically where to decrease or increase across a row. Other times it will only tell you the specific number of stitches to decrease or increase, and will need to do so evenly. You do not want the decreases or increases together at one end but spread out as evenly as possible across the entire row. Otherwise, it will cause your knitting to pucker and flare.

DIRECTIONS ARE FOR SMALLEST SIZE WITH LARGER SIZES IN PARENTHESES: When the pattern is given for more than one size, all through the pattern the smallest size is given first then the other sizes are shown in parentheses afterward. For example, "bind off 6 (9, 12) stitches" means to bind off 6 stitches for the smallest size, 9 stitches for the middle size, and 12 stitches for the largest size.

DOUBLE INCREASE: An increase of two stitches. Knit 1 through the back loop (k1 tbl), then knit the same stitch in the front loop, then insert left-hand needle point behind the vertical strand that runs downward from between the 2 stitches just made, and k1 tbl into this strand to make the 3rd stitch of the group.

DOUBLE NEEDLE CAST-ON: Hold two needles together and make slipknot around needles. When all the stitches are cast on, slip the 2nd needle back out of the loops.

END WITH A RIGHT SIDE (RS) OR WRONG SIDE (WS) ROW: The pattern is indicating the side which to make the last row worked on.

FAGOTING: A variation of lace knitting in which every stitch is a yarn over or a decrease.

FASTEN OFF: After you have finished binding off, pull the end of the yarn through the last loop on the needle, pull tight, and cut.

FROM BEGINNING: You often see this when you are to measure your piece. It means to measure from where you began the piece, including any edgings.

G: Gram(s)

GARTER STITCH: Works on any number of stitches. In flat knitting: Knit (or purl) every row. In circular knitting: Knit one round, purl the next round.

GAUGE: The number of stitches and rows that measure one inch. Patterns often give this measurement for four inches or 10 centimeters.

I-BOBBLE: Step 1: Knit 3 stitches into next stitch. Slip these 3 stitches back to left-hand needle and knit. Step 2: Knit 2 stitches into first stitch, knit 1 stitch, knit 2 stitches into last stitch. Slip these 5 stitches back to left-hand needle and knit. [Repeat Step 2 for a larger bobble.] Step 3: Knit 1, VDD (vertical double decrease), knit 1. Slip stitches back to left-hand needle and knit. [Repeat Step 3 until 3 stitches remain.] Step 4: VDD last 3 stitches.

I-CORD: Cast on 3, 4, 5, or 6 stitches using double-pointed needles. Step 1: Knit, do not turn. Step 2: Slide the stitches back to the beginning of the needle. Repeat steps one and two until you have a short length of knitting, pulling down on the cord and the gap at the back will close. Repeat until the cord is the length you desire. Thread the yarn through the stitches and pull firmly.

I-CORD BIND-OFF: Also known as APPLIED I-CORD. I-cord that is worked on the bind-off row. This makes a decorative edging that is firm and has a nicely finished appearance. Cast on 3 stitches, using the cable cast-on. Step 1: Knit two stitches, and then knit two stitches together through the back loop (K2tog tbl). Step 2: Slip the three worked stitches back onto the left-hand needle, then pull the working yarn tightly across the back of those 3 stitches. Repeat

steps one and two. The result is a raised I-cord edging running perpendicular to the body of knitting.

I-CORD CAST-ON: Cast on 3 stitches. Knit these 3 stitches and slip them back onto the left-hand needle. Step 1: Make one (m1) increase by knitting in front and back of first stitch (Kfb), knit 2. Step 2: Slip last 3 stitches to left-hand needle purlwise. Repeat steps one and two until you have cast on the stitches required plus 2 additional stitches. Slip last 3 stitches from right-hand needle to left-hand needle, knit 2 stitches together, knit one stitch. Slip last 2 stitches from right-hand needle to left-hand needle, knit 2 stitches together.

INCREASE 1 OR INCREASE IN NEXT STITCH (KFB): On a knit row, knit first into the front of the stitch normally, then, before slipping it off the needle, knit again into the back of the same stitch, and slip the stitch off. The same method is applied to a purl row; in this case, you purl into the front then the back of the stitch.

INVISIBLE CAST-ON: Knot your working yarn to your contrasting yarn. Then, with needle and knot in your right hand, pull both strands with your left hand until you achieve tension. Make sure to separate the strands using the fingers of your left hand. Yarn over with working yarn in front of waste yarn.

JOIN(ING) IN THE ROUND: Having all your stitches on your cast-on needle to be able to work them in the round so you can make a tube.

K (KNIT): Insert the right needle into the front of the stitch from front to back.

K1 (KNIT ONE STITCH): Create a stitch by inserting the needle through the stitch from the front to the back, wrapping yarn around the needle and pulling loop through.

(K1, YO, K1) BIND-OFF: Knit 1 stitch, *yarn over, knit 1 stitch. Pick up first knit stitch and yarn over and pass both off the needles, leaving 1 stitch remaining on right-hand needle; repeat from * until only 1 stitch remains on the right-hand needle. Fasten off. The extra yarn over between bind-off stitches adds extra length to your final stitches and gives you extra stretch for the blocking stage.

K1B (KNIT ONE INTO THE STITCH BELOW): A nearly invisible single increase. Knit the stitch below the top stitch on your left needle. This is a more awkward method of increasing and tends to make the stitches tighter if not careful while you knit the increase.

K1, P1 RIB (KNIT ONE, PURL ONE RIBBING): Any odd number of stitches. Row 1 (RS): Knit one, *purl one, knit one; repeat from * to end. Row 2: Purl one, *knit one, purl one; repeat from * to end. Repeat rows 1 and 2.

K1 TBL (KNIT ONE STITCH THROUGH BACK LOOP): Also known as K TBL. Insert the right needle into the back of the stitch from the front to back and knit the stitch.

K1 TBL-YO-K1: Knit one stitch through the back loop, wrap the yarn over the right needle, and then knit through the front loop of the same stitch.

K2, P2 RIB (KNIT TWO, PURL TWO RIBBING): Multiple of 4 stitches + 2 extra. Row 1 (RS): Knit two, *purl two, knit two; repeat from * to end. Row 2: Purl two, *knit two, purl two, repeat from * to end. Repeat rows 1 and 2.

K2TOG (KNIT TWO STITCHES TOGETHER) (over 2 stitches): Also known as K2TOGR. This is a right-slanting, single decrease when used on the right side of the work. Knit two stitches together as though they were one stitch.

K2TOG-K3TOG-PSO (over 5 stitches): This is a decrease of 5 stitches at once. Knit the first two stitches together, knit the next three stitches together, and then pass the first decrease stitch over the one just made and off the needle.

K2TOGL (KNIT TWO STITCHES TOGETHER WITH LEFT SLANT) (over 2 stitches): Also known as SSK, K2TOG TBL, or SL1-K1-PSSO (SKP) and is a single decrease when used on the right side of the work. Knit two stitches together through the back loop as if they were one stitch.

K2TOGR (KNIT TWO STITCHES TOGETHER WITH RIGHT SLANT) (over 2 stitches): Also known as K2TOG and is a single decrease when used on the right side of the work. Knit two stitches together as though they were one stitch.

K2TOG PICOT BO (KNIT TWO TOGETHER PICOT BIND-OFF): This can also be worked with a crochet hook in lieu of the left-hand needle to add picot chain stitches to the k2tog bind-off. Step 1: Knit 2 stitches together left (k2togL or k2tog tbl), and slip the stitch created back onto the left needle. Step 2: Knit this stitch, then slip the stitch just created back onto the left-hand needle (repeat once or as many times as required for picot chain). Repeat Steps 1 and 2 along row until the last two stitches, knit 2 stitches together left, fasten off.

K3TOG (KNIT THREE STITCHES TOGETHER) (over 3 stitches): Also known as K3TOGR. This is a right-slanting double decrease when used on the right side of the work. Knit three stitches together as if they were one stitch.

K3TOGL (KNIT THREE STITCHES TOGETHER WITH LEFT SLANT) (over 3 stitches): Also known as K3TOG TBL and is a double decrease. Knit three stitches together through the back loop as if they were one stitch.

K3TOGR (KNIT THREE STITCHES TOGETHER WITH RIGHT SLANT) (over 3 stitches): Also known as K3TOG and is a double decrease when used on the right side of the work. Knit three stitches together as if they were one stitch.

KFB (KNIT INTO THE FRONT AND BACK OF ONE STITCH) INCREASE: Also known as K1 F&B or BAR INCREASE. On a knit row, knit first into the front of the stitch normally, then, before slipping it off the needle, knit again into the back of the same stitch, and slip the stitch off. The same method is applied to a purl row; in this case, you purl into the front then the back of the stitch.

KEEPING TO PATTERN: If knitting a stitch pattern, follow the instruction for each row as long as you keep working over the same number of stitches. However, as you shape a project, such as a sleeve or a neckline, you will find that you need to increase or decrease the number of stitches you are knitting. This changes where you will begin and end each row.

KITCHENER STITCH: Also known as GRAFTING. Preparation: Cut the yarn that you have been knitting with, leaving a long tail. Thread the tail onto a yarn needle. Place the needles with the stitches on them on top of each other, so that the wrong sides of the work are facing in toward each other. Slide the yarn needle through the first stitch on the front needle as if to purl, leaving the stitch on the needle and pulling the yarn snug all the way through the stitch. Now take the needle and slide it through the first stitch on the back needle as if to knit, again not slipping the stitch off the needle and pulling the yarn snug all the way through the stitch. Now you are ready to begin the grafting. Step 1: Slide the yarn needle into the first stitch on the front needle as if to knit, this time slipping the stitch off the knitting needle and pulling tight. Step 2: The now first stitch on the front needle is stitched next, with the yarn needle going in as if to purl, and without slipping the stitch off the needle. Pull the yarn all the way through. Step 3: Slide yarn needle into the first stitch on the back needle as if to purl and slide that stitch off the needle and pull snug. Step 4: Slide the yarn needle into what is now the first stitch on the back needle as if to knit, leaving the stitch on the needle. As usual, pull the yarn all the way through. Steps one to four completes one round of Kitchener Stitch. Repeat Steps one to four on each of the following stitches.

KNITTED CAST-ON: Place slipknot on left needle if there are no established stitches. Step 1: With right needle, knit into first stitch (or slipknot) on left needle and place new stitch onto left needle. Step 2: With right needle, knit into last stitch made on left needle and place new stitch onto left needle. Repeat Step 2 for desired number of stitches to cast on.

KNITTED CAST-ON INCREASE: Knit the next stitch but do not drop the stitch from the left needle. Slip the new stitch onto the left needle. This will result in a slanted stitch.

KNITTED LACE: A type of open stitchwork when the stitch pattern rows are alternated with rows of plain knit or purl stitches.

KNITWISE: Also known as K-WISE or AS IF TO KNIT. Insert right needle into the stitch as if to knit it.

LACE KNITTING: A type of open stitchwork when the stitch pattern rows are worked on both right- and wrong-side rows.

LEFT SIDE: The part of the garment that is on your left side when you are wearing it.

LIFTED INCREASE: This is a right-slanting single increase. Insert right needle downward into the back of the stitch (the purl nub) in the row below the first stitch on left-hand needle, and knit, then knit the stitch on the needle.

LONG-TAIL CAST-ON: Also known as DOUBLE CAST-ON or 2-STRAND CAST-ON. Step 1: Place a slipknot several inches into a strand of yarn (roughly 1" [2.5 cm] for each stitch to be cast on). Place the slipknot on a knitting needle and hold the needle in your right hand. Be sure to keep the tail toward you and the live end of the yarn away from you. Step 2: With the needle in your right hand, slip your left thumb and index finger between the two strands of yarn and separate them. Hold both strands of yarn securely in your left hand. Step 3: Spread your thumb and index finger and turn your palm upward. Touch the tip of your needle to your palm and slide the needle up your thumb, under the yarn. Step 4: Move the tip of the needle toward your index finger and grab the strand that is wrapped around that finger. Return to the thumb and slide the tip of the needle back down the thumb toward the palm. Step 5: Allow the loop around your thumb to slip off, separating the two strands to tighten the cast-on stitch just created. Repeat Steps 2 to 5 for desired number of stitches to cast on.

M: Meter(s)

M1 (MAKE ONE STITCH): This is a single increase. It utilizes the running thread between two live stitches to create a new stitch. This increase can lean to the left (M1L) or to the right (M1R) depending on which direction you pick up the new stitch. If the method is not specified, use whichever increase you like.

M1L (MAKE ONE LEFT): This is a left-slanting single increase. Lift the horizontal thread between your needles with your left needle tip from front to back. Knit this newly lifted stitch through the back loop. You will be twisting the stitch to keep the space below the new stitch tidy and prevent a hole from forming.

M1R (MAKE ONE RIGHT): This is a right-slanting single increase. Lift the horizontal thread between your needles with your left needle tip from back to front. Knit this newly lifted stitch through the front loop. You will be twisting the stitch to keep the space below the new stitch tidy and prevent a hole from forming.

MM: Millimeter(s)

MAGIC LOOP: A technique for small circumferences using one circular needle. It is an alternative method for using double-pointed needles. Using a long circular needle (the length of the circular needle used should be about three to four times the circumference of the knitting), cast on the number of stitches needed to begin project, then slide them to the cable portion of the circular needle. With all of the stitches still on the cable, count until you reach approximately the halfway point in your total number of stitches and bend the cable to pull a section of cable out between the stitches. Continue pulling the loop of cable as you slide the divided stitches onto each needle. The excess cable is pulled out in between the divided stitches and each half of the stitches are on a needle. Join the stitches to form a ring, making sure the stitches are facing the proper way and are not twisted. Begin knitting in the round according to instructions

MULTIPLE OF STITCHES: A stitch multiple is the number of stitches you need to have for one complete repeat of a stitch pattern. A multiple of 5 stitches means you should cast on any number of stitches that is divisible by 5. A multiple of 6 + 1 means you should cast on any number of stitches that is divisible by 6 plus 1 extra stitch.

NEXT ROW (RS) OR (WS): Sometimes given at the end of a series of instructions and refers to which side your next row should be.

OZ: Ounce(s)

P (PURL): Insert the right needle into the front of the stitch from right to left.

P1 (PURL ONE STITCH): Create a stitch by inserting the needle through the stitch from the back to the front, wrapping yarn around the needle and pulling loop back through.

P1 TBL (PURL ONE STITCH THROUGH BACK LOOP): Also known as P TBL or P1B. Insert the right needle into the back of the stitch from back to front and purl the stitch.

P2TOG (PURL TWO STITCHES TOGETHER) (over 2 stitches): Also known as P2TOGR. This is a right-slanting single decrease when used on the wrong side of the work. Purl two stitches together as though they were one stitch.

P2TOG TBL (PURL TWO STITCHES TOGETHER THROUGH BACK LOOP) (over 2 stitches): Also known as P2TOGL. This is a left-slanting single decrease when used on the wrong side of the work.

Turn the work over slightly and insert the needle from the left-hand side into the back loops of the second and the first stitches, in that order, then wrap the yarn around the needle in front to complete the purl stitch.

P2TOGL (PURL TWO STITCHES TOGETHER WITH A LEFT SLANT) (over 2 stitches): Also known as P2TOG TBL. This is a left-slanting single decrease when used on the wrong side of the work. Turn the work over slightly and insert the needle from the left-hand side into the back loops of the second and the first stitches, in that order, then wrap the yarn around the needle in front to complete the purl stitch.

P2TOGR (PURL TWO STITCHES TOGETHER WITH A RIGHT SLANT) (over 2 stitches): Also known as P2TOG. This is a right-slanting single decrease when used on the wrong side of the work. Purl 2 stitches together so that they slant to the left when viewed from right side of the work.

P3TOG (PURL THREE STITCHES TOGETHER) (over 3 stitches): This is a right-slanting double decrease (two stitches for one stitch) when used on the wrong side of the work. Purl three stitches together as though they were one stitch.

PICK UP AND KNIT [PICK UP STITCHES]: To add more stitches to an existing piece of knitting in order to knit in another direction or to finish it off. Insert needle into fabric, wrap yarn around tip of needle and draw through fabric.

PICOT BIND OFFS: The cast-on stitches in the methods below form the picots.

Method One:

Step 1: Bind off 2 stitches, put remaining stitch on right needle back on left needle as if to purl. Step 2: Cast on one stitch using cable cast-on, then bind off three stitches (picot made). Step 3: Place remaining stitch on right needle back on left needle as if to purl. Repeat Steps 2 and 3 until all stitches are bound off.

Method Two:

Step 1: Cast on 3 stitches using cable cast-on and bind off 6 stitches (picot made). Step 2: Slip last stitch back to left needle. Repeat Steps 1 and 2 until all stitches are bound off.

Method Three:

Step 1: Cast on 2 stitches using the knitted cast-on method. Bind off the 2 stitches by knitting the 1st stitch, then knitting the 2nd stitch (you now have 2 stitches on the right hand needle). Using your left-hand needle, slip the 1st stitch over the 2nd stitch on the right-hand needle, leaving one stitch. Step 2: Knit one more stitch from the left-hand needle to the right-hand needle (2 stitches). Slip the 1st stitch over the 2nd stitch on the right-hand needle, leaving one stitch (picot made). Step 3: Bind off the next three stitches from the left-hand needle normally, and then slip the last stitch back onto your left needle. Repeat Steps 1 to 3 until all stitches are bound off.

K2TOG PICOT BO (KNIT TWO TOGETHER PICOT BIND OFF): This can also be worked with a crochet hook in lieu of the left-hand needle to add picot chain stitches to the k2tog bind-off. Step 1: Knit 2 stitches together left (K2togL or K2tog tbl), and slip the stitch created back onto the left needle. Step 2: Knit this stitch, then slip the stitch just created back onto the left-hand needle (repeat once or as many times as required for picot chain). Repeat Steps 1 and 2 along row until the last two stitches, knit 2 stitches together left, fasten off.

PLACE MARKER: Put a (stitch) marker or a piece of yarn at the place or places suggested in the directions.

PSP: This is a left-slanting single decrease when used on the wrong side of the work. Purl 1 stitch, slip stitch back to left needle, and pass the 2nd stitch over the first stitch.

PSSO: Pass the slipped stitch over.

PURLWISE: Also known as P-WISE or AS IF TO PURL. Insert right needle down into the front loop, or up into the back loop for tbl (through back loop).

PROVISIONAL CAST ON (STANDARD): Also known as INVISIBLE CAST ON. The waste yarn used can be pulled out later to continue the knitting in the opposite direction. Holding the ends of a waste yarn and the working yarn, make an overhand knot. Place a needle held in the left hand between the two yarns, with the knot below, the waste yarn held underneath and parallel to the needle out to the right, and the working yarn up and in front of the needle. Bring the working yarn down behind the needle and in front of the waste yarn; up behind the waste yarn and over-and-up then down in front of the needle; down behind the waste yarn; then up in front of the needle. Repeat for each two stitches. When desired number of stitches is reached, loosely fasten the waste yarn and work as usual with the working yarn. To take out the provisional cast-on, unfasten the end of the waste yarn and carefully pull it out, picking up the now-loose loops on a needle and working from the opposite direction of previous work.

PROVISIONAL CAST-ON (CROCHET): Generally worked with a piece of scrap or waste yarn, a provisional cast-on allows the knitter to remove the cast-on row and pick up the newly live stitches in the first row and work them. With a piece of waste yarn and a crochet hook slightly larger than the knitting needle, create a crochet chain, one chain for each cast-on stitch. Insert the knitting needle into the back loop of each chain. Use the loops on the needle as your cast-on row. When you want to release the first row and re-use them, carefully undo the last chain stitch, then pull the waste yarn to pull out the crochet chain and release the first row of knitting. Pick up these stitches and work as directed.

RS (RIGHT SIDE): The outside or public side of a sweater. Also stated to indicate which side is facing you when carrying out instructions.

REP BETWEEN *and *: Repeat whatever it says to do between the two asterisks.

REP . . . . TIMES MORE: Do whatever it says that many times more, in addition to the first time.

REV ST ST (REVERSE STOCKINETTE STITCH): In flat knitting: Purl on right side; knit on wrong side. In circular knitting: Purl every round on right side.

RIB: Also known as RIBBING. Vertical columns of knit and purl stitches, side by side, as in K1, P1 ribbing.

RING CAST-ON: To begin a center in circular knitting. Make a loose slipknot on the double-pointed needle, (k1, yo) into the slipknot four times and join.

ROUNDS (RNDS): In circular knitting, a "row" is called a "round."

ROW(S): Knitting back and forth in flat, noncircular knitting.

SKP (SL1-K1-PSSO) (over 2 stitches): Also known as SLIP, KNIT, And PASS. This is a left-slanting single decrease when used on the right side of the work. Slip one stitch onto right needle knitwise, knit the next stitch, then use the left needle tip to lift the slipped stitch over the knitted stitch and off the needle.

SK2P (SL1-K2TOG-PSSO) (over 3 stitches): This is a left-slanting double decrease when used on the right side of the work. Slip one stitch knitwise, knit two stitches together, and pass the slipped stitch over the two stitches knitted together.

S2KP2 (SL2-K1-P2SSO): Also known as CDD (CENTER DOUBLE DECREASE) or VDD (VERTICAL DOUBLE DECREASE). This is a centered double decrease when used on the right side of the work. Slip two stitches together knitwise, knit one stitch, and pass the two slipped stitches together over the knitted stitch and off the right-hand needle.

S2PP2 (SL2-P1-P2SSO) (over 3 stitches): This is a centered double decrease when used on the wrong side of the work. Slip two stitches knitwise one at a time, return two slipped stitches to left needle. Insert right needle though back loops of the second and the first slipped stitches, and slip them together off left needle. Purl next stitch and with left needle, pass the two slipped stitches over the purl stitch.

SP2P (SL1-P2TOG-PSSO) (over 3 stitches): This is a left-slanting double decrease when used on the wrong side of the work. Slip one stitch knitwise, purl two stitches together, and pass the slipped stitch over the two stitches purled together.

SSK (SLIP, SLIP, and KNIT TWO STITCHES TOGETHER) (over 2 stitches): This is a left-slanting single decrease when used on the right side of the work. Slip first stitch knitwise, slip second stitch knitwise, pass left needle back through these two stitches, so that the left needle is in front of the right needle. Wrap yarn as usual around right needle and knit the two stitches together.

SSK IMPROVED (SLIP, SLIP, and KNIT TWO STITCHES TOGETHER) (over 2 stitches): This is a left-slanting single decrease when used on the right side of the work. Slip first stitch knitwise, slip second stitch purlwise, pass left needle back through these two stitches, so that the left needle is in front of the right needle. Wrap yarn as usual around right needle and knit the two stitches together.

SSK AND PASS (over 3 stitches): This is a double decrease. Ssk over first two stitches, return the resulting stitch to left-hand needle and with point of right-hand needle pass the next stitch on the left

needle over the returned stitch and off the needle. then slip the returned stitch back to the right-hand needle.

SSP (SLIP, SLIP, PURL TWO STITCHES TOGETHER) (over 2 stitches): A single decrease, usually done on the purl side. Slip the next two stitches from left needle, one at a time, knitwise. Place these stitches back onto the left needle, insert right needle from left to right into the back of the two slipped stitches, and purl these two stitches together. Drop these two stitches as purled off the left needle.

SL1-K1-PSSO (SKP) (over 2 stitches): Also known as SLIP, KNIT, And PASS. This is a left-slanting single decrease when used on the right side of the work. Slip one stitch onto right needle knitwise, knit the next stitch, then use the left needle tip to lift the slipped stitch over the knitted stitch and off the needle.

SLIP 1, K2, PSSO (over 3 stitches): This is a single decrease. Slip one stitch knitwise, knit next two stitches individually, and pass the slipped stitch over the two knitted stitches.

SL1-K2TOG-PSSO (SK2P) (over 3 stitches): This is a left slanting double decrease when used on the right side of the work. Slip one stitch knitwise, knit two stitches together, and pass the slipped stitch over the two stitches knitted together.

SL1-P1-PSSO (SPP) (over 2 stitches): This is a right-slanting single decrease. Slip one stitch purlwise, purl one stitch, and pass the slipped stitch over the purled stitch and off the right needle.

SL1-P2TOG-PSSO (SP2P) (over 3 stitches): This is a left slanting double decrease when used on the wrong side of the work. Slip one stitch knitwise, purl two stitches together, and pass the slipped stitch over the two stitches purled together.

SL2-K1-P2SSO (S2KP2): Also known as CDD (CENTER DOUBLE DECREASE) or VDD (VERTICAL DOUBLE DECREASE). This is a centered double decrease when used on the right side of the work. Slip two stitches together knitwise, knit one stitch, and pass the two slipped stitches together over the knitted stitch and off the right hand needle.

SL2-K2TOG-P2SSO (S2K2P2) (over 4 stitches): This is a left-slanting triple decrease. Slip two stitches together knitwise, knit two stitches together, and pass the two slipped stitches over the two stitches knitted together.

SL2-P1-P2SSO (S2PP2) (over 3 stitches): This is a centered, double decrease when used on the wrong side of the work. Slip two stitches knitwise one at a time, return two slipped stitches to left needle. Insert right needle though back loops of the second and the first slipped stitches, and slip them together off left needle. Purl next stitch and with left needle, pass the two slipped stitches over purl stitch.

SCHEMATIC: The little line drawing included in most patterns, which tells the measurements of the different parts of your project before sewing together, and how each piece should look when completed.

SELVEDGE: Also known as SELVAGE. All knitting has a selvedge on each side—the first and last stitches. If there is seaming, these are the stitches that will be used to seam the piece together; they will no longer be visible when it is sewn. With knitting projects such as scarves and afghans where there are no seams, but only selvedge. Sometimes a pattern will tell you to work the first and last stitch in a specific way, such as slipping the first stitch and knitting the last stitch. This creates a neat selvedge on each side that enhances the look of the project.

SHIR: Gather

SHORT ROW: A row that is only partially knitted where the work is turned before reaching the end of the row. Short rows of knitting are used to shape or curve sections or to compensate for patterns with different row gauges. Wrap and Turn (W&T) is the most common way of creating short rows. Bring the yarn to the front of the work (as if to purl), and slip one stitch from the left needle to the right (again, as if to purl). Then, turn the work over. The yarn is now again at the back of the piece and the left and right needles have changed places. Bring the yarn to the front, and slip one stitch from the left to the right needle. The wrap and turn is now complete; if the next stitch is a knit stitch, remember to return the yarn to the back of the piece before beginning.

SHRIMP STITCH: Also known as REVERSE SINGLE CROCHET (RSC) or CRAB STITCH. Step 1: After completing a row of single crochet, do not turn the work around. Step 2: Working from left to right, insert the crochet hook into the next stitch to the right, yarn over and draw up a long loop. (Keep the length of loop consistent through your row). Yarn over and pull through both loops on the hook. Repeat Step 2 for remaining stitches.

SINGLE CROCHET (SC): Step 1: Keeping working yarn behind work, insert crochet hook into the spot indicated by the instruction. Yarn over to create a loop on the hook (wrap yarn around hook from back to front into hook opening). Step 2: Pull loop on hook through so that there are now two loops on the hook. Step 3: Bring yarn over hook again, from back to front so that yarn engages in hook opening. Step 4: Draw loop through so that only one loop remains on the hook. This completes the single crochet stitch.

SLIP (SL): Stitches are slipped without working from the right needle to the left needle. They can be slipped either purlwise or knitwise. If the pattern instructions do not specify which way, slip the stitch or stitches purlwise.. If slipping stitch(es) when decreasing and instructions do not specify, then slip it knitwise on the knit rows, and purlwise on the purl rows.

SLIPKNOT: An adjustable loop, used to begin many cast-on methods. To make a slipknot using a knitting needle: Step 1: Make a loop with the yarn, making sure that the tail of the yarn is behind the loop. Step 2: Insert the needle through the loop, moving under the tail and back out the loop. Step 3: Grab the tail and pull to create slipknot on needle. The slipknot is completed. To make a slipknot without using a knitting needle: Step 1: After pulling yarn for the tail, make a loop (you should see an 'X'). Step 2: Grab hold of the strand of yarn that is on the top of the 'X' and bring this strand behind and through the loop that was made. Step 3: Pull this new loop through the old loop and pull down to create your slipknot. Once you have your slipknot you are ready to cast on. The slipknot counts as your first cast on stitch.

SLIP MARKER: Move a marker from the left needle to the right needle as you knit or purl the row.

SLIP . . . STITCH(ES): Pass the number of stitches instructed from the left needle to the right needle without knitting them.

SLIP STITCH (SL ST): Used in crochet. Insert the crochet hook in the next stitch to be worked, wrap the yarn or thread over the hook, pull the yarn or thread through both the stitch to be worked and the loop already on the hook, all at the same time.

SLIP STITCHES TO HOLDER: Take the stitches off the needle and put them on to a holder or thread them onto a piece of yarn.

SPRAY (MIST) BLOCKING: IMPORTANT: Check yarn label care instructions before proceeding. For a minimal stretch, place the item on a blocking surface, stretch to desired size and shape, and pin in place. Lightly mist the surface with a spray bottle of water or a combination of water and gentle wool wash. Leave to dry undisturbed. Once dry, your item will maintain its blocked shape.

STEAM BLOCKING: IMPORTANT: Check yarn label care instructions before proceeding. Gently lay your piece out on the blocking board. Spread your piece out to the correct dimensions without distorting the direction of the stitches. Use the schematic for reference and the grid as a guide, start at the center. Pin and smooth all pieces. Hold a steam iron over the piece about ½ inch (13mm) away from the surface. Steam to penetrate the piece without the weight of the iron pressing down on it. If your knitting is cotton, you can let the iron touch the fabric very lightly, but keep it moving and do not let the full weight of the iron lay on the surface. After steaming, let your piece rest and dry for at least 30 minutes. Make sure the piece is dry before working with it further.

STOCKINETTE STITCH (ST ST): In flat knitting: Knit on right side; purl on wrong side. In circular knitting: Knit every round on right side.

SWATCH: A piece of knitting done in the yarn and in the stitch pattern you are going to use on your project.

TBL: Through the back loop(s)

TWISTED CORD: Measure a length of yarn 4 times longer than the desired length of the cord. Fold the strand in half and make a slipknot at the cut ends. Pass the slipknot over a doorknob and stand far enough away that the yarn hangs in midair and does not touch the ground. Slip a crochet hook into the loop you are holding in your hand and pull the cord taut so that the hook rests perpendicular to your fingers, allowing the hook to slip between your middle and pointer finger. Begin turning the hook—similar to the way that the propeller on a toy airplane twists a rubber band— to twist the strands of yarn. Continue twisting until the yarn is quite taut and evenly twisted. When relaxed slightly, the twisted yarn will want to kink up. Still holding one end of the yarn in your left hand, with your right hand pinch the twisted strand midway between yourself and the doorknob. Bring the ends of the yarn together by moving toward the doorknob, but do not let go of the

middle of the twisted yarn. When the piece is folded in half, release the middle of the cord. You will notice the yarn twisting around itself, forming a plied cord. Still holding tightly to the looped end, loosen the slipknot end from the doorknob and tie both ends together. Run your finger between the cords to even out the twists if necessary.

VDD (VERTICAL DOUBLE DECREASE) (over 3 stitches): Also known as CDD (CENTER DOUBLE DECREASE) or SL2-K1-P2SSO (S2KP2). This is a centered double decrease when used on the right side of the work. Slip two stitches together knitwise, knit one stitch, and pass the two slipped stitches together over the knitted stitch and off the right-hand needle.

W&T (WRAP AND TURN): This is the most common way of creating short rows. Bring the yarn to the front of the work (as if to purl), and slip one stitch from the left needle to the right (again, as if to purl). Then, turn the work over. The yarn is now again at the back of the piece and the left and right needles have changed places. Bring the yarn to the front, and slip one stitch from the left to the right needle. The wrap and turn is now complete; if the next stitch is a knit stitch, remember to return the yarn to the back of the piece before beginning.

WS (WRONG SIDE): The inside or non-public side of a sweater. Also stated to indicate which side is facing you when carrying out instructions.

WYIB (WITH YARN IN BACK): Move the yarn away from you to the back of the work. **Note:** Back may not be the wrong side of the work.

WYIF (WITH YARN IN FRONT): Move the yarn toward you for the next step. **Note:** Front may not be the right side of the work.

WASTE YARN: A length of waste yarn other than the actual yarn used in the garment, that is removed later to reveal "live" stitches, which are then placed back on the needle and knit in the opposite direction.

WEAVE IN ENDS: To sew in the excess yarn ends when a project is finished so that it is not seen.

WET BLOCKING: IMPORTANT: Check yarn label care instructions before proceeding. Soak the finished item in lukewarm water (preferably with a gentle wool wash) until it is completely wet. Wait 30-45 minutes to allow the water to absorb thoroughly. It will float until the trapped air releases and water is completely absorbed. Remove the item from the bath and gently press the water out. Do not wring! Wringing your swatch or finished piece can unevenly stretch or warp the stitches and even felt it. Place the item on a blocking surface and stretch it into shape. A blocking surface could be a carpeted floor covered in fresh towels, a mattress, or a blocking board you purchase. Use rustproof pins and/or blocking wires to secure your desired shape. Leave to dry undisturbed. Once dry the item will maintain its blocked shape.

WITH RIGHT SIDE (RS) FACING: You will often see this term when you are about to pick up stitches along an edge but you may see it at other times as well. The right side or the public side when it is completed, should be facing you as you work.

WORK EVEN: Continue knitting without increasing or decreasing.

YD: Yard(s)

YARN OVER (YO): Also known as YARN FORWARD. Making a yarn over is a simple way to increase stitches or create a hole in the knitting and is popularly combined with a decrease such as knit two together to keep the number of stitches the same across the row. Working a yarn over is the same whether you are knitting or purling the next stitch. When knitting, wrap the yarn around the needle and leave it in the back; when purling, wrap it all the way around the needle so the yarn is back in front where it needs to be to purl. To work a yarn over increase at the beginning of a knit row, bring your yarn to the front of your work and knit the first stitch of the row. To knit that first stitch, you move the yarn from the front to the back over the top of the right needle tip while it is inserted into the first stitch. To work a yarn over increase at the beginning of a purl row, bring your yarn to the back of your work and purl the first stitch of the row. You will bring the yarn from the back to the front over the right needle to purl this first stitch.

YARN OVER (DOUBLE): Also known as YO2, YO TWICE or YARN OVER TWICE. To make a double yarn over, wrap the yarn around the right-hand needle from back to front counterclockwise twice before knitting the next stitch. Then just work the next stitch as normal. When you get to the yarn overs on the next row, work yarn overs as specified in instructions.

Resources

Artyarns
www.artyarns.com
914-428-0333

Berroco Yarn
www.berroco.com
508-278-2527

Cascade Yarns
www.cascadeyarns.com
800-548-1048

Debbie Bliss
www.debbieblissonline.com

Elsa Sheep and Wool Company
www.wool-clothing.com
970-884-2145

Foxfire Fiber
www.foxfirefiber.com
413-625-6121

Frog Tree
www.frogtreeyarns.com
508-385-9476 (fax)

Karabella Yarns
www.karabellayarns.com
800 550 0898

Koigu
www.koigu.com
1-888-765-WOOL

Wollmeise
Distributed by The Loopy Ewe
www.theloopyewe.com

Lorna's Laces
www.lornaslaces.net
773-935-3803

Malabrigo Yarn
www.malabrigoyarn.com
786-866-6187

Plymouth Yarn Co.
www.plymouthyarn.com
215-788-0459

Rowan Yarns
Distributed by Westminster
Fibers
www.knitrowan.com
800-445-9276

Takhi Stacy Charles
www.tahkistacycharles.com
800-338-9276

Tilli Tomas
www.tillitomas.com
617-524-3330

Wooly West
www.woolywest.com
888-487-9665

Standard Yarn Weight System

Categories of yarn, gauge ranges, and recommended needle sizes

Yarn Weight Symbol & Category Names	**0** LACE	**1** SUPER FINE	**2** FINE	**3** LIGHT	**4** MEDIUM	**5** BULKY
Type of Yarns in category	Fingering	Lace, Fingering, Sock	Sport	DK, Light Worsted	Worsted, Aran	Chunky
Knit Gauge Range* in Stockinette Stitch to 4 inches	33–40** sts	27–32 sts	23–26 sts	21–24 sts	16–20 sts	12–15 sts
Recommended Needle in US Size Range	000–1	1–3	3–5	5–7	7–9	9–11
Recommended Needle in Metric Size Range	1.5–2.25mm	2.25–3.25mm	3.25–3.75mm	3.75–4.5mm	4.5–5.5mm	5.5–8mm

* GUIDELINES ONLY: The above reflect the most commonly used gauges and needle or hook sizes for specific yarn categories.

** Lace weight yarns are usually knitted or crocheted on larger needles and hooks to create lacy, openwork patterns. Accordingly, a gauge range is difficult to determine. Always follow the gauge stated in your pattern.

ACKNOWLEDGMENTS

This book would not have been possible without the beautiful lace work of some of our favorite knitters. A heartfelt thanks goes out to Lisa Lloyd, Annie Modesitt, Berta Karapetyan, Phoenix Bess, Melissa Matthay, Shelia January, Elanor Lynn, Jackie Erickson-Schweitzer, Anne Lorenz-Panzer, Cheryl Niamath, and Bethany Kok.

The editors also wish to acknowledge the valuable contributions of Jeannie Chin in the development of this compendium.

Last but not least, a special thanks goes out to Kristin Omdahl, for her valuable work and insight above and beyond the patterns, and Clara Parkes.

INDEX

Photo credits and Copyright ◇◇◇◇◇◇◇◇◇◇◇◇◇◇◇◇◇◇◇◇◇◇◇◇◇◇◇◇◇◇◇◇◇◇

Portions of this work were originally published in the following:

A Fine Fleece by Lisa Lloyd, copyright © 2008 by Lisa Lloyd, photographs by Alexandra Grablewski, photos copyright © 2008 by Potter Craft, a division of Random House, Inc.

It Girl Knits by Phoenix Bess, copyright © 2008 by Phoenix Bess, photographs by Dan Howell, photos copyright © 2008 by Dan Howell

Knits Three Ways by Melissa Matthay, copyright © 2007 by Melissa Matthay, photographs by Alan Foreman, photos copyright © 2007 by Alan Foreman

The Knitter's Book of Yarn by Clara Parkes, copyright © 2007 by Clara Parkes, photographs by Alexandra Grablewski, photos copyright © 2007 by Potter Craft, a division of Random House, Inc.

Romantic Hand Knits by Annie Modesitt, copyright © 2007 by Annie Modesitt, photographs by Thayer Allyson Gowdy, photos copyright © 2007 by Thayer Allyson Gowdy

Runway Knits by Berta Karapetyan, copyright © 2007 by Berta Karapetyan, photographs by Justin William Lin, photos copyright © 2007 by Justin William Lin

Published in the United States by Potter Craft, an imprint of the Crown Publishing Group, a division of Random House, Inc., New York.

www.crownpublishing.com
www.pottercraft.com

POTTER CRAFT and colophon is a registered trademark of Random House, Inc.

Library of Congress Cataloging-in-Publication Data

The art of knitted lace : with complete lace how-to and dozens of patterns / [compiled by Potter Craft]. — 1st ed.

    p. cm.

  Includes index.

  ISBN 978-0-307-46493-4

  1. Potter Craft (Firm)

  TT805.K54A78 2010

  746.43'2--dc22

    2009053096

Printed in China

Design by Chi Ling Moy

10 9 8 7 6 5 4 3 2 1

First Edition

Thanks to the Craft Yarn Council of America (www.yarnstandards.com) for their Standard Yarn Weight System chart, which appears on page 173.